Schriften zur Restrukturierung

edited by

Prof. Dr. Stephan Madaus
Prof. Dr. Bettina Nunner-Krautgasser
Prof. Dr. Christoph G. Paulus, LL.M.
RA Wolfgang Zenker

Volume 38

Abbas Abbasov

Recognition of Restructuring Plans under the UNCITRAL Model Law on Cross-Border Insolvency

Modified Universalism, the Gibbs Rule, and the "Adequate Protection" Safeguard

Nomos

The publication of this work was supported by the Publication Fund of Martin Luther University Halle-Wittenberg, the Volkswagen Foundation, and the German-British Lawyers' Association.

The Deutsche Nationalbibliothek lists this publication in the Deutsche Nationalbibliografie; detailed bibliographic data are available on the Internet at http://dnb.d-nb.de

a.t.: Halle-Wittenberg, Univ., Diss., 2025

Original title: Recognition of Foreign Restructuring Plans under the UNCITRAL Model Law on Cross-Border Insolvency: A Fair Balance Between the Interests of the Debtor and Dissenting Foreign Creditors

1st Edition 2026

Published by
Nomos Verlagsgesellschaft mbH & Co. KG
Waldseestraße 3–5 | 76530 Baden-Baden
www.nomos.de

Production of the printed version:
Nomos Verlagsgesellschaft mbH & Co. KG
Waldseestraße 3–5 | 76530 Baden-Baden

ISBN 978-3-7560-3612-7 (Print)
ISBN 978-3-7489-6767-5 (ePDF)

DOI https://doi.org/10.5771/9783748967675

Online Version
Nomos eLibrary

To my parents

Acknowledgements

This work is the final version of the doctoral thesis accepted by Martin Luther University Halle-Wittenberg. The defence took place on 10 September 2025.

First and foremost, I would like to express my sincere gratitude to my academic supervisor, Prof. Dr. Stephan Madaus, for introducing me to this topic, for his guidance and support throughout my research, and for his invaluable first review of my thesis. I am also grateful to Prof. Dr. Christoph G. Paulus, LL.M., for his insightful second review of my work.

Furthermore, I would like to acknowledge the institutions and individuals who supported my research and its publication, including the Ministry of Science and Education of the Republic of Azerbaijan, the Volkswagen Foundation, the Publication Fund of Martin Luther University Halle-Wittenberg, the German-British Lawyers' Association, and ADA University. I am particularly thankful to Prof. Dr. Azar Aliyev for his support throughout this process.

In addition, I am grateful to my colleagues from Prof. Dr. Stephan Madaus's research team for the memorable moments we shared over the years. I am glad to now call many of them friends. I would also like to extend my heartfelt thanks to my close friends, whose support I am fortunate to have in all aspects of my life.

Last but not least, I owe my deepest gratitude to my family. I am especially thankful to my father, Kazim Abbasov, and mother, Leyla Abbasova, for their unwavering dedication to my personal and professional growth. I am deeply grateful to my wife and son, who have been firsthand witnesses to this journey and a constant source of motivation throughout it. I would also like to thank my siblings, particularly my sister, for their support. Finally, I would like to express my gratitude to my uncle Vakil Abbasov for always encouraging me to pursue my goals with dedication and perseverance.

Halle (Saale), 06 November 2025 *Abbas Abbasov*

Table of Contents

List of Abbreviations

APR	Absolute priority rule
BC	Bankruptcy Code (US)
BIT	Best interests test (BC)
CBIR	Cross-Border Insolvency Regulations 2006 (UK)
CJEU	Court of Justice of the European Union
COMI	Centre of main interests
CPC	Civil Procedure Code (Azerbaijan)
CVA	Company Voluntary Arrangement
EGBGB	Einführungsgesetz zum Bürgerlichen Gesetzbuche (Introductory Act to the Civil Code, Germany)
EIR	European Insolvency Regulation (recast) (EU, 2015/848)
EU	European Union
EU BIT	Best-interest-of-creditors test (PRD)
EWCA	Court of Appeal (England and Wales)
EWHC	High Court (England and Wales)
IBA	International Bank of Azerbaijan
InsO	Insolvenzordnung (Insolvency Code, Germany)
LB	Law on Banks (Azerbaijan)
LIB	Law on Insolvency and Bankruptcy (Azerbaijan)
MLCBI	Model Law on Cross-Border Insolvency (UNCITRAL)
MLIJ	Model Law on Recognition and Enforcement of Insolvency-Related Judgments (UNCITRAL)
PRD	Preventive Restructuring Directive (EU, 2019/1023)
RPR	Relative priority rule
SDNY	Southern District of New York

UK	United Kingdom
UKSC	Supreme Court of the United Kingdom
UNCITRAL	United Nations Commission on International Trade Law
US	United States
USSC	Supreme Court of the United States

A. Introduction

I. Introduction to the Topic

The restructuring of distressed companies is a delicate matter. It is a complex process that may involve measures such as reducing principal amounts, extending maturity dates, and transferring equity to creditors in order to achieve the objectives of a restructuring.[1] In the absence of a specific framework, a restructuring would require the consent of all affected claimants under general principles of private law, as is the case with contractual workouts.[2] However, a collective framework based on the unanimous support of the affected claimants has its shortcomings. Some claimants, known as *free riders,* may withhold their consent to receive better treatment at the expense of others.[3] This could obstruct the collective benefits that would be generated if the restructuring went through, commonly referred to as the *holdout problem* in the literature.[4] Lawmakers' response to prevent such unjustified holdout scenarios is creating specific restructuring frameworks that can bind all affected claimants, including holdouts.[5]

That said, such a binding effect may also give rise to opportunities for abuse and misuse.[6] That is to say, holdout behaviour is not always unjustified and may reflect legitimate opposition to an unfair distribution under

1 For a discussion of possible restructuring measures, see Riz Mokal, 'The Goals, Contents, and Structure of the Plan' (with help from Charles G. Case and Lorenzo Stanghellini) in Lorenzo Stanghellini and others (eds), *Best Practices in European Restructuring: Contractualised Distress Resolution in the Shadow of the Law* (Wolters Kluwer 2018) s 3.

2 Jennifer Payne, 'The Role of the Court in Debt Restructuring' (2018) 77 CLJ 124, 127.

3 Stephan Madaus, 'The Cross-border Effects of Restructurings' in Katharina de la Durantaye and others (eds), *Festschrift für Christoph G. Paulus zum 70. Geburtstag* (CH Beck 2022) 472.

4 Stephan Madaus, 'Leaving the Shadows of US Bankruptcy Law: A Proposal to Divide the Realms of Insolvency and Restructuring Law' (2018) 19 EBOR 615, 633ff.

5 Madaus, 'The Cross-border Effects of Restructurings' (n 3) 472. See also Payne, 'The Role of the Court' (n 2) 127-28.

6 Payne, 'The Role of the Court' (n 2) 129-131. For a more detailed discussion of fairness concerns in different scenarios of debt-restructuring, see generally Sarah Paterson, 'Debt Restructuring and Notions of Fairness' (2017) 80 MLR 600.

the restructuring plan. Most jurisdictions provide fairness frameworks to assess whether holdout behaviour is justified before binding holdout creditors to the plan.[7] Such an assessment is generally conducted by the court prior to sanctioning the plan or when the plan is challenged on the respective grounds, as the case may be.[8] Different jurisdictions apply varying tests and priority rules in this regard.[9]

The restructuring becomes even more delicate when cross-border elements are involved. A typical example involves a plan that contemplates the non-consensual discharge of a foreign law-governed debt. Here, more than the confirmation of the local court is needed to fully implement the plan, particularly in relation to the dissenting foreign creditor. To prevent that creditor from enforcing the original claim in foreign jurisdictions (e.g. in the jurisdiction whose law governs the creditor's original claim), the plan and its binding effect should be recognised in the eyes of those jurisdictions. Several additional issues arise concerning such cross-border recognition.

First and foremost, it is essential to identify which route to use for cross-border recognition. This, in turn, refers to the much more complex issue of determining the legal nature of a restructuring plan. As this work will outline in section B.I, there is no consensus in the literature regarding these matters. The same section of this work will also demonstrate that the majority in academia view restructuring proceedings as insolvency proceedings and, therefore, support achieving their cross-border effects through the existing cross-border insolvency frameworks. After briefly taking a stance on the legal nature of restructuring proceedings in that section, this work will not argue against the respective route of achieving the cross-border effects of restructuring plans. Section B.III of this work will indeed indicate that the cross-border insolvency frameworks examined therein expressly include restructuring proceedings.

II. Research Problem

The fact that restructuring proceedings fall within the existing cross-border insolvency frameworks does not eliminate the uncertainty surrounding the

7 For a more detailed discussion, see s E.II.
8 For a more detailed discussion, see sub-s D.II.1.c).
9 For a more detailed discussion, see s E.II.

cross-border effects of restructuring plans. That is to say, even jurisdictions that otherwise apply the progressive universalist approach to foreign insolvency proceedings, like England,[10] may adopt an over-protective approach to giving effect to foreign restructuring plans.[11] That is particularly true when recognising the discharge of a foreign law-governed debt under the plan. Since discharge is a central aspect of restructuring,[12] this matter is of high importance.

The recognition of restructuring plans depends on the cross-border insolvency framework in question. For example, the European Insolvency Regulation ("EIR")[13] establishes a framework for automatic recognition of insolvency proceedings, which generally include restructuring proceedings.[14] Despite such recognition being subject to the public policy exception, the EIR can generally be considered an effective tool for recognising the cross-border effects of restructuring plans within the EU. Nonetheless, the current EU example does not reflect the global reality as it relies on mutual trust among a closed group of a limited number of countries with harmonised laws in several key areas. For example, the Preventive Restructuring Directive ("PRD")[15] aims to harmonise, to a certain extent, critical aspects of national restructuring laws across the EU.[16]

10 English courts' universalist approach towards cross-border insolvencies goes back to the 18th century. See, eg, *Solomons v Ross* (1764) 1 HBI 131. For a more detailed discussion, see generally K. H. Nadelmann, 'Solomons v. Ross and International Bankruptcy Law' (1946) 9 MLR 154. See also Tom Smith, 'Recognition of Foreign Corporate Insolvency Proceedings at Common Law' in Richard Sheldon (ed) *Cross-Border Insolvency* (4th edn, Bloomsbury Professional 2015), paras 6.4-15. For a more detailed discussion of the universalist approach to cross-border insolvency in general, see sub-s B.II.3.

11 For a more detailed discussion of the English approach in this context, see sub-s C.II.1.

12 Jay Lawrence Westbrook, 'Comity and Choice of Law in Global Insolvencies' (2019) 54 Tex Intl L J 259, 270.

13 Regulation (EU) 2015/848 of the European Parliament and of the Council of 20 May 2015 on insolvency proceedings (recast) ("EIR").

14 For a more detailed discussion of the EIR, see sub-s B.III.1.

15 Directive (EU) 2019/1023 of the European Parliament and of the Council of 20 June 2019 on preventive restructuring frameworks, on discharge of debt and disqualifications, and on measures to increase the efficiency of procedures concerning restructuring, insolvency and discharge of debt, and amending Directive (EU) 2017/1132 (Directive on restructuring and insolvency) ("PRD").

16 For a more detailed discussion of the PRD, see sub-s E.II.3.

In this context, a quite different perspective is presented under the UNCITRAL Model Law on Cross-Border Insolvency ("MLCBI").[17] To begin with, it provides a model that does not rely on mutual trust. Nor does it require reciprocity.[18] Therefore, this model allows the recognition of eligible proceedings from all jurisdictions. Furthermore, the MLCBI can easily be incorporated into national legislation without the consent of other states.[19] It has been implemented, in one or another form, in over 60 jurisdictions worldwide, representing different continents and legal systems, ranging from the US to Saudi Arabia, from Japan to Zimbabwe, from Australia to Chile, and so forth.[20] Additionally, the MLCBI is underpinned by the principle of modified universalism, developed as a fitting interim solution for the current world reality.[21]

Although the MLCBI generally encompasses restructuring proceedings, it does not expressly mention the recognition of restructuring plans. Such recognition does not come automatically upon recognition of foreign restructuring proceedings and may only be available as post-recognition relief under the MLCBI.[22] That said, the lack of express reference to the recognition of restructuring plans in the text of the MLCBI and the discretionary nature of such relief give rise to uncertainty. That is to say, jurisdictions that have implemented the MLCBI apply different approaches and tests to the respective matter. That holds true for England and the US, even though

---

17 UNCITRAL adopted the Model Law on Cross-Border Insolvency ("MLCBI") in 1997 and revised its Guide to Enactment and Interpretation ("Guide to the MLCBI") in 2013. See UNCITRAL, *Model Law on Cross-Border Insolvency with Guide to Enactment and Interpretation* (UN 2014) <https://uncitral.un.org/sites/uncitral.un.org/files/media-documents/uncitral/en/1997-model-law-insol-2013-guide-enactment-e.pdf> accessed 21 October 2025. For a summary of its origins and legislative history, see Adrian Walters, 'Modified Universalisms & the Role of Local Legal Culture in the Making of Cross-Border Insolvency Law' (2019) 93 Am Bankr LJ 47, 56.

18 Walters, 'Modified Universalisms' (n 17) 60. It is noteworthy that South Africa included a reciprocity requirement in its local version of the MLCBI. Christoph G. Paulus, 'Civil Law Codificationalism vs. UNCITRAL's Soft Law Approach in the Context of Insolvency Law' in Ángel María Ballesteros Barros and David Amable Morán Bovio (eds), *Insolvency Law in UNCITRAL: Instruments and Comments* (Editorial Aranzadi 2023), 392.

19 For a more detailed discussion of the MLCBI, see sub-s B.III.2.

20 For the status of the MLCBI, see UNCITRAL, 'Status: UNCITRAL Model Law on Cross-Border Insolvency (1997)' <https://uncitral.un.org/en/texts/insolvency/modellaw/cross-border_insolvency/status> accessed 21 October 2025.

21 For a more detailed discussion, see sub-s B.II.4.

22 For a more detailed discussion of the automatic effects of recognition and post-recognition relief under the MLCBI, see sub-s B.III.2.c).

they belong to the same legal system and have a common legal history. The English approach prioritises the protection of creditors by not recognising a discharge under a foreign restructuring plan (e.g. one confirmed in the debtor's home jurisdiction) unless it constitutes a valid discharge under the law governing the debt in question (the Gibbs rule).[23] By contrast, the American approach is more favourable to the debtor. It allows recognising a discharge (including that of a US law-governed debt) under a foreign plan, with certain safeguards in place.[24]

This work will thoroughly analyse the approaches mentioned above and seek to strike a fair balance between the interests of the debtor and dissenting foreign creditors in the recognition of restructuring plans under the MLCBI. For that purpose, particular attention will be given to the *adequate protection* safeguard under article 22 (1) of the MLCBI.

III. Definitions and Limitations

In this work, the term *restructuring proceedings* encompasses all formal rescue procedures that involve the restructuring of claims held by the distressed debtor's existing claimants, with binding effect on holdouts. Whether these procedures occur within insolvency proceedings or as stand-alone processes and what they are called (rehabilitation, reorganisation, restructuring, and similar terms) are irrelevant. The term *restructuring plan* should be construed accordingly. For the avoidance of doubt, plans that contemplate the ultimate liquidation of the debtor or its going-concern sale to third parties are excluded.

Throughout this work, the term *requisite majority* refers to a majority in number and/or in value in the meeting of all claimants or any specific group of them, as required by the applicable law for approval of a particular type of restructuring plan. A *dissenting* or *holdout creditor* is a creditor who has not supported the proposed plan, whether by voting against it, abstaining from voting, or not participating in the vote. The term *discharge* in relation to a dissenting creditor refers to any non-consensual modification of the original claim of that creditor in restructuring proceedings. In this work, the term *governing law of the contract* refers to the law applicable to a contract as determined under private international law rules.

23 For a more detailed discussion, see sub-s C.II.1.
24 For a more detailed discussion, see sub-s C.II.2.

This work will focus on the problem described above and, therefore, will not address related side issues. That is to say, for the purpose of this work, the *debtor* should be considered as a single, non-regulated company. Hence, individuals, whether merchants or consumers, are excluded. Furthermore, this research will not address issues related to the restructuring of groups, whether in a domestic or cross-border context. Additionally, this work will not delve into the matters specific to the restructuring of regulated companies, such as credit institutions and insurance undertakings. Although third-party releases will be touched on while discussing the US case law on the recognition of foreign restructuring plans, the focus of this work will be on the claims against the debtor itself. Therefore, the concept of third-party releases in restructuring will not be analysed.

This work will focus on fairness issues in recognising foreign restructuring plans under the MLCBI framework. Therefore, it will not address choice-of-forum and choice-of-law rules for cross-border restructuring cases. However, under the MLCBI, a *foreign main proceeding* is considered to take place in the state where the debtor's centre of main interests ("COMI") is located, as will be evident in subsection B.III.2 of this work. Therefore, for the purposes of this work, it will be assumed that the main restructuring proceedings take place in the jurisdiction where the debtor's COMI is located. Throughout this work, this jurisdiction may also be referred to as the *debtor's home country* or *jurisdiction.* Additionally, this work will assume that the court in the debtor's home jurisdiction applies the law of the forum (the *lex fori concursus*) to procedural and substantive matters.[25]

IV. Structure of the Research

As stated, this work will focus on striking a fair balance between the interests of the debtor and dissenting foreign creditors when recognising restructuring plans. It was also noted that this work will describe and analyse the research problem using a model based on the MLCBI. That said, other frameworks, such as the EIR, may also be referred to, e.g. for comparison.

This work comprises five main parts. Part B will provide an introduction to cross-border restructuring, considering several crucial aspects. This

25 The MLCBI is silent on the matter. Nevertheless, this is generally the case under the principles of universalism and modified universalism (see sub-ss B.II.3 and B.II.4, respectively) and the EIR (see sub-s B.III.1.b)).

includes discussing the academic debate and taking a stance on the legal nature of restructuring proceedings as well as their cross-border effects, examining underlying principles and modern mechanisms of the cross-border insolvency system.

Part C will provide a comparative analysis and outline the preliminary findings. As mentioned earlier, the focus of this work will be on the interpretation of the MLCBI in England and in the US regarding the recognition of restructuring plans. There are several reasons for selecting these jurisdictions. First, both England (London) and the US (New York) are widely known as *financial hubs* hosting major financial institutions and stock exchanges. This ultimately affects the choice of governing law for most international debt instruments, which, in turn, influences the number of recognition proceedings in these jurisdictions. In addition, both jurisdictions are also *restructuring hubs* equipped with advanced statutory mechanisms and case law principles, as well as competent judges who apply the law. These factors naturally impact litigation involving cross-border restructuring issues in these jurisdictions in terms of well-established principles and the competence of judges. Finally, the rule protecting creditors, which has been touched on earlier, is almost specific to English law. On the other hand, American courts have a long record of granting comity to foreign insolvency and restructuring proceedings.[26] The fact that the recognition of the restructuring proceedings of the International Bank of Azerbaijan ("IBA"), an exemplary case that will be discussed in section C.I, was sought in these two jurisdictions is also a relevant factor. After analysing those jurisdictions, this work will suggest a middle-ground model drawing primarily on the American approach.

Part D will examine the traditional safeguards in recognising foreign judgments as part of this model, namely, public policy and procedural fairness. This work will discuss several important aspects of each safeguard, mainly in the context of recognising restructuring plans under the MLCBI.

Then, this work will turn to the analysis of substantive fairness. Part E will generally analyse substantive fairness in restructuring proceedings without considering a cross-border context. It will also examine how the concept is implemented in different jurisdictions. Part F will develop a framework to ensure substantive fairness in considering the recognition of restructuring plans under the MLCBI as part of the model suggested in this

26 See sub-s C.II.2.

work. As already noted, the *adequate protection* safeguard under article 22 (1) of the MLCBI will be closely examined in this context.

B. Introduction to Cross-Border Restructuring

As already identified, the problem of this research concerns fairness in achieving the cross-border effects of restructuring plans. Before delving into the research problem, it is essential to discuss the foundations of debt restructuring with a particular focus on its cross-border aspects. Part B will aim to accomplish this goal. Section B.I will be devoted to the legal nature of restructuring proceedings. This analysis will reveal that most scholars view restructuring proceedings as insolvency proceedings and see these proceedings, in one form or another, within the existing cross-border insolvency system. This work, too, will conclude that the use of cross-border insolvency frameworks to achieve the cross-border effects of restructuring proceedings is, in principle, acceptable. Sections B.II and B.III, therefore, will further explore the underlying principles and instruments of cross-border insolvency law, respectively. Section B.IV will summarise the points discussed in this Part.

I. Legal Nature of Restructuring Proceedings

Insolvency law governs the collective satisfaction of claims against an insolvent debtor.[27] This is done by administering and realising the debtor's entire asset pool and distributing the proceeds among creditors under statutory distribution rules.[28] By preventing individual actions, insolvency law aims, *inter alia*, to maximise the value of the debtor's estate, ultimately benefiting creditors as a general body.[29] In situations where the debtor has a going concern value, keeping the business intact is more advantageous for creditors as a whole.[30] One way to achieve this is to sell the entire business to a third party and distribute the proceeds from the sale among

27 Ian F. Fletcher, *The Law of Insolvency* (5th edn, Sweet & Maxwell 2017) paras 1-007-08.

28 ibid para 1-008.

29 Kristin van Zwieten (ed), *Goode on Principles of Corporate Insolvency Law* (5th edn, Sweet & Maxwell 2018) para 2-04.

30 Douglas G. Baird, 'Priority Matters: Absolute Priority, Relative Priority, and the Costs of Bankruptcy' (2016) 165 U Pa L Rev 785, 789

the existing claimants.[31] However, it is essential to acknowledge that finding a third-party buyer willing or able to pay a price close to the going concern value of the business may be challenging for different reasons.[32] In such instances, the going concern value can be best preserved by restructuring existing claims against the debtor.[33] Modern restructuring frameworks are designed to facilitate this process.

That said, the legal nature of restructuring proceedings is far from clear. Several doctrinal approaches have been suggested in that regard. The debate is mainly about whether the same set of rules and principles should be applied to both insolvency and restructuring proceedings and, if not, what rules and principles should govern the latter. The PRD, which envisages the availability of restructuring mechanisms for not-yet-insolvent debtors, led to a more intense debate on the issue, particularly regarding the cross-border effects of such proceedings.[34] The matter is particularly relevant from the perspective of debt discharge, as these two proceedings do not treat discharge similarly. That is to say, insolvency proceedings affect the enforcement of pre-insolvency entitlements rather than discharging them outright in the eyes of substantive law.[35] Restructuring proceedings, on the contrary, can directly modify creditors' entitlements under the original debt instruments.[36] Under some frameworks, there is no way back, even if the debtor fails to fulfil the obligations under the confirmed plan. The reorganisation procedure under the US Bankruptcy Code ("BC"),[37] more specifically, under Chapter 11 of the BC ("Chapter 11"), is a notable example in this context: once the restructuring plan has been confirmed and become final, the debtor is discharged of all the original debts and can be sued

---

31 ibid.

32 ibid 789-90.

33 ibid.

34 See, eg, generally Dominik Skauradszun and Walter Nijnens, 'Brussels Ia or EIR Recast? The Allocation of Preventive Restructuring Frameworks' (2019) 16 Int Corp Res 193; Irit Mevorach and Adrian Walters, 'The Characterization of Pre-Insolvency Proceedings in Private International Law' (2020) 21 EBOR 855.

35 Generally, discharge only occurs once insolvency proceedings have been terminated and the debtor has been liquidated. Even in this scenario, one cannot talk about full discharge since creditors may still enforce the unpaid part of their claims against the debtor's assets discovered after the latter's liquidation. See, eg, German Insolvency Code (Insolvenzordnung ["InsO"]), s 201. For a more detailed discussion, see Riz Mokal, 'What is an Insolvency Proceeding? *Gategroup* Lands in a Gated Community' (2022) 31 Intl Ins Rev 418, 422.

36 Madaus, 'The Cross-border Effects of Restructurings' (n 3) 480.

37 Title 11 of the US Code ("BC").

by the creditors only for the breach of the plan, not the original debt contracts.[38]

Section B.I will first summarise two main doctrinal approaches to the legal nature of restructuring proceedings in a purely domestic context, i.e. without considering a cross-border setting (B.I.1). It will then outline the cross-border implications of the respective approaches (B.I.2). This work will also briefly take a stance on the nature of restructuring proceedings in both contexts (B.I.3).

1. Restructuring Proceedings in a Domestic Setting

Below, this work will summarise two main approaches to the nature of restructuring proceedings. For the purposes of this work, they will be referred to as the *insolvency* and *contractual* approaches.

a) The Insolvency Approach

The insolvency approach, championed by most scholars and practitioners from across the globe, views restructuring proceedings as a form of insolvency proceedings. The idea is prevalent in the US, where the Constitution prohibits non-consensual impairment of debt under the contract law of individual states.[39] US scholars such as Thomas Jackson[40] and Douglas Baird[41] define restructuring as a form of insolvency proceedings in which the business is hypothetically sold as a going concern to the existing claimants (e.g. creditors) of the debtor instead of a third party. This definition is given as part of the *Creditors' Bargain Theory* on insolvency law, which suggests that insolvency law mirrors the mechanism that creditors would themselves *ex ante* agree upon for the insolvency scenario of the debtor, *inter alia*, to avoid dismantling the insolvent business through

38 Rodrigo Olivares-Caminal and others, *Debt Restructuring* (3rd edn, OUP 2022) para 3.130.

39 The Constitution of the US, art I, s 10, cl 1. For a more detailed discussion, see Madaus, 'A Proposal to Divide the Realms of Insolvency and Restructuring Law' (n 4) 628-29.

40 Thomas H. Jackson, 'Bankruptcy, Non-Bankruptcy Entitlements, and the Creditors' Bargain' (1982) 91 Yale LJ 857, 893ff.

41 Douglas G. Baird, 'The Uneasy Case for Corporate Reorganizations' (1986) 15 (1) J Legal Stud 127, 139.

individual advantage-taking creditor actions (thus, responding to the *common pool* problem).[42] Another US scholar, Jay Westbrook, who extensively publishes on cross-border insolvency matters, underscores *in rem* nature of restructuring proceedings based on insolvency (bankruptcy) theory on restructuring.[43]

The concept has strong support outside the US as well. Dutch scholar Rolef de Weijs defines restructuring as an alternative to liquidation under insolvency law but addressing the problem of *anticommons* rather than that of *common pool.*[44] English scholar and practitioner Riz Mokal suggests the purposive and contextual classification of insolvency law under which a restructuring proceeding shall be considered an insolvency proceeding when the proceeding operates pursuant to a law that is able to respond to 'circumstances peculiar to insolvency' and with respect to a 'sufficiently insolvent' (or 'insufficiently solvent') debtor.[45] To him, the fact that such proceeding may also be applied to a solvent debtor, as in the case of the English scheme of arrangement,[46] is irrelevant for the purposes of the classification.[47] Singaporean judge Kannan Ramesh criticises the contractual approach to debt discharge in restructuring proceedings, highlighting policy considerations behind such discharge.[48] Although he defines a scheme of arrangement 'as a statutory mechanism for the adjustment of contractual rights not predicated on the insolvency of the corporation', he underscores the circumstances

42 See generally Jackson (n 40). It should be noted that several alternative theories have also been advanced in US scholarship. See, eg, generally Robert K. Rasmussen, 'Debtor's Choice: A Menu Approach to Corporate Bankruptcy' (1992) 71 Tex L Rev 51 (*Menu Approach*); Anthony J. Casey, 'Chapter 11's Renegotiation Framework and the Purpose of Corporate Bankruptcy' (2020) 120 Colum L Rev 1709 (*New Bargaining Theory*).

43 Westbrook, 'Comity and Choice of Law' (n 12) 263. See also Jay Lawrence Westbrook, 'Interpretation Internationale' (2015) 87 Temp L Rev 739, 748; Jay Westbrook, 'Ian Fletcher and the Internationalist Principle' (2015) 3 NIBLeJ 30 565 <https://ssrn.com/abstract=3064868> accessed 21 October 2025, 566.

44 Rolef de Weijs, 'Too Big to Fail as a Game of Chicken with the State: What Insolvency Law Theory Has to Say About TBTF and Vice Versa' (2013) 14 EBOR 201, 210-12.

45 Mokal, 'What is an Insolvency Proceeding?' (n 35) 429.

46 For a more detailed discussion of the English scheme of arrangement, see sub-s E.II.2.b).

47 In relation to such debtor, the proceeding should not be considered as an insolvency proceeding as per Riz Mokal's classification. See Mokal, 'What is an Insolvency Proceeding?' (n 35) 429.

48 Kannan Ramesh, 'The Gibbs Principle - A Tether on the Feet of Good Forum Shopping' (2017) 29 SAcLJ 42, para 21ff.

in light of which these proceedings typically occur.[49] To him, they are sought mainly by insolvent corporations as a debtor-in-possession regime to restructure debt obligations, and this context should not be disregarded while considering the legal nature of schemes of arrangement.[50] Hence, he underscores the insolvency underpinnings of schemes of arrangement.[51] Kannan Ramesh's criticism of the (mis)characterisation of discharge as a contractual (rather than an insolvency law) matter is supported by US bankruptcy judge Martin Glenn.[52]

These examples are illustrative of the global support for the insolvency approach.

b) The Contractual Approach

Stephan Madaus provides a detailed exposition of the contractual approach, which offers a different perspective.[53] He draws a normative distinction between insolvency and restructuring proceedings and argues against applying insolvency law rules and principles to the latter.[54] In his view, the main purpose of insolvency law is to prevent the overuse, through uncoordinated creditor actions, of the insufficient common pool of the debtor's remaining assets.[55] Restructuring proceedings, says Stephan Madaus, whether they respond to a present common pool problem or aim to prevent one, focus on the debtor's future income, which is not part of the common pool of the debtor's remaining assets.[56] Here, the purpose is, according to him, to prevent an underuse of common goods (the *anticommons* problem).[57] Stephan Madaus, thus, argues that:

> Any solution that goes beyond the common pool requires an agreement between the debtor and (most of) his creditors (about future income). Such a solution is always a contractual

49 ibid para 28.
50 ibid.
51 ibid.
52 *In re Agrokor dd* 591 BR 163, 195 (Bankr SDNY 2018) (*Agrokor*).
53 See generally Madaus, 'A Proposal to Divide the Realms of Insolvency and Restructuring Law' (n 4).
54 ibid.
55 ibid 619-21, 623-24.
56 ibid 621-623.
57 ibid 633ff.

> solution and, consequently, any legal framework supporting the conclusion of such agreements (restructuring law) should be based on contract and company law principles instead of those of a liquidation (insolvency principles).[58]

In simple terms, Stephan Madaus defines restructuring proceedings as a court-assisted execution of a contract.[59] As to the issue of binding holdouts under contract law, which would otherwise contradict the core contract law principle of party autonomy, he suggests referring to other contract law principles (doctrines) such as hardship, abuse of rights, bad faith, self-contradictory behaviour as a solution.[60]

2. Restructuring Proceedings in a Cross-Border Setting

Restructuring proceedings can be purely domestic. This is the case when the debtor has no business and assets abroad, all stakeholders, including creditors, are local, and all claims against the debtor are governed by local law and so on. Such proceedings generally do not require legal action abroad. That said, globalisation and the internet bring increasingly international elements to previously purely local businesses. The COVID-19 pandemic has undoubtedly accelerated this trend, particularly for online services that do not adhere to borders. Once an international element is involved, one can no longer talk about the purely domestic nature of the restructuring. That is to say, the restructuring is now considered to be of an *international* or *cross-border* nature.

In restructuring proceedings, international elements often involve foreign creditors with claims governed by foreign laws and/or the presence of assets located abroad.[61] Domestic restructuring laws generally apply to restructuring proceedings in a scenario with one or more international elements, too. Nonetheless, once restructuring proceedings "cross" borders, a number of additional cross-border issues arise. These include determining which state's court should administer the case, under which law substantive

58 ibid 618.

59 ibid 637.

60 ibid 629-30, 637-38.

61 For a more detailed discussion of the features of internationality in insolvency (restructuring) proceedings, see van Zwieten (ed), *Principles of Corporate Insolvency Law* (n 29) para 16-02.

rights should be modified, and how to bind dissenting creditors in other jurisdictions.[62]

The varying opinions within the academic community regarding the legal nature of restructuring proceedings also apply in a cross-border context. More to the point, there is no global consensus in scholarship as to whether the existing cross-border insolvency frameworks should extend to the recognition and enforcement of restructuring plans. If not, a secondary question to answer is what the other options are.

a) The Insolvency Approach

For scholars who are fully committed to the insolvency approach in a domestic context, the answer to the first question above is straightforward: affirmative.[63] Since they view restructuring proceedings as insolvency proceedings, it logically follows that such proceedings fall within the scope of cross-border insolvency frameworks.

Some scholars support, in principle, the idea of cross-border insolvency instruments applying to restructuring proceedings but with some qualifiers, albeit different in each case. Horst Eidenmuller suggests limiting cross-border insolvency frameworks only to the fully collective restructuring proceedings, i.e. ones that affect all creditors.[64] As already noted, according to Riz Mokal, restructuring proceedings shall fall within the scope of cross-border insolvency instruments when they pertain to an insolvent debtor.[65] Irit Mevorach and Adrian Walters are in favour of the inclusion of pre-insolvency restructurings in the existing cross-border insolvency system built mainly upon the principle of modified universalism but generally stress the importance of safeguards (such as *public policy* and *adequate protection*) under such a system to address unique aspects of those proceedings.[66]

62 For a more detailed discussion of the issues of cross-border insolvency and restructuring (from the angle of English law), see ibid para 16-03.

63 See, eg, generally Westbrook, 'Internationalist Principle' (n 43); Westbrook, 'Comity and Choice of Law' (n 12) 263.

64 Horst Eidenmuller, 'What Is an Insolvency Proceeding' (2018) 92 Am Bankr LJ 53, 65ff.

65 Mokal, 'What is an Insolvency Proceeding?' (n 35) 442. See also text to nn 45, 47.

66 Mevorach and Walters (n 34) 877ff.

b) The Contractual Approach

Stephan Madaus defends his contractual approach in a cross-border context, too, by generally favouring international civil procedure or contract law frameworks.[67] He opposes the use of cross-border insolvency frameworks, which are designed for asset-oriented insolvency proceedings, in the context of restructuring proceedings, highlighting the debt-oriented nature of the latter.[68] Accordingly, Stephan Madaus suggests a new framework for the recognition of the cross border effects of restructuring plans, which stipulates that a restructuring of substantive rights should be conducted under the law with the 'closest connection', namely, the governing law of the contract (in the case where the affected contracts are governed by several laws: a law governing 'a clear majority' of these contracts or agreed as such by 'a qualified majority' of creditors) and should be recognised globally through general private international law mechanisms (both the applicable law and judgement recognition routes).[69] In the event that it is not possible to determine a specific law with the closest connection, in his view, a foreign debt may be modified under the *lex fori concursus*, but 'substantive limits' of the governing law of the contract should be respected (establishing, thus, a 'sufficient connection' to that law) in order to achieve the cross-border effects through the judgement recognition route.[70] Without such sufficient connection, according to him, any cross-border effect should not be expected.[71]

---

67 Madaus, 'A Proposal to Divide the Realms of Insolvency and Restructuring Law' (n 4) 643-44.

68 Madaus, 'The Cross-border Effects of Restructurings' (n 3) 479-82.

69 ibid 483-84.

70 ibid 484-86. This work will return to this point in sub-s F.II.2.b)dd). See also Stephan Madaus, 'Corporate Reorganisation Law and the Shaping Powers of Market Realities and Doctrinal Concepts' (2022) 42 OJLS 1195, 1211, where Stephan Madaus concludes that the cross-border effects of the plan should be denied in the respective jurisdictions with respect to rights of stakeholders if '(i) the impairment under the foreign plan is not in line with the policy choice of the *lex causae* and (ii) the impaired stakeholders are worse off under the plan compared to a restructuring under the *lex causae*'.

71 Madaus, 'The Cross-border Effects of Restructurings' (n 3) 485.

3. Position on the Legal Nature of Restructuring Proceedings

Below, this work will briefly present its own perspective on the legal nature of restructuring proceedings, both in a domestic setting and concerning cross-border effects.

a) Domestic Context

To begin with, this work fully agrees with the argument that, unlike asset-oriented insolvency proceedings, restructuring proceedings are mainly debt-oriented.[72] That is to say, the primary focus of these proceedings is not the collective satisfaction of claimants (of the debtor) by realising the debtor's assets. Instead, they aim to preserve the going concern value of the debtor for the collective benefit of the claimants by modifying the latter's claims with a binding effect on holdouts. Hence, if the restructuring proves successful, the debtor will not be liquidated and will generally continue to trade (with assets remaining wholly or partly untouched but original obligations being permanently discharged), which can even lead to a profitable business over the years.[73] Against this backdrop, this work does not consider restructuring proceedings of a purely insolvency nature.

72 ibid 479-80.

73 Take the IBA as an example. After successfully restructuring some of its liabilities (see s C.I) and as a result of other rescue measures implemented in Azerbaijan, such as the transfer of its non-performing loan portfolio to a state-owned corporation (see Decree of the President of the Republic of Azerbaijan on the measures for rehabilitation related to the preparations for privatising the state-owned shares of "the International Bank of Azerbaijan" [No 507, dated 15 July 2015]), the IBA turned out to be a viable business generating profits (For the IBA's IFRS financial statements, see International Bank of Azerbaijan, 'Reports' <https://abb-bank.az/en/hesabatlar> accessed 21 October 2025). In the context of questioning the US bankruptcy approach to restructuring (viewing restructuring as a hypothetical sale to creditors), Sarah Paterson also highlights that 'if one class retains equity after the restructuring then ... it has the chance to benefit from potentially unlimited future upside if the company returns to profitability. ... other creditors may see their claims written down or even written off completely, in a way that certainly does crystallise their loss' Sarah Paterson, 'The Conceptual Foundation of Cross-class Cramdown' (18 September 2024) <https://papers.ssrn.com/sol3/papers.cfm?abstract_id=4959732> accessed 21 October 2025, 15.

That said, this work does not characterise restructuring proceedings as purely contractual either.[74] Hence, this work agrees with the arguments that under restructuring frameworks, the modification of obligations does not occur in the ordinary course of circumstances.[75] Besides the process (of the modification of obligations), its background (the debtor's distress) is also a crucial factor to consider. In most cases, the alternative to the restructuring is the debtor's asset-oriented insolvency, whether through going concern or piecemeal sale. In this alternative scenario, claimants of the debtor would not be able to enforce their original claims according to general rules of private law but rather seek some recovery (if any) from the existing assets of the debtor under the statutory order of distribution.[76] It is not a coincidence that fairness tests under restructuring frameworks generally look at the alternative scenario as a comparator, which, again, is the debtor's insolvency in most cases.[77] Accordingly, the insolvency-related background of restructuring proceedings should not be disregarded.

Furthermore, general rules and principles of contract law might be limited in addressing all the issues that arise from restructuring, in particular, binding holdouts to the will of the majority (assessing fairness in this context) and moratoriums (as the case may be). In addition, restructuring frameworks are driven by broader policy objectives, such as maintaining

74 While questioning the US bankruptcy (insolvency) approach to restructuring and underscoring that 'Restructurings require a new bargain, achieved either through private bargaining or court order…', Sarah Paterson also notes that 'This does not require us to equate a restructuring squarely with contract law, or to draw divisions between fully inclusive or selective corporate restructurings'. Sarah Paterson, 'A Qualified Defence of the Rule in Gibbs' (15 April 2025) LSE Legal Studies Working Paper 6/2025 <https://papers.ssrn.com/sol3/papers.cfm?abstract_id=5218429> accessed 21 October 2025, pt III. This approach builds on her earlier proposition that restructuring law and insolvency law should be treated as distinct branches of what she refers to as 'the law of corporate distress'. See generally Sarah Paterson, 'Rethinking the Role of the Law of Corporate Distress in the Twenty-First Century' (2014) LSE Law, Society and Economy Working Papers 27/2014 <https://eprints.lse.ac.uk/60583/1/WPS2014-27_Paterson.pdf> accessed 21 October 2025. In the US context, while describing Chapter 11 as a framework for the renegotiation of incomplete contracts in financial distress as part of his New Bargaining Theory of bankruptcy, Anthony Casey argues that general contract law is not the appropriate venue for addressing the problem (of incomplete contracts in financial distress) due to, *inter alia*, the ubiquity of the issue. Casey (n 42) pt II.

75 See, eg, text to nn 48, 49, 50.

76 For a more detailed discussion, see sub-s E.I.1.

77 For a discussion of the fairness tests under US and English laws as well as the PRD, see s E.II.

the stability of the financial sector and economy as a whole and preventing the loss of jobs or know-how.[78] Addressing these broader objectives goes beyond the goals and capabilities of contract law.

Hence, restructuring proceedings should be characterised as neither purely contractual nor purely insolvency-related but rather as *sui generis*. While being primarily debt-oriented procedures, restructuring proceedings may have rules and principles peculiar to them or employ those of insolvency law necessary to achieve their objectives. The matter, however, will not be explored further in this work.[79] That is because this work focuses mainly on the cross-border aspects of restructuring proceedings. The cross-border model suggested in this work, built on the *sui generis* nature of restructuring proceedings, will also function under both the insolvency and contractual approaches to restructuring. However, some compromises will be necessary from each approach, as will become evident as this work unfolds.

b) Cross-Border Effects

In light of the position outlined above, this work, in principle, does not argue against achieving the cross-border effects of restructuring proceedings through cross-border insolvency frameworks, given the advantages that the respective route offers.[80] However, restructuring proceedings should be differentiated from asset-oriented insolvency proceedings and the debt-oriented nature of the former should not be disregarded. Hence, the interests of the parties to the debt in question (the debtor and the dissenting foreign creditor) should be balanced in recognising restructuring plans through cross-border insolvency frameworks. This work will attempt to determine whether it is possible under those frameworks. For the reasons articulated in section A.II, the present work will use the MLCBI framework as a model for this discussion. Hence, this work will deeply explore the MLCBI and

78 See, eg, MLCBI (n 17) Preamble (e); PRD (n 15), recs 2-3. See also Paterson, 'The Conceptual Foundation' (n 73) 20.

79 That said, the differences between restructuring and insolvency proceedings or distinction from the pure contractual approach may be discussed throughout this work in different contexts.

80 For a discussion of the advantages, see particularly sub-s B.II.3.a).

the safeguards thereunder to determine whether these safeguards suffice to strike the respective balance.[81]

II. Principles of Cross-Border Insolvency Law

As identified earlier, this work will focus on the cross-border effects of restructuring plans within the cross-border insolvency system, in particular under the MLCBI. Below, this work will outline the fundamental principles underpinning the existing cross-border insolvency system. This work will first discuss the comity doctrine from which some of the important principles of cross-border insolvency stem. Then, it will turn to more specific principles of cross-border insolvency law, particularly those relevant to the focus of this work. Some of those principles compete with each other, i.e. unity versus plurality and universality versus territoriality. This work will mainly focus on the ones (out of each pair) with overwhelming scholarly support and that are reflected in the modern instruments of cross-border insolvency.

1. Comity

Under the doctrine of territorial sovereignty, insolvency or restructuring proceedings (judgments issued in the framework of such proceedings) in one state have effect only within that state, unless other states accept their cross-border effects.[82] Hence, a foundation should be in place for recognising the effect of a law or a judgment (including one associated with insolvency or restructuring proceedings) belonging to one jurisdiction in other jurisdictions. An essential concept playing a crucial role in this context is the *comity* doctrine, initially developed by Dutch scholars in the seventeenth century[83] and later introduced and widely invoked in common

81 This aligns with Irit Mevorach and Adrian Walter's general idea of using safeguards under the MLCBI to address the peculiarities of pre-insolvency restructurings (see text to n 66).

82 Fletcher (n 27) paras 28-020-21.

83 For a discussion of the origins of the doctrine, see generally Hessel E. Yntema, 'The Comity Doctrine' (1966) 65 Mich L Rev 9; Joel R. Paul, 'Comity in International Law' (1991) 32 Harv Intl L J 1, 12-17.

law jurisdictions such as England and the US.[84] Despite having been frequently invoked in these jurisdictions, particularly in the US, the doctrine is also known for its ambiguity.[85] In *Hilton v. Guyot*, the US Supreme Court ("USSC") famously redefined the doctrine as follows:

> No law has any effect, of its own force, beyond the limits of the sovereignty from which its authority is derived. The extent to which the law of one nation, as put in force within its territory, whether by executive order, by legislative act, or by judicial decree, shall be allowed to operate within the dominion of another nation, depends upon what our greatest jurists have been content to call "the comity of nations." Although the phrase has been often criticised, no satisfactory substitute has been suggested.
>
> "Comity," in the legal sense, is neither a matter of absolute obligation, on the one hand, nor of mere courtesy and good will, upon the other. But it is the recognition which one nation allows within its territory to the legislative, executive or judicial acts of another nation, having due regard both to international duty and convenience, and to the rights of its own citizens or of other persons who are under the protection of its laws.[86]

Comity was also defined by US courts as a rule of 'practice, convenience, and expediency' rather than 'a rule of law'.[87] It has also been stated that US courts consider 'the interests of the United States, the interests of the foreign state or states involved, and the mutual interests of the family of nations in just and efficiently functioning rules of international law' while

84 For a discussion of the history of the introduction of the doctrine and further developments in the mentioned jurisdictions, see generally D. J. Llewelyn Davies, 'The Influence of Huber's De Conflictu Legum on English Private International Law' (1937) 18 Brit YB Intl L 49; generally Kurt H. Nadelmann, 'Introduction - The Comity Doctrine' (1966) 65 Mich L Rev 1; Paul (n 83) 17-24; William S. Dodge, 'International Comity in American Law' (2015) 115 Colum L Rev 2071, 2084-98.

85 Paul (n 83) 8-11; Dodge (n 84) 2073-76.

86 *Hilton v. Guyot*, 159 US 113, 163-64 (1895).

87 *Ad Hoc Group of Vitro Noteholders v. Vitro S.A.B. de C.V.*, 701 F.3d 1031, 1044 (5th Cir 2012) (*Vitro*) (citations omitted).

applying comity.[88] These definitions, particularly the one given by the *Hilton* court, have been scrutinised in the literature.[89]

The doctrine of comity has significantly shaped the evolution of modern cross-border insolvency law. It has been suggested that the concept of modified universalism, which is one of the key principles of modern cross-border insolvency law, is essentially an expansion of the doctrine of comity specific to cross-border insolvency.[90] In a cross-border insolvency context, too, the doctrine has been widely invoked particularly in common law jurisdictions.[91] As it will be observed in subsection C.II.2 of this work, US courts extensively refer to the doctrine while exercising their discretion to defer to foreign insolvency or restructuring proceedings. The following remarks by a US Circuit Court illustrate the importance of the comity doctrine in cross-border insolvency:

> The rationale underlying the granting of comity to a final foreign judgment is that litigation should end after the parties have had an opportunity to present their cases fully and fairly to a court of competent jurisdiction. The extending of comity to a foreign bankruptcy proceeding ... has a somewhat different rationale. The granting of comity to a foreign bankruptcy proceeding enables the assets of a debtor to be dispersed in an equitable, orderly, and systematic manner, rather than in a haphazard, erratic or piecemeal fashion.[92]

---

88 ibid 1053 (citations omitted).

89 For a critical analysis of this definition, see Paul (n 83) 8-11; Dodge (n 84) 2074-75.

90 Westbrook, 'Comity and Choice of Law' (n 12) 260.

91 Andrew Godwin, Timothy Howse and Ian Ramsay. 'The Inherent Power of Common Law Courts to Provide Assistance in Cross-Border Insolvencies: From Comity to Complexity' (2017) 26 Intl Ins Rev 5, 7-9.

92 *Cunard Steamship Co. v. Salen Reefer Services AB*, 773 F2d 452, 457-58 (2d Cir 1985). For a more detailed discussion of this case, see Douglass G. Boshkoff, 'United States Judicial Assistance in Cross-Border Insolvencies'(1987) 36 Intl Comp LQ 729, 731-35.

2. Unity Versus Plurality

The principle of unity envisages a single set of proceedings governing the debtor's insolvency.[93] According to the principle, the court of the state with which the debtor has the strongest legal connection has such exclusive jurisdiction, and all other states recognise this exclusivity.[94] The competing principle is plurality, which allows multiple proceedings, such as when the debtor's assets are located in more than one state.[95] Although a single set of (unified) proceedings is desirable from a theoretical point of view,[96] several practical factors may necessitate additional proceedings.[97]

3. Universality (Universalism) Versus Territoriality (Territorialism)

The principle of universality envisages the universal effect of proceedings governing the debtor's insolvency to encompass its assets worldwide.[98] As the purpose of the principle of unity cannot be achieved without such universal effect, these two principles are closely connected,[99] together forming what is known as *universalism*.[100] The competing principle is territoriality, according to which the effect of insolvency proceedings opened in one state

---

93 Reinhard Bork, *Principles of Cross-Border Insolvency Law* (Intersentia 2017) para 2.2; Fletcher (n 27) para 28-004. See also van Zwieten (ed), *Principles of Corporate Insolvency Law* (n 29) para 16-04; Irit Mevorach, *The Future of Cross-Border Insolvency: Overcoming Biases and Closing Gaps* (OUP 2018) 3.

94 van Zwieten (ed), *Principles of Corporate Insolvency Law* (n 29) para 16-04 (fn 9 therein and accompanying text).

95 Bork, *Principles of Cross-Border Insolvency Law* (n 93) para 2.2; Fletcher (n 27) para 28-004. See also van Zwieten (ed), *Principles of Corporate Insolvency Law* (n 29) para 16-04, Mevorach, *The Future of Cross-Border Insolvency* (n 93) 4.

96 For a discussion of the advantages of the principle of the unity over the principle of plurality, see Bork, *Principles of Cross-Border Insolvency Law* (n 93) paras 2.3-4.

97 Bork, *Principles of Cross-Border Insolvency Law* (n 93) paras 2.5-6; Fletcher (n 27) para 28-004.

98 Bork, *Principles of Cross-Border Insolvency Law* (n 93) para 2.8; Fletcher (n 27) para 28-004; See also van Zwieten (ed), *Principles of Corporate Insolvency Law* (n 29) para 16-04; Mevorach, *The Future of Cross-Border Insolvency* (n 93) 3.

99 That said, they are not interchangeable. For a more detailed discussion, see Bork, *Principles of Cross-Border Insolvency Law* (n 93) para 2.12; van Zwieten (ed), *Principles of Corporate Insolvency Law* (n 29) para 16-04.

100 Jay Lawrence Westbrook, 'A Global Solution to Multinational Default' (2000) 98 Mich L Rev 2276, 2297. See also Mevorach, *The Future of Cross-Border Insolvency* (n 93) 3.

shall be confined to the assets located in that state.[101] *Territorialism* is a concept based on the principles of territoriality and plurality.[102] Despite being the historical approach[103] and the multi-fold advantages of universalism as will be summarised below, territorialism still preserves its relevance globally because states are often reluctant to relinquish all of their sovereign powers and prefer to maintain its certain elements.[104]

a) Advantages of Universalism

The system rooted in the concept of single proceedings coupled with universal effect offers numerous benefits such as value maximisation, just treatment of all creditors worldwide, enhanced chances of rescue, and a higher level of predictability and, thus, elevates the core objectives of insolvency law to a global scale.[105] As to the advantages in relation to restructurings specifically, Jay Westbrook notes that 'a sufficient guarantee of legal certainty' is of utmost importance for a successful restructuring plan, which is possible only in a single system settling the legal rights of all stakeholders with binding effect on all of them.[106]

101 Fletcher (n 27) para 28-004; van Zwieten (ed), *Principles of Corporate Insolvency Law* (n 29) para 16-04.

102 Mevorach, *The Future of Cross-Border Insolvency* (n 93) 4. For a summary of both approaches (universalism and territorialism) and current theories emerging from their convergence, see Edward S. Adams and Jason K. Finche, 'Coordinating Cross-Border Bankruptcy: How Territorialism Saves Universalism' (2008) 15 Colum J Eur L 43, 47ff; van Zwieten (ed), *Principles of Corporate Insolvency Law* (n 29) paras 16-04-07. See also Paul J. Omar, 'The Landscape of International Insolvency Law' (2002) 11 Intl Ins Rev 173, 176-181.

103 Adams and Finche (n 102) 47.

104 Frederick Tung, 'Is International Bankruptcy Possible' (2001) 23 Mich J Intl L 31, pt II; Adams and Finche (n 102) 53; Fletcher (n 27) para 28-020; van Zwieten (ed), *Principles of Corporate Insolvency Law* (n 29) para 16-05.

105 Westbrook, 'A Global Solution' (n 100) 2292-94. See also Mevorach, *The Future of Cross-Border Insolvency* (n 93) 5ff. For a comparative analysis of the advantages of universalism and the disadvantages of the concurrent proceedings with territorial effect, see van Zwieten (ed), *Principles of Corporate Insolvency Law* (n 29) para 16-05.

106 Westbrook, 'A Global Solution' (n 100) 2285-86. For a discussion of the advantages of the universalist system concerning restructuring proceedings, see also Mevorach, *The Future of Cross-Border Insolvency* (n 93) 11-12; Westbrook, 'Comity and Choice of Law' (n 12) 266.

b) Main Features of Universalism

Jay Westbrook identifies two distinct pivotal aspects of universalism: a single court controlling and a single law governing each cross-border insolvency case.[107] According to him, either of these elements can be achieved by two different approaches: (i) the establishment of a single international court system and bankruptcy law (the more desirable option, according to him) or (ii) the development of a uniform set of choice-of-forum and choice-of-law rules.[108]

Reinhard Bork summarises the main features of the principle of universalism (which largely corresponds to Jay Westbrook's second approach outlined above) as follows: (i) exclusive international jurisdiction (to open main insolvency proceedings) of the state within the territory of which the debtor is domiciled; (ii) the law of this state to govern the proceedings; (iii) the worldwide effect of such insolvency proceedings; (iv) unlimited control of the insolvency practitioner over the assets, including those located in a foreign state; (v) extension of the effects of the proceedings to the complete legal relationship between the debtor and its creditors; (vi) acceptance the features mentioned above by all other states; and (vii) cooperation and assistance of foreign states.[109]

c) Implementation of Universalism: A Need for a Global Consensus

As noted above, a concept based on a single set of proceedings with universal effect offers numerous advantages. That said, to properly function in the real world, it requires the agreement of all states as dictated by the doctrine of legal sovereignty.[110] Claiming the universal effect of proceedings opened in one jurisdiction is only one element of universalism (outgoing universalism).[111] There is, however, another element that is not less important: acceptance of such universal effect by all other affected jurisdictions

107 Westbrook, 'A Global Solution' (n 100) 2292.
108 ibid. However, he describes any form of the latter approach as *lesser universalism* (ibid 2315-18).
109 Bork, *Principles of Cross-Border Insolvency Law* (n 93) para 2.16.
110 See text to n 82.
111 Bork, *Principles of Cross-Border Insolvency Law* (n 93) paras 2.8-9.

(incoming universalism).[112] As already mentioned, it is the latter that is challenging to achieve in reality.[113]

4. Modified Universalism

As noted above, achieving full universalism would require a global consensus, which is unlikely to occur in the near future.[114] Until such a consensus is reached (if ever), an interim principle is needed to guide administering cross-border insolvency cases. Several solutions have been suggested to address this need, with the most prominent one being *modified universalism* by Jay Westbrook.[115]

Under the principle of modified universalism, the debtor's default is dealt with from a global perspective (a single court and a single law), as in the case of universalism, on the one hand.[116] On the other hand, deference to the proceedings in the debtor's home jurisdiction occurs only after evaluating the respective proceedings (and applicable law thereto) and 'practical finding of fairness and rough similarity' by courts of all other affected jurisdictions.[117] This allows foreign courts to ensure, *inter alia,* that foreign creditors have been fairly treated in the debtor's home jurisdiction.[118]

As stated earlier, modified universalism is commonly perceived as an interim solution operational in the real world until full universalism is attained. That said, it has also been suggested that modified universalism be reconceptualised from an interim solution into a 'stand-alone norm' (by separating from universalism).[119]

---

112 ibid para 2.10.

113 See text to n 104.

114 Westbrook, 'A Global Solution' (n 100) 2299; Bork, *Principles of Cross-Border Insolvency Law* (n 93) para 2.11.

115 Westbrook, 'A Global Solution' (n 100) 2299ff. Other solutions include (but not limited to) cooperative territoriality (see Lynn M. LoPucki, 'Cooperation in International Bankruptcy: A Post-Universalist Approach' (1998-1999) 84 Cornell L Rev 696, 742ff), universal proceduralism (see Edward J. Janger, 'Universal Proceduralism' (2007) 32 Brook J Intl L 819, 834ff) and an approach based on the debtor's *ex ante* selection of the jurisdiction for the administration of its insolvency (see Robert K. Rasmussen, 'A New Approach to Transnational Insolvencies' (1997) 19 Mich J Intl L 1, 32ff).

116 Westbrook, 'A Global Solution' (n 100) 2301.

117 ibid.

118 van Zwieten (ed), *Principles of Corporate Insolvency Law* (n 29) para 16-06.

119 Mevorach, *The Future of Cross-Border Insolvency* (n 93) 108ff.

This work will later identify that the principle of modified universalism lies at the core of the MLCBI and, therefore, is of the utmost relevance for the purposes of this research. Hence, it is something to be returned to in greater detail as this work progresses.

5. Mutual Trust

One of the fundamental principles of a cross-border insolvency system based on universalism (through a uniform set of choice-of-law and choice-of-forum rules) is mutual trust.[120] Without mutual trust in one another's legal system, it is difficult to imagine a group of states agreeing to the automatic, group-wide recognition of the effects of insolvency (restructuring) proceedings opened in a state within the group, whether or not subject to certain exceptions. The EIR expressly states that mutual trust is the basis for the recognition of judgments within the EU, and this also applies to disputes among Member States regarding jurisdiction to open insolvency proceedings.[121]

The principle implies reciprocity since one is talking about *mutual* trust.[122] This explains why frameworks like the MLCBI, which do not require reciprocity and are not implemented in the form of agreement between states, do not refer to the principle. The ultimate effect is that the MLCBI does not provide for automatic recognition but rather requires ancillary recognition proceedings.

Mutual trust applies to substantive laws, too.[123] The principle, however, does not imply that the respective substantive laws should be identical. Rather, it refers to having a general trust in the fairness of the legal systems, both in substance and procedure.[124] That said, there may be irreconcilable differences within a framework based on mutual trust. Such differences, however, can be addressed with the public policy exception since the states in question are free to agree on the level of trust.[125] In that regard, Reinhard Bork distinguishes different levels of trust, such as *general* (*unconditional*)

120 Bork, *Principles of Cross-Border Insolvency Law* (n 93) para 2.33.
121 EIR (n 13) rec 65.
122 Bork, *Principles of Cross-Border Insolvency Law* (n 93) para 2.34.
123 ibid para 2.36.
124 ibid para 2.33.
125 This work will analyse the public policy exception in s D.I.

or *sceptical* (e.g. qualified by the public policy exception as mentioned above) trust.[126]

III. Modern Instruments of Cross-Border Insolvency

Provisions on the cross-border effects, whether incoming or outgoing, of insolvency proceedings are commonly found in domestic legislation[127] since it is the sovereign right of each state to determine the scope of such effects, particularly the incoming ones.[128] However, there are several international and regional legal instruments in place to address the different aspects of this matter. Section B.III of this work will briefly examine three notable frameworks in that respect. Subsection B.III.1 will touch on the EIR, which is a hard law EU instrument directly applicable in all Member States, with the exception of Denmark.[129] Subsections B.III.2 and B.III.3 will outline two UNCITRAL model laws ("Model Laws"): the MLCBI and the Model Law on Recognition and Enforcement of Insolvency-Related Judgments ("MLIJ"),[130] respectively.

1. The EIR

a) Objectives and Scope

The main objectives of the EIR, which was adopted in 2015, are to efficiently and effectively administer cross-border insolvency cases and prevent forum shopping across the EU.[131] In addition to traditional insolvency proceedings like bankruptcy and winding-up of insolvent companies, the EIR also encompasses restructuring proceedings, with a focus on those aiming

---

126 Bork, *Principles of Cross-Border Insolvency Law* (n 93) para 2.35.

127 See, eg, InsO (n 35) ss 335ff.

128 See text to n 82.

129 On the position of Denmark, see EIR (n 13) rec 88.

130 UNCITRAL adopted the Model Law on Recognition and Enforcement of Insolvency-Related Judgments ("MLIJ") with its Guide to Enactment ("Guide to the MLIJ") in 2018. See UNCITRAL, *Model Law on Recognition and Enforcement of Insolvency-Related Judgments with Guide to Enactment* (UN 2019) <https://uncitral.un.org/sites/uncitral.un.org/files/media-documents/uncitral/en/ml_recognition_gte_e.pdf> accessed 21 October 2025.

131 EIR (n 13) recs 3, 5.

at rescuing companies that are not yet insolvent and those providing for a debtor-in-possession regime.[132] It is also noteworthy that, in order to be considered within the scope of the EIR, proceedings in each Member State must be expressly designated as such in Annex A thereto.[133]

The EIR excludes, *inter alia*, proceedings that are confidential and those that are not confined to insolvency situations.[134] That said, another EU private international law instrument, namely, the Brussels I bis Regulation,[135] may facilitate achieving the EU-wide cross-border effects of such proceedings.[136] It, however, should be noted that the discussion of the EU perspective in section B.III of this work will be limited to the EIR, as the present section focuses on the instruments specific to cross-border insolvency. Accordingly, this work treats the EIR as the sole suitable EU instrument in this context and as the one most comparable to the Model Laws.

b) Choice-of-Forum and Choice-of-Law

The principle of universalism is central to the EIR, which establishes uniform choice-of-forum and choice-of-law rules for insolvency proceedings within the EU.[137] That is to say, the jurisdiction to open main insolvency proceedings with universal scope and encompassing the debtor's entire asset pool within the EU is allocated to a Member State in the territory of which the debtor has its COMI, i.e. the place where the debtor is regularly administered and which third parties can ascertain.[138] Although the debtor's registered office is presumed to be its COMI, this presumption

132 ibid recs 7, 10, art 1 (1).

133 ibid rec 9, arts 1 (1), 2 (4).

134 ibid recs 12-13, 16.

135 Regulation (EU) No 1215/2012 of the European Parliament and of the Council of 12 December 2012 on jurisdiction and recognition and enforcement of judgments in civil and commercial matters (recast) (Brussels I bis Regulation).

136 A typical example in this context was the English scheme of arrangement which was arguably considered to fall within the scope of the Brussels I bis Regulation in the pre-Brexit era. See Dominik Skauradszun and Walter Nijnens, 'The Toolbox for Cross-Border Restructurings Post-Brexit - Why, What & Where?' (2019) 7 NIBLeJ 1 1 <https://www.ntu.ac.uk/media/documents/research-documents/1.pdf> accessed 21 October 2025, 2 (and cited sources in fn 4 therein). See also Paterson, 'A Qualified Defence of the Rule in Gibbs' (n 74) pt VI.

137 EIR (n 13) rec 23. For a more detailed discussion of the elements of universalism under the EIR, see Bork, *Principles of Cross-Border Insolvency Law* (n 93) para 2.17.

138 EIR (n 13) rec 23-28, art 3 (1).

can be rebutted.[139] The proceedings shall be governed by the *lex fori concursus*,[140] subject to several exceptions.[141] This law applies to an extensive, non-exhaustive list of matters, including the effects of the proceedings on the existing contracts of the debtor, the distribution of proceeds, the priority of claims, and subsequent creditor rights.[142]

Despite its universalist aspirations, the EIR provides several significant exceptions in that regard. That is to say, apart from the exceptions relating to applicable law, the EIR allows, subject to the fulfilment of certain conditions, opening of territorial or secondary proceedings in a Member State other than the one where the debtor's COMI is situated.[143] These proceedings, however, are confined to the assets in that other Member State.[144]

c) Cross-Border Effects Within the EU

Based on the principle of mutual trust,[145] the EIR grants automatic recognition within the EU to a judgment opening main insolvency proceedings in one Member State.[146] Such recognition generally yields the same effects as under the *lex fori concursus*, including conferring on the insolvency practitioner appointed in the main proceedings a wide range of powers exercisable in other Member States.[147] Other judgments related to the main insolvency proceedings are also recognised in all other Member States without any formalities.[148] The automatic recognition effect constitutes a crucial aspect of the universalist ambitions of the EIR. Nonetheless, the EIR provides an exception also with respect to this aspect of universalism, namely, the public policy exception.[149]

---

139 ibid rec 30, art 3 (1).
140 ibid art 7.
141 ibid arts 8-14, 16-18.
142 ibid art 7 (2).
143 ibid art 3 (2-3).
144 ibid art 3 (2).
145 See text to n 121.
146 EIR (n 13) art 19.
147 ibid arts 20-21.
148 ibid art 32.
149 ibid art 33.

2. The MLCBI

a) Objectives and Scope

UNCITRAL adopted the MLCBI as a soft law instrument of cross-border insolvency law in 1997.[150] It comes into effect when a state[151] adopts it as domestic law.[152] The MLCBI provides a comprehensive framework for administering cross-border insolvency cases. Such cross-border cases may occur, for example, when the debtor has assets in multiple states or some creditors from a state other than that where the insolvency proceedings have been initiated.[153] The primary goals of the MLCBI include enhancing cooperation between courts and other bodies of the enacting state and all other affected states, increasing legal certainty for global commerce, ensuring just and effective management of cross-border insolvency proceedings with a focus on protecting creditors and other involved parties, maximising value of the debtor's estate, and expediting rescue of distressed businesses.[154] The MLCBI focuses on the following four key aspects: access to the courts of the enacting state (for representatives of foreign insolvency proceedings, creditors, etc.); recognition of specific foreign court orders; assistance to foreign proceedings; and cooperation among the courts of the affected states and coordination of concurrent proceedings.[155] A *foreign proceeding* is defined under the MLCBI as 'a collective judicial or administrative proceeding ... pursuant to a law relating to insolvency in which proceeding the assets and affairs of the debtor are subject to control or supervision by a foreign court, for the purpose of reorganization or liquidation'.[156] As can be seen, the definition is broad and expressly pertains to proceedings aimed at the debtor's restructuring.

---

150 See n 17 and accompanying text.

151 Throughout this work, such a state will be referred to, depending on the context, as the *enacting state* or the *receiving state*.

152 Guide to the MLCBI (n 17) paras 19-20.

153 ibid para 1.

154 MLCBI (n 17) preamble.

155 Guide to the MLCBI (n 17) para 24. For a more detailed discussion, see ibid paras 25-45. See also Gerard McCormack and Wan Wai Yee, 'The UNCITRAL Model Law on Cross-Border Insolvency Comes of Age: New Times or New Paradigms' (2019) 54 Tex Intl L J 273, 276-77; Walters, 'Modified Universalisms' (n 17) 57-58.

156 For the full definition of *foreign proceeding*, see MLCBI (n 17), art 2 (a).

b) Choice-of-Forum

The MLCBI defines a foreign proceeding taking place in the state where the COMI of the debtor is located as a *foreign main proceeding*.[157] As to the COMI, the MLCBI provides for a rebuttable presumption in favour of the debtor's registered office.[158] A *foreign non-main proceeding* is defined as a foreign proceeding, which is not a foreign main proceeding, commenced in a state in the territory of which the debtor has an establishment.[159]

Like the EIR, the MLCBI does not attempt to harmonise substantive laws applicable to cross-border insolvency cases.[160] Neither does it, unlike the EIR, establish uniform choice-of-law rules in that respect.[161]

c) Recognition and Its Effects

Under the MLCBI, subject to the fulfilment of the conditions as to *foreign proceeding* and *foreign representative*[162] as well as a few procedural requirements regarding the application itself, foreign proceedings shall be recognised as such (either as a foreign main proceeding or a foreign non-main proceeding) upon application of the foreign representative to the designated court of the enacting state.[163] Once recognition is granted with respect to a foreign main proceeding, it produces several automatic, albeit limited and procedural in nature, effects under article 20 of the MLCBI, such as a stay of actions and execution concerning the debtor's assets in the territory of the enacting state.[164] Additionally, the court may, upon request, grant additional post-recognition relief under article 21 of the MLCBI, which sets out a non-exhaustive list of such reliefs. Furthermore, the court may provide assistance under other laws of the enacting state pursuant to article 7 of the MLCBI.

---

157 ibid art 2 (b).
158 ibid art 16 (3).
159 ibid art 2 (c). For the definition of *establishment*, see ibid art 2 (f).
160 Guide to the MLCBI (n 17) para 3.
161 Irit Mevorach, 'On the Road to Universalism: A Comparative and Empirical Study of the UNCITRAL Model Law on Cross-Border Insolvency' (2011) 12 EBOR 517, 523-24; Walters, 'Modified Universalisms' (n 17) 59.
162 For the definition of *foreign representative*, see MLCBI (n 17) art 2 (d).
163 ibid arts 15-17.
164 ibid art 20.

d) Modified Universalism and the MLCBI

The MLCBI contains certain safeguards regarding the actions noted above. To begin with, like the EIR, it contains the public policy exception to all possible actions under the MLCBI, including the ones mentioned above.[165] Apart from that, post-recognition relief under article 21 is of a discretionary nature and subject to the *adequate protection* safeguard pursuant to article 22 (1) of the MLCBI. As it can be seen, modified universalism underpins the MLCBI.[166] On the one hand, it provides for deference to main proceedings in the debtor's home jurisdiction even without requiring reciprocity. On the other hand, such deference does not occur automatically but through the cooperation of the court in the enacting state, with some safeguards in place.[167]

As stated earlier, this work focuses on a cross-border system based on the MLCBI. Hence, the safeguards outlined above are at the core of the present research and will be discussed in greater detail as this work progresses.

---

165 ibid art 6.

166 For a more detailed discussion, see Jay L. Westbrook, 'Global Insolvency Proceedings for a Global Market: The Universalist System and the Choice of a Central Court' (2018) 96 Tex L Rev 1473, 1478ff; Irit Mevorach, 'Overlapping International Instruments for Enforcement of Insolvency Judgments: Undermining or Strengthening Universalism?' (2021) 22 EBOR 283, 289-93; Gerard McCormack, 'UK Contracts and Modification under Foreign Law: Time to Consign the Gibbs Rule to Legal History?' (2024) 2023 (4) J Bus L 290 (a repository copy: <https://eprints.whiterose.ac.uk/198398/3/Modification%20of%20English%20law%20contracts.pdf> accessed 21 October 2025), pt 2. See also McCormack and Wan (n 155) 276; Walters, 'Modified Universalisms' (n 17) 64 (and cited sources in fn 77 therein).

167 That said, it is worth noting that *cooperation* is not exclusively attributable to a system based on modified universalism and may play a pivotal role also in the case of several territorial proceedings concerning the same debtor. Bork, *Principles of Cross-Border Insolvency Law* (n 93) para 2.45; Stephan Madaus, 'Article 25: Cooperation and Direct Communication Between a Court of This State and Foreign Courts or Foreign Representatives' in Reinhard Bork and Michael Veder (eds), *The UNCITRAL Model Laws on Cross-Border Insolvency and on the Recognition and Enforcement of Insolvency-Related Judgments: An Article-by-Article Commentary* (Edward Elgar 2025) para 1.25.02.

3. The MLIJ

a) Objectives and Scope

The MLIJ was adopted by UNCITRAL in 2018.[168] As its title suggests, the MLIJ provides a harmonised framework for the recognition and enforcement of insolvency-related judgments.[169] The MLIJ has several objectives, such as enhancing certainty, avoiding concurrent proceedings, promoting comity and cooperation, maximising the asset pool of the debtor, and complementing the MLCBI (as the case may be).[170]

Like the MLCBI, the MLIJ is a soft law instrument requiring enaction into domestic legislation to be applicable.[171] Unlike the MLCBI, it has not been implemented in any jurisdiction thus far.[172] One possible reason for this is that in some jurisdictions (like the US[173]), the recognition of foreign insolvency-related judgments falls within the scope of the adopted version of the MLCBI, making additional implementation of the MLIJ unnecessary. Accordingly, the MLIJ is particularly relevant for jurisdictions where the MLCBI is not interpreted broadly, like England.[174] In fact, the MLIJ is, *inter alia*, a response to the uncertainty of whether insolvency-related judgments can be recognised and enforced under article 21 of the MLCBI.[175] Hence, the MLIJ also contains an article (Article X) that gives the states enacting the MLCBI an option to address this uncertainty in relation to article 21 of the MLCBI.[176]

In order to fall within the scope of the MLIJ, an insolvency-related judgment needs to be handed down in proceedings taking place in a state other

---

168 See n 130 and accompanying text.

169 Guide to the MLIJ (n 130) para 1.

170 For the full list, see MLIJ (n 130) preamble.

171 Guide to the MLIJ (n 130) para 15.

172 Unlike the MLCBI, there is no information regarding the implementation of the MLIJ on the website of UNCITRAL.

173 For a more detailed discussion of the implementation of the MLCBI in the US, see sub-s C.II.2.

174 For a more detailed discussion of the implementation of the MLCBI and a government consultation on the implementation of the MLIJ (Article X) in Great Britain, see sub-s C.II.1.

175 Guide to the MLIJ (130) para 2. For a discussion of the relationship between the MLIJ and the MLCBI, see ibid paras 35-41. For a discussion of overlaps and inconsistencies concerning these two frameworks, see Mevorach, 'Overlapping International Instruments' (n 166) 298-304.

176 Guide to the MLIJ (n 130) paras 126-27.

than the enacting state.[177] Under the MLIJ, an *insolvency-related judgment* is defined as 'a judgment that a. Arises as a consequence of or is materially associated with an insolvency proceeding …; and b. Was issued on or after the commencement of that insolvency proceeding', excluding, however, judgments initiating insolvency proceedings.[178] As to the definition of an *insolvency proceeding*, the MLIJ defines it in a manner similar, if not identical in key aspects, to the definition of a *foreign proceeding* under the MLCBI,[179] thus, encompassing restructuring proceedings.[180] Furthermore, the Guide to the MLIJ makes it clear that the definition of an *insolvency-related judgment* encompasses a judgment 'confirming or varying a plan of reorganization' or 'granting a discharge of the debtor or of a debt'.[181] It should also be noted that article 14 *(f)* of MLIJ expressly refers to the respective types of judgment.

The MLIJ allows the enacting states, which have implemented the MLCBI, to opt for a provision that enables them to refuse to recognise and enforce judgments from states whose proceedings are not eligible for recognition under the MLCBI, e.g. due to a lack of COMI or an establishment, subject to some exceptions.[182]

b) Recognition and Enforcement

An insolvency-related judgment shall, upon request, be recognised and enforced by the designated court of the enacting state, subject to the fulfilment of certain conditions concerning the effect and enforceability of the judgment in the originating state, the applicant's standing, and a few procedural requirements.[183] As to the effects of such recognition and enforcement, the MLIJ presents two options: the insolvency-related judgment shall be given

177 MLIJ (n 130) art 1 (1).

178 For the full definition of *judgment* and *insolvency-related judgment*, see MLIJ (n 130) art 2 (*(c)*, *(d)*).

179 See n 156 (and accompanying text) and text thereto.

180 For the full definition of *insolvency proceeding*, see MLIJ (n 130) art 2 *(a)*.

181 Guide to the MLIJ (n 130) para 60 (e). See also Michael Veder, 'Article 2: Definitions' in Reinhard Bork and Michael Veder (eds), *The UNCITRAL Model Laws on Cross-Border Insolvency and on the Recognition and Enforcement of Insolvency-Related Judgments: An Article-by-Article Commentary* (Edward Elgar 2025) paras 2.2.34-35.

182 MLIJ (n 130) art 14 (h). See also Guide to the MLIJ (n 130) paras 39, 116-120.

183 MLIJ (n 130) arts 9-11, 13.

the same effect it has in the state where it has been issued or would have had if it had been handed down by a court of the enacting state.[184]

c) Safeguards and Their Relevance for the Research

The MLIJ also sets out several grounds to refuse the recognition and enforcement of insolvency-related judgments, such as public policy, fraud, lack of due notice, and inadequate protection of the interests of the involved parties.[185] While not currently in effect in any jurisdiction, the MLIJ is a valuable source for this work. Later in this work, it will become clear that the MLIJ employs more detailed and advanced language and structure regarding the respective safeguards and, therefore, will be helpful in interpreting similar ones under the MLCBI. Accordingly, some of the grounds for refusal under the MLIJ will be revisited later in this work.

IV. Summary

Part B of this work provided an introduction to cross-border restructuring. It began by briefly examining the legal nature of restructuring proceedings (B.I). It summarised two main doctrinal approaches to the nature of restructuring proceedings and their cross-border effects. The analysis revealed that most scholars generally view restructuring proceedings as insolvency proceedings and, therefore, within the scope of cross-border insolvency frameworks. That said, the contractual nature of restructuring proceedings is also highlighted in the literature. This work presented its perspective on the matter by underscoring the *sui generis* nature of restructuring proceedings. It also stressed that achieving the cross-border effects of restructurings through cross-border insolvency frameworks might be feasible. However, this work highlighted the importance of exercising caution in that regard, in particular, taking into account the debt-oriented nature of restructuring proceedings and, thus, fairly balancing the interests of the parties to the debt in question.

Part B also briefly examined the underlying principles (B.II) and three notable frameworks (B.III) of cross-border insolvency, which will be re-

184 ibid art 15. For rationale behind both options, see Guide to the MLIJ (n 130) para 121.

185 MLIJ (n 130) arts 7, 14.

ferred to throughout this work in various contexts. The examination showed that the scope of the frameworks is broad enough to encompass restructuring proceedings. It has also been noted that these frameworks (particularly the Model Laws) contain certain safeguards that might be of importance for striking a fair balance between the respective interests.

C. Recognition of Restructuring Plans under the MLCBI: A Comparative Analysis and Preliminary Findings

Part C of this work will be dedicated to the recognition of restructuring plans under the MLCBI. As noted earlier, the MLCBI is not applied in a similar manner with respect to the recognition of restructuring plans, even though it is designed as a model law with the goal of harmonising the respective area in the enacting states.[186] For the reasons already provided (A.IV), Part C will examine two jurisdictions, namely, England and the US, in this regard. Although the MLCBI has been implemented in both jurisdictions, there are variations in the respective texts and even greater differences in how local courts interpret these texts.[187] This is best exemplified by the restructuring proceedings of the IBA ("IBA restructuring proceedings"), which were recognised as a foreign main proceeding in both jurisdictions. That is to say, the IBA's restructuring plan ("IBA plan"), which had been confirmed by the Azerbaijani court in the framework of the IBA restructuring proceedings, was fully recognised and enforced in the US but was not granted the same treatment in England.

Part C will first summarise the IBA restructuring proceedings (C.I). It will then examine the national versions of the MLCBI as implemented in England and in the US with respect to the recognition of restructuring plans (C.II). This will be followed by an assessment of the approaches adopted in the respective jurisdictions, focusing on their advantages and disadvantages (C.III). Based on this assessment, the present work will suggest a balanced model for the recognition of restructuring plans under the MLCBI (C.IV). A brief summary will conclude this Part (C.V).

---

186 Guide to the MLCBI (n 17) para 1.

187 For a discussion of the implementation of the MLCBI in these jurisdictions in light of the differences in their cross-border insolvency system, see Walters, 'Modified Universalisms' (n 17) s III. See also generally Gerard McCormack, 'US Exceptionalism and UK Localism? Cross-border Insolvency Law in Comparative Perspective' (2016) 36 Legal Studies 136; Daniel M. Glosband, 'Common Law Perspective on UNCITRAL Instruments on Insolvency Law' in Ángel María Ballesteros Barros and David Amable Morán Bovio (eds), *Insolvency Law in UNCITRAL: Instruments and Comments* (Editorial Aranzadi 2023) 406-09.

I. The IBA Restructuring Proceedings

This section will discuss the IBA restructuring proceedings.[188] It will first touch on the applicable Azerbaijani law (C.I.1), which will be followed by a summary of the facts of the case (C.I.2). This section will then turn to the recognition of the IBA restructuring proceedings in England and in the US (C.I.3).

1. Applicable Azerbaijani Law

a) Nature of Proceedings

Restructuring of banks is governed by the Law on Banks ("LB")[189] and the Civil Procedure Code ("CPC"),[190] as the general insolvency regime (and rehabilitation procedure within that regime) does not apply to banks.[191] The voluntary restructuring procedure under the LB may (but must not) be initiated by a bank that is unable (or under threat of it) to meet its obligations before creditors due to the lack or shortage of funds or impossibility of the usage of funds on other grounds.[192] As the name of the procedure implies, the process is voluntary and cannot be initiated by creditors. Although the proceedings are generally supervised by the Central Bank of the Republic

188 For a brief summary of the IBA restructuring proceedings (Azerbaijani law, facts, and the recognition abroad) by the author of this work, see also Abbas Abbasov, 'Protection of Dissenting Creditors' Interests: Direct Application of the "Substantive Fairness" Test While Considering the Recognition of Foreign Restructuring Plans' (2022) Richard Turton Award Paper 2021 <https://insol.azureedge.net/cmsstorage/insol/media/documents_files/richard%20turton%20award%20papers/richard-turton-award-final-paper-2021.pdf> accessed 21 October 2025 (Overview: Eurofenix [Aut 2022] 32; INSOL World [4th qtr 2022] 42), pt I.

189 Law of the Republic of Azerbaijan on Law on Banks (dated 16 January 2004) ("LB"). For voluntary restructuring of banks generally, see ch VIII-I thereof.

190 Civil Procedure Code of the Republic of Azerbaijan (entry into force: 01 September 2000) ("CPC"). For voluntary restructuring of banks generally, see ch 40-5 thereof.

191 The Law of the Republic of Azerbaijan on Insolvency and Bankruptcy (dated 13 June 1997) ("LIB"), art 2 (2).

192 LB (n 189) art 57-11.2.

of Azerbaijan ("Central Bank")[193] and the court,[194] the bank's management retains control and the bank is allowed to carry on its ordinary trade, subject to the limitations outlined in the LB and the restructuring plan itself.[195]

The bank may restructure some or all of its obligations, excluding those owed to insured depositors.[196] The LB does not provide specific criteria for determining which obligations to be restructured and which to remain unaffected, nor does it expressly require such selection to be justified in the restructuring plan. Although the LB does not specify restructuring measures either, it mandates that they be listed in the plan.[197] Furthermore, the LB does not provide any distribution or priority framework. It is also noteworthy that the bank has the right to suspend fulfilling the obligations affected by the restructuring plan, as well as those arising from contracts involving the sale, gifting, exchange, or other disposition of its assets, starting from the date the court order commencing the restructuring proceedings becomes final.[198]

To summarise, this procedure provides banks facing illiquidity with an opportunity to restructure their liabilities while continuing to trade, thus resolving liquidity issues and avoiding liquidation. Subject to the general supervision of the Central Bank and the court, banks are granted a wide range of powers regarding several key matters, such as the selection of liabilities to be restructured, the determination of restructuring measures, and the classification of creditors (liabilities) for the purpose of entitlements to be received as a result of restructuring.

193 The legislative provisions under which the IBA restructuring proceedings were commenced provided for the supervision of the Financial Markets Supervisory Authority. However, this function was transferred to the Central Bank following the former's dissolution by a Presidential Order dated 28 November 2019.

194 For the role of the Central Bank and the court, see generally LB (n 189) ch VIII-I. It is difficult to assess the actual effectiveness of such supervision due to its general nature, lack of guidelines and further cases so far.

195 ibid arts 57-11.15.4, 57-11.21.

196 ibid art 57-11.1.

197 ibid art 57-11.15.3.

198 ibid art 57-11.8.

b) Plan Content, Voting, and Confirmation

The bank's proposed restructuring plan shall include, *inter alia*, the purpose and duration of the restructuring, a list of the affected obligations, the restructuring measures, and any limitations to be imposed on the bank's activity in the course of the proceedings.[199] The draft plan must be approved by the Central Bank before the bank can apply to the court for the commencement of the proceedings.[200]

Once the court grants the application and the respective court order becomes final,[201] the information regarding the restructuring shall be advertised in local and international media as well as on the bank's website within seven working days.[202] The bank shall then convene a creditors' meeting,[203] where the affected creditors will vote as a single class despite the possibility of being treated differently under the plan.[204] At least two-thirds of the affected creditors in value must approve the plan at the meeting.[205] It is also noteworthy that insiders' votes are not expressly prohibited from being counted towards the requisite majority.

Once the plan has been duly approved by the requisite majority, the bank shall inform the Central Bank and apply to the court for the confirmation of the plan.[206] Upon receiving such an application, the court shall schedule a hearing within thirty days and send a notification of the hearing to all interested parties.[207] The court order confirming the plan, once issued, becomes effective immediately[208] and may be appealed according to the general rules for appeals in the CPC.[209] However, filing an appeal does not stay the implementation of the order.[210]

---

199 ibid art 57-11.5.
200 ibid arts 57-11.4-6.
201 For the procedural aspects, see CPC (n 190) arts 355-15-17.
202 LB (n 189) art 57-11.7.
203 ibid art 57-11.9.
204 The LB does not expressly provide for such a possibility. Nor does it prohibit such differential treatment. In fact, creditors were treated differently under the IBA plan (sub-s C.I.2).
205 LB (n 189) art 57-11.11.
206 ibid arts 57-11.12-13.
207 CPC (n 190) arts 355-18.2-18.3.
208 ibid art 355-18.4.
209 ibid ch 41.
210 ibid art 355-18.4.

c) Effects of Confirmation

Once the restructuring plan has been duly approved by the creditors and confirmed by the court, it has a binding effect on all obligations listed in the plan, including the ones before the dissenting creditors.[211] These obligations are considered duly fulfilled upon the termination of the proceedings on the grounds of the full implementation of the restructuring plan.[212]

During the implementation period, the enforcement or fulfilment of the claims arising out of the obligations to be restructured is suspended.[213] The restructuring proceedings, thus, the implementation of the plan, may last for up to 180 days from the date the court order commencing the proceedings becomes final.[214] However, this period may be extended by the court for up to 180 days, each time upon application of the bank, which, in turn, shall be pre-agreed upon with the Central Bank.[215] There is no limit to the number of such extensions.[216]

d) Creditor Rights

Creditors, whether local or foreign, enjoy a number of rights, mostly procedural in nature, in the framework of restructuring proceedings of banks. First and foremost, creditors' right to be heard is generally respected. That is to say, as already identified, the commencement of the restructuring proceedings should be advertised in the local and international media and on the website of the bank.[217] The affected creditors may receive a copy of the restructuring plan and the court decision commencing the restructuring proceedings.[218] Additionally, nothing prevents these creditors from proposing amendments to the plan, as the law expressly permits making

211 LB (n 189) art 57-11.12.
212 ibid art 57-11.18.
213 ibid art 57-11.14.
214 ibid art 57-11.6.
215 ibid.
216 ibid. Under the initial text of the respective article, the period of extension was limited to up to 90 days and any further extension was not allowed. For the respective amendment, see the Law of the Republic of Azerbaijan (970-VQD) dated 29 December 2017.
217 See text to n 202.
218 LB (n 189) art 57-11.7.

amendments to the proposed plan.[219] These amendments, however, shall be approved by the Central Bank and separately publicised.[220] Furthermore, the affected creditors are entitled to attend the creditors' meeting and vote on the restructuring plan or appoint a proxy to do so in their stead.[221] These creditors shall be notified of the court hearing on the confirmation of the plan.[222] They, thus, are entitled to attend the court hearing, present their case before the court, and raise objections to the confirmation of the restructuring plan in accordance with the general provisions of the CPC.[223] The affected creditors also have the right to appeal the court order confirming the plan.[224]

To sum up, the rights mentioned are procedural and are meant primarily to ensure due process. The LB, however, does not address how the substantive rights of the affected creditors, particularly those who disagree, should be properly protected. Furthermore, no well-established principles have been developed in Azerbaijani case law to address this issue.[225]

2. Facts

The brief facts of the IBA restructuring proceedings were as follows.[226] The IBA, the largest bank in Azerbaijan, initiated restructuring proceedings in 2017 to address financial difficulties stemming primarily from mismanage-

219 ibid art 57-11.9.

220 ibid arts 57-11.9-10.

221 ibid art 57-11.11.

222 See text to n 207.

223 See CPC (n 190) art 306.1, which provides for the application of the rules for general proceedings to such kind of special proceedings.

224 ibid art 357.1.

225 This is primarily due to the lack of actual cases. In fact, the IBA restructuring proceedings are the first and, thus far, the only case under the respective chapter of the LB. As to case law under the general insolvency regime in Azerbaijan, which despite being not applicable to banks could be used as an analogy, it should be noted that there are only a few actual cases. In fact, this work could not reach any court judgment addressing the issue of the protection of dissenting creditors' rights under the general insolvency regime.

226 Unless another source is cited, all the facts outlined in sub-s C.I.2 of this work are taken from the reserved judgment of Mr. Justice Hildyard in *In the Matter of the OJSC International Bank of Azerbaijan* [2018] EWHC 59 (Ch). For a more detailed summary of the undisputed facts of the case, see ibid [4]-[8], [30]-[42].

ment and the devaluation of the Azerbaijani manat.[227] The proceedings were commenced under the then newly introduced chapters to the LB and the CPC (C.I.1). The IBA plan contemplated restructuring the IBA's financial indebtedness, roughly amounting to 3.34 billion US Dollars. According to the IBA plan, the obligations to be restructured were divided into three categories, each receiving different treatment. The IBA plan provided for all affected obligations to be discharged in full and exchanged for various new entitlements. These entitlements mainly consisted of new debt securities, such as bonds issued by the Government of Azerbaijan or the IBA itself.

The IBA plan was approved by 99.7 per cent of those voting at the meeting of a single class of creditors, who held 93.9 per cent of the value of the affected obligations. Subsequently, the Azerbaijani court confirmed the IBA plan in an unopposed hearing.

3. Recognition Abroad

a) Recognition in England

Shortly after the commencement of the proceedings in Azerbaijan, the IBA applied to the High Court of England and Wales ("EWHC") for an order recognising the IBA restructuring proceedings as a foreign main proceeding under the Cross-Border Insolvency Regulations 2006 ("CBIR"),[228] which is the British version of the MLCBI. The court granted the order sought, which was unopposed.[229] The court also imposed a moratorium[230] pursuant to article 21 of Schedule 1 to the CBIR instead of the automatic effects under article 20.[231] The moratorium temporarily prevented creditors

227 International Bank of Azerbaijan, 'ABB Launches Debt Restructuring Offer to its Creditors' (2017) <https://abb-bank.az/en/maliyye-ve-investisiya/diger-melumatlar/press-relizler/londonda-azerbaycan-beynelxalq-bankinin-xarici-kreditorlari-ile-gorus-kecirilib> accessed 21 October 2025.

228 Cross-Border Insolvency Regulations 2006, SI 2006/1030 ("CBIR").

229 *In the Matter of OJSC International Bank of Azerbaijan* [2017] EWHC 2075 (Ch) [25]. An anonymous group of creditors was initially considering opposing the application but then chose not to do so at that stage (ibid [18]-[21]).

230 The moratorium granted was similar to that under the Insolvency Act 1986, sch B1 (Administration), para 43.

231 *International Bank of Azerbaijan* [2017] EWHC 2075 (Ch) (n 229) [14]-[16], [21], [23], [25]. Under the CBIR (sch 1, art 20), the automatic effects of recognition are only reserved for the proceedings analogous to the winding-up of companies under the Insolvency Act 1986. The discretionary relief in this case was, thus, requested

from commencing or continuing any legal proceedings against the IBA and its assets without the permission of the court.[232]

Later in 2017, the foreign representative of the IBA applied to the EWHC for the continuation of the already imposed moratorium for an indefinite period.[233] Two dissenting creditors, who had their debts governed by English law, opposed the application and filed cross-applications to lift the moratorium.[234] The IBA, in turn, opposed their cross-applications.[235] The issues raised in these three applications are also at the heart of the present work. Specifically, the focus was on the relationship between the principle of modified universalism and the rule of English private international law known as the Gibbs rule.[236] According to this rule, which will be thoroughly examined later in this work, English law recognises a discharge of a debt in foreign insolvency proceedings only when it is a discharge under the governing law of the contract. It was not contested by the IBA that, for the purposes of the applications at hand, the court was bound by the rule.[237] Nor did the IBA dispute that the IBA plan had not discharged the debts in question in the eyes of English law or the Azerbaijani court order confirming the IBA plan could not be directly recognised and enforced under the CBIR.[238]

Nonetheless, the IBA argued that, if granted, the permanent moratorium requested would not result in the discharge of the debts in question and, therefore, the Gibbs rule would still be formally observed.[239] Hence, the IBA suggested distinguishing the issue of the permanent impediment to the enforcement of a right from its discharge.[240]

The respondents (the dissenting creditors), by referring to the Gibbs rule, opposed the IBA's application, arguing that their claims had not been discharged under the IBA plan and that the permanent moratorium sought

and granted by the court under the CBIR, sch 1, art 21, as the aim of the IBA restructuring proceedings was the rescue of the IBA rather than its liquidation.

232 n 230 and accompanying text.

233 *International Bank of Azerbaijan* [2018] EWHC 59 (Ch) (n 226) [12]-[13].

234 ibid [3], [14], [20]. For more about the identity of the opposing creditors and their claims, see ibid [9]-[11], [38]-[39].

235 ibid [13].

236 ibid [1]-[2].

237 ibid [16].

238 ibid [16]-[17].

239 ibid [60]-[75].

240 ibid.

would prevent them from enforcing their English law rights.[241] The court agreed with the respondents' position, holding that the relief requested would, if granted, have had practically the same effect as a discharge,[242] as had generally been predicted in the literature.[243] Consequently, the previously imposed moratorium was lifted (that lifting being subject to stay pending the IBA's appeal).[244]

The IBA appealed the EWHC judgment and this appeal was dismissed by the Court of Appeal of England and Wales ("EWCA").[245] The EWCA held that article 21 or any other provision of the MLCBI (as incorporated in the CBIR) cannot be used to bypass the substantive rights of English law creditors under the Gibbs rule and, therefore, English courts lack jurisdiction to grant the moratorium sought.[246] The EWCA also pointed out the possibility of the initiation of analogous proceedings in England by the IBA, which had not been the case.[247]

b) Recognition in the US

In 2017, the IBA also submitted a petition to the US Bankruptcy Court for the Southern District of New York ("SDNY"), seeking the recognition of the IBA restructuring proceedings as a foreign main proceeding under Chapter 15 of the BC ("Chapter 15"), which is the US version of the MLCBI.[248] The application was objected to by an ad hoc group of noteholders.[249] The objection was based on the arguments that the applicable Azerbaijani law does not adequately protect creditors, particularly foreign ones, and does not ensure procedural and substantive fairness, thus violat-

241 ibid [14].

242 ibid [142]-[147].

243 Adrian Walters, 'Giving Effect to Foreign Restructuring Plans in Anglo-US Private International Law' (2015) 3 NIBLeJ 20 375 <https://irep.ntu.ac.uk/id/eprint/11905/1/220288_2492.pdf> accessed 21 October 2025, 388.

244 *In the Matter of the OJSC International Bank of Azerbaijan* [2018] EWHC 792 (Ch).

245 *Re OJSC International Bank of Azerbaijan* [2018] EWCA Civ 2802 (*IBA*).

246 ibid [83]-[101].

247 ibid [88].

248 *In re International Bank of Azerbaijan* 17-11311 (JLG) (Bankr SDNY, entered 7 July 2017)

249 Elena D. Lobo and Daniel J. Soltman, 'Azeri Restructuring Could Test Limits of Chapter 15 Foreign Plan Enforcement' (2018) 5 (Winter 2017-2018) Emerg Mark Rest J 37, 38-39.

ing the public policy of the US.[250] These arguments were supported, *inter alia*, by the claims that under Azerbaijani law, there are no restrictions on considering insider votes towards the requisite majority, and no provisions for preventing fraudulent transactions.[251] Additionally, the objection pointed out the possibility of different treatment of creditors who vote as a single class under Azerbaijani law.[252]

Despite these objections, the bankruptcy court granted the IBA's petition by recognising the IBA restructuring proceedings as a foreign main proceeding and expressly confirming the automatic effects under article 20.[253] The court overruled the objection, considering it premature, and pointed out that the respective issues would be better addressed while deciding on possible post-recognition relief on the recognition and enforcement of the IBA plan.[254] According to the court, the mere recognition would not violate the public policy of the US.[255]

A few months later, the foreign representative of the IBA indeed filed a motion to the same court to request the recognition and enforcement of the IBA plan, along with a permanent moratorium (injunctive relief) in the US, referring to, *inter alia*, sections 1507 and 1521 of the BC.[256] The court granted the relief requested and overruled any objections thereto.[257] It is not entirely clear, however, whether or not the same objections were in place when the court considered the IBA's request. As a result, the IBA plan (as well as the court order confirming the IBA plan) was recognised and entitled to full force and effect and any claim arising out of the debt discharged thereunder became permanently unenforceable in the US.[258] This included the unenforceability of judgments and being barred from commencing or continuing proceedings against the IBA and its assets in the US.[259]

250 ibid.
251 ibid 39
252 ibid.
253 *International Bank of Azerbaijan* 17-11311 (JLG) (Bankr SDNY, entered 7 July 2017) (n 248).
254 See Lobo und Soltman (n 249) 39.
255 ibid.
256 *In re International Bank of Azerbaijan* Case No 17-11311 (JLG) (Bankr SDNY, entered 23 January 2018).
257 ibid.
258 ibid.
259 ibid.

The court based its decision on several general arguments, such as preventing harm to the creditors of the IBA and other stakeholders involved in the IBA restructuring proceedings.[260] Such harm could arise, according to the court, due to potential individual actions against the IBA and its assets in the US in the absence of the relief requested.[261] The court also held that granting relief was consistent with the principle of comity, necessary for the purposes of Chapter 15, and did not contradict the public policy of the US.[262]

II. Interpretation of the MLCBI in England and in the US with Respect to the Recognition of Restructuring Plans

After discussing the IBA restructuring proceedings as an illustrative example of the different interpretations of the MLCBI in England and in the US with respect to the cross-border effects of restructuring plans, this work will below analyse the matter in each jurisdiction separately. Subsection C.II.1 will examine the English (British) version of the MLCBI, while subsection C.II.2 will focus on the American version. Subsection C.II.3 will provide a comparative summary.

1. England

a) Introduction to the CBIR

The CBIR is a statutory instrument implementing the MLCBI in Great Britain in 2006.[263] Schedule 1 to the CBIR contains the modified text of the MLCBI.[264] One of the main modifications relates to article 20 of the MLCBI. That is to say, in the case of non-individual debtors, the automatic effects of recognition under article 20 can only take place with respect to foreign main proceedings that are analogous to the winding-up of a company under the Insolvency Act 1986, i.e. proceedings commenced for

260 ibid.
261 ibid.
262 ibid.
263 CBIR (n 228) s 2 (1).
264 ibid.

the purpose of liquidating the debtor.[265] Hence, foreign proceedings aimed at rescuing the debtor as a going concern rather than liquidating it, upon being recognised as a foreign main proceeding, do not enjoy the automatic effects of recognition under the CBIR. This is the reason why the IBA restructuring proceedings were not granted automatic relief under article 20 upon recognition as a foreign main proceeding under the CBIR, but rather a similar relief under the British version of article 21 of the MLCBI.[266] That said, article 21 is not construed generously by English courts, as will become evident as subsection C.II.1 of this work progresses.

b) The Gibbs Rule

Below, this work will discuss the Gibbs rule, which significantly shapes the English approach to the matter.

aa) *Antony Gibbs*

The rule derives its name from the 19th-century case of *Antony Gibbs & Sons Ltd v La Société Industrielle et Commerciale des Métaux.*[267]

(1) Facts

The main facts of the case were as follows.[268] The case involved a dispute over contracts for the sale of copper governed by English law. The buyer under the contracts was a French company which eventually went into judicial liquidation in France and refused to accept cooper under the contracts. The seller brought an action against the buyer in England for damages due to the non-acceptance of the copper (including the non-acceptance of the copper that became due only after the pronouncing of the judicial liquidation in France) under the contracts. The defendants (buyer) argued that the pronouncement of the liquidation under French law then in force had the

265 ibid sch 1, art 20 (2) (a).
266 See n 231 and accompanying text.
267 *Antony Gibbs & Sons Ltd v La Société Industrielle et Commerciale des Métaux* [1890] LR 25 QBD 399 (CA).
268 For the facts of the case, see ibid 399-401.

effect of the company existing only for the purposes of liquidation, with all its assets and affairs being vested in the liquidator and of the dissolution of the liability to be sued on the contracts. As to the breaches of the obligation (non-acceptance) under the contracts that had not become due until after the announcement of liquidation, the defendants further submitted that the contracts had been cancelled by operation of law then in force in France and, therefore, no liability could arise due to the non-performance of the contracts after such announcement. The defendants further argued that the law of England then in force recognised and gave effect to a foreign bankruptcy or liquidation in accordance with the respective principles of international law. According to the defendants, the effect of the liquidation in France, thus, constituted a bar to the action in England or at least a ground for a stay of proceedings and the seller should not be allowed to have access to the assets of the defendants in England, which, in turn, should be vested in the liquidator in France and administered accordingly.

(2) Reasoning

The EWCA unanimously dismissed the appeal against the judgment in favour of the claimants.[269] Lord Esher, who delivered the judgment of the EWCA, held that a contract cannot be discharged by foreign insolvency proceedings, referring to a general rule that the issue of a discharge of a contract is governed only by its proper law.[270] He highlighted the importance of respecting the agreement of contracting parties in this context by asking his oft-quoted rhetoric question: 'Why should the plaintiffs be bound by the law of a country to which they do not belong, and by which they have not contracted to be bound?'.[271] Lord Esher further noted that the non-recognition of a foreign bankruptcy discharge (other than one under the governing law of the contract) of a contract in England was not confined to English law-governed contracts only:

> I should say, too, that, if the contract had been made in any foreign country other than France, the plaintiffs could sue upon it in this country, and their action would not be affected

269 ibid 409-11.
270 ibid 405-06.
271 ibid 406.

> by the law of France. In that case the law of such other foreign country would govern the contract.[272]

The court decided the issue of the stay of proceedings against the defendants as well.[273]

bb) English Private International Law Rule on the Recognition of a Foreign Bankruptcy Discharge

The English private international law rule on the recognition of a foreign bankruptcy discharge is often associated with Lord Esher's reasoning summarised above and, thus, known as the Gibbs rule. However, it should be noted that the reasoning itself did not develop a new rule and was based on the settled case law.[274] The respective rule states that: 'A discharge from any debt or liability under the bankruptcy law of a foreign country outside the United Kingdom is a discharge therefrom in England if, and only if, it is a discharge under the law applicable to the contract'.[275] It is worth noting that the rule is not without exception. That is to say, the Gibbs rule does not afford protection to a creditor submitting to foreign bankruptcy proceedings[276] and whether the submission has taken place is construed broadly by English courts.[277]

As can be seen, both Lord Esher's reasoning and the definition of the rule are not confined to English law alone but rather apply to the governing law of the contract generally. Most recently, the EWCA reaffirmed this position in *IBA*.[278] That said, the Gibbs rule is primarily associated with

272 ibid 406-407.

273 ibid 409.

274 See, eg, the case referred to in the reasoning: *Smith v. Buchanan* (1800) 1 East, 6. For a summary of the earlier case law, see Andrew Grossman, 'Conflict of Laws in the Discharge of Debts in Bankruptcy' (1996) 5 Int Ins Rev 1, 15-18; Riz Mokal, 'Shopping and Scheming, and the Rule in Gibbs' [2017 March] South Square Digest 58, 58; McCormack 'UK Contracts and Modification under Foreign Law' (n 166) pt 2.

275 Lord Collins of Mapesbury and Jonathan Harris (eds), *Dicey, Morris & Collins on the Conflict of Laws* (16th edn, Sweet & Maxwell 2022) vol 2, Rule 211, para 31R-105 (footnote omitted).

276 *IBA* (n 245) [28]. For a more detailed discussion of the exception, see McCormack 'UK Contracts and Modification under Foreign Law' (n 166) s 3.a.

277 See text to nn 356, 357.

278 *IBA* (n 245) [30].

English law-governed contracts in practice. However, the rule may theoretically be invoked in relation to a discharge of a debt governed by a law other than English law. In that respect, this work will below discuss four scenarios illustrating the position of English law on bankruptcy discharge involving foreign elements.[279]

(1) Recognition of a Foreign Bankruptcy Discharge of an English Law-Governed Debt

This is the most prominent area of the application of the Gibbs rule, and there is no uncertainty surrounding this scenario. As was the case in *Antony Gibbs*[280] itself and *IBA*,[281] English courts do not recognise a discharge of an English law-governed debt in foreign insolvency or restructuring proceedings unless the English creditor has submitted to those proceedings.

(2) Recognition of a Foreign Bankruptcy Discharge of a Debt Governed by That Foreign Law

Not much uncertainty is involved also in this scenario. It perfectly aligns with the Gibbs rule, as the debt in question has been discharged by its proper law. Lord Esher's *dicta* in *Antony Gibbs* suggests that a discharge in this scenario would be recognised in England.[282] Hence, the Gibbs rule should not be a bar to recognising such a foreign discharge in the eyes of English law.[283] In *IBA*, too, the EWCA expressly stated in *dicta* that 'if they [the relevant contracts] had been governed by Azeri law, the English court would have recognised the effect of the restructuring'.[284]

279 For the purpose of this discussion, bankruptcy discharge also includes discharge in restructuring proceedings.

280 *Antony Gibbs* (n 267).

281 *IBA* (n 245).

282 *Antony Gibbs* (n 267) 406.

283 Lord Collins and Harris (n 275) paras 31-107 (see cited cases in fn 280 therein), 31-112 (Illustration 1 therein).

284 *IBA* (n 245) [30].

(3) Recognition of a Foreign Bankruptcy Discharge of a Debt Governed by Another Foreign Law

Things are slightly complex in this scenario. Imagine a case where a New York law-governed debt is discharged by a restructuring plan under German law without the New York law creditor submitting to the German proceedings. Would English courts recognise and give effect to the German plan in England despite the objection of the New York law creditor? Here, a preliminary question to answer is whether or not the German discharge is valid in the eyes of New York law. If the answer is affirmative, the Gibbs rule should not be an obstacle and English courts would likely to recognise the discharge in the German proceedings since it is also a valid discharge under the governing law of the contract (New York law).[285] The same does not hold if the answer to the preliminary question is negative, i.e. New York law itself does not recognise the discharge in the German proceedings.[286] According to this work, English courts do not have jurisdiction to recognise such a discharge under the Gibbs rule and they would unlikely to grant recognition in such a case. Deciding otherwise would contradict Lord Esher's *dicta* in *Antony Gibbs* expressly referring to such a scenario[287] and its reaffirmation by the EWCA in *IBA* by stating 'that questions of discharge of a contractual liability are governed by the proper law of the contract, whether or not that law is English law'.[288] That said, this work could not reach any English case applying the Gibbs rule in a similar situation.

(4) English Bankruptcy Discharge of a Foreign Law-Governed Debt

Technically, this scenario does not fall within the scope of the Gibbs rule, as it does not involve the recognition of a foreign bankruptcy discharge. Instead, it pertains to an English bankruptcy discharge of a foreign law-governed debt. However, Lord Esher's reasoning in *Antony Gibbs* was predicated on the general principle that a debt can only be discharged under its proper law.[289] Hence, one would logically expect English law to confine English bankruptcy discharge to English law-governed debts

285 Lord Collins and Harris (n 275) paras 31-111, 31-112 (Illustration 4).
286 ibid.
287 See text to n 272.
288 *IBA* (n 245) at [30].
289 See text to nn 270, 271.

only. However, English law surprisingly takes the opposite approach. That is to say, an English bankruptcy discharge (section 281 of the Insolvency Act 1986) is a discharge in England, irrespective of the governing law of the contract.[290] Furthermore, English courts generally sanction schemes of arrangement under Part 26 of the Companies Act 2006 modifying foreign law-governed debts if satisfied that the scheme will be given effect in the respective foreign jurisdictions, i.e. the scheme 'will achieve its purpose'.[291] That holds true for the recently introduced restructuring framework under Part 26A of the same act.[292]

290 Lord Collins and Harris (n 275) Rule 205 (para 31R-069) and Comment thereto (paras 31-070-73). This aspect constitutes one of the key arguments of critics of the Gibbs rule. See n 312 (and accompanying text) and text thereto.

291 See, eg, *in the matter of Magyar Telecom B.V. Magyar Telecom B.V.,* [2013] EWHC 3800 (Ch) [16]. In that case, the EWHC sanctioned a scheme modifying New York law-governed notes after being convinced that the scheme would be given effect in the US under Chapter 15 (ibid [16]-[25]. Indeed, recognition was subsequently granted under Chapter 15, along with permanent injunctive relief. See Walters, 'Giving Effect to Foreign Restructuring Plans' (n 243) 378-81. See also *in re Avanti Commc'ns Grp. PLC*, 582 BR 603 (Bankr SDNY 2018) (*Avanti*), where an English scheme of arrangement modifying New York law-governed notes was recognised and given effect in the US under Chapter 15. For a more detailed discussion of this case, see sub-s C.II.2.d)bb). See also Robert van Galen, 'The Scheming Brits' in Katharina de la Durantaye and others (eds), *Festschrift für Christoph G. Paulus zum 70. Geburtstag* (CH Beck 2022) 215.

292 See, eg, *in the matter of AGPS Bondco Plc* [2023] EWHC 916 (Ch), where the EWHC sanctioned a plan amending the terms of German law-governed notes (in the framework of the restructuring of a group of companies with parent company in Luxembourg and assets in Germany) after being satisfied 'that there is at the very least a reasonable prospect that the Plan will be recognised under both German law and the law of Luxembourg' (ibid [332]). The decision, however, was subsequently set aside by the EWCA following a successful appeal (but not over the jurisdiction issue, instead due to fairness matters). For a more detailed discussion of this case, see sub-s E.II.2.c)bb)(2)(b). For a discussion of the recognition of plans under Part 26A of the Companies Act 2006 in Germany, see, on the one hand, generally Stephan Madaus, 'Are Non-EU Preventive Restructuring Plans Effective in Germany?' (2025) 22 Int Corp Res 198, on the other hand, generally Dominik Skauradszun, Johannes Schröder, and Jeremias Kümpel, 'Why a Sanction Order Pursuant to Part 26A UK CA Cannot Be Recognised in Germany: Part One' (2024) 21 Int Corp Res 349; generally Dominik Skauradszun, Johannes Schröder, and Jeremias Kümpel, 'Why a Sanction Order Pursuant to Part 26A UK CA Cannot Be Recognised in Germany: Part Two' (2025) 22 Int Corp Res 7.

cc) The Gibbs Rule and the CBIR

The CBIR further (in addition to the court's power to assist a trustee in foreign bankruptcy proceedings under common law[293]) diminishes the effect of the Gibbs rule in relation to foreign insolvency proceedings. Once recognised in England as such, foreign main insolvency proceedings enjoy the automatic effects of recognition under the British version of article 20 of the MLCBI. Additionally, the court has the discretion to assign the administration, realisation, or distribution of some or all of the debtor's assets in Great Britain to the foreign representative (subject to adequate protection of the interests of local creditors).[294] Hence, although their English law claims remain undischarged,[295] English creditors may be permanently prevented from enforcing their claims against the debtor's assets in Great Britain. As critics of the rule state, had *Antony Gibbs*[296] been decided with the CBIR in force, the stay sought by the defendants in that case would have been granted under the CBIR.[297]

The situation is quite different with respect to foreign restructuring proceedings. As already mentioned, one of the main distinctions is that the automatic effects of recognition under the British version of article 20 are not available for foreign restructuring proceedings. However, the court may grant similar relief in such cases under the British version of article 21 of the MLCBI, as it did upon the recognition of the IBA restructuring proceedings as a foreign main proceeding.[298] That said, article 21 is constructed narrowly by English courts and is generally confined to procedural matters rather than affecting substantive rights. That is to say, based on the Gibbs rule, English courts not only refuse to recognise a discharge of an English law-governed debt in foreign restructuring proceedings but also do not allow a moratorium that would permanently prevent English creditors from

293 See text to nn 302, 313.

294 CBIR (n 228) sch 1, art 21((1) (e), (2)).

295 As already identified, that is because insolvency proceedings, unlike restructuring proceedings, do not directly discharge pre-insolvency entitlements. See n 35 (and accompanying text) and text thereto.

296 *Antony Gibbs* (n 267).

297 Look Chan Ho, *Cross-Border Insolvency: Principles and Practice* (Sweet & Maxwell 2016) para 4-031; Ramesh (n 48) para 32.

298 See nn 230, 231 (and accompanying text) and text thereto.

enforcing their rights under English law.[299] As they do so due to the lack of jurisdiction, it is not even a matter of discretion.[300]

dd) Academic Reception

The Gibbs rule has been the subject of academic debate, particularly in recent decades. This is because restructurings became a global trend only a few decades ago. As mentioned earlier, discharge is particularly important in restructuring proceedings and operates in a significantly different way from discharge in insolvency proceedings.[301] Besides, under another rule of English private international law, the debtor's movables may vest in the foreign trustee in foreign insolvency proceedings, resulting in the debtor remaining liable under an English law-governed debt in England but without assets there.[302] This significantly reduces the impact of the Gibbs rule regarding foreign insolvency proceedings. As already noted, things are different in restructuring proceedings, which are not asset-oriented proceedings and generally do not focus on marshalling and the realisation of the assets of the debtor.[303] Therefore, the Gibbs rule is of particular importance in relation to restructuring proceedings.

Additionally, two events in the 21st century have sparked discussions around the rule. One is the adoption of the MLCBI, underpinned by modified universalism, in Great Britain. The other one is a consultation commenced by the UK Government regarding, *inter alia*, the implementation of Article X of the MLIJ.[304]

---

299 See text to n 246.

300 ibid.

301 See nn 35, 36 (and accompanying text) and text thereto.

302 Lord Collins and Harris (n 275) para 31-111 (referring to Rule 208, para 31R-086). See also Fletcher (n 27) para 29-064; Ramesh (n 48) para 34.

303 See sub-s B.I.3.a).

304 Insolvency Service (UK), 'Implementation of Two UNCITRAL Model Laws on Insolvency Consultation' (published 7 July 2022, updated 10 July 2023) <https://www.gov.uk/government/consultations/implementation-of-two-uncitral-model-laws-on-insolvency/implementation-of-two-uncitral-model-laws-on-insolvency-consultation> accessed 21 October 2025. It should be noted that it was not the Government's intent to override the Gibbs rule. In fact, the consultation states that one of the reasons for not implementing the MLIJ in full is that the full implementation would override the Gibbs rule. Besides, one of the factors suggested by the Government in the consultation that courts may take into account in denying recognition of a foreign judgment under the MLCBI after implementing Article X is:

Below, this work will summarise the reception of the Gibbs rule.

(1) Arguments Against the Gibbs Rule

The Gibbs rule has been roundly criticised in the literature. Its application in relation to discharges under foreign restructuring plans was already being questioned in the mid-20th century.[305] Those critics differentiate *compositions*[306] from bankruptcy (insolvency) discharges in that respect.[307] They argue that, unlike bankruptcy discharge, which is in the interests of the debtor only, compositions, negotiated and assented by the majority of cred-

'The defending party did not submit to the foreign jurisdiction and the originating court did not otherwise exercise jurisdiction on a basis that is compatible with UK law'. That said, most of the responses to the consultation raised concerns about the uncertainty regarding the effect of the implementation Article X over the Gibbs rule. See Insolvency Service (UK), 'Implementation of Two UNCITRAL Model Laws on Insolvency: Summary of Consultation Responses and Government Response' (updated 10 July 2023 <https://www.gov.uk/government/consultations/implementation-of-two-uncitral-model-laws-on-insolvency/outcome/implementation-of-two-uncitral-model-laws-on-insolvency-summary-of-consultation-responses-and-government-response#:~:text=On%207%20July%202022%20the,Law%20> 21 October 2025.

305 See, eg, Kurt H. Nadelmann, 'Compositions: Reorganizations and Arrangements: In the Conflict of Laws' (1948) 61 Harv LR 804, 819ff; 'Bankruptcy in English Private International Law. II: Foreign Adjudications' (1955) 4 Intl & Comp LQ 1 (published online by CUP in 2008), 20ff.

306 *Composition* is defined, in the respective context, as 'an agreement of an insolvent debtor ... with his creditors in a judicial proceeding whereby a proposed agreement is accepted by a majority of the creditors ... and made binding on all creditors by the decision of the court'. See 'Bankruptcy in English Private International Law' (n 305) 20. Thus, in the sources cited in n 305, for the purpose of the differentiation from bankruptcy discharges, the term *composition* was defined broadly to include then-existing analogues of modern restructuring frameworks (reorganisations, arrangements). However, one type of composition was distinguished and likely to be excluded: 'where the debtor assigns all his assets and receives, in return, a release from his debt'. Nadelmann, 'Compositions: Reorganizations and Arrangements' (n 305) 823. The respective exclusion, however, is not relevant to this work since the mentioned type does not qualify as a *restructuring plan* for its purposes. Except for the discussion herein, examining origins, legal nature, and types of compositions falls outside the scope of this work.

307 Nadelmann, 'Compositions: Reorganizations and Arrangements' (n 305) 819ff, 'Bankruptcy in English Private International Law' (n 305) 20ff.

itors, are in the interests of a general body of the creditors, too.[308] According to them, the non-recognition of the binding effect of compositions in foreign jurisdictions equals giving vetoing power to the dissenting individual creditors, who are otherwise expected to be bound by the outcome.[309] This is unfair to the assenting majority bound by this outcome and can even jeopardise the execution of the composition, which would be against the interests of creditors as a whole, say critics.[310] It is also noteworthy that the rule was applied with respect to compositions at least in two cases in the late 19th - early 20th century.[311]

The more recent criticism of the Gibbs rule is mainly about its non-conformity with modern trends in cross-border insolvency law and the principle of (modified) universalism. Therefore, the rule has faced significant criticism from the universalist front in particular. English law's conflicting position towards the effect of a bankruptcy discharge (universal effect for an English discharge versus territorial effect for a foreign discharge) is often highlighted by opponents. Ian Fletcher, one of the harshest critics of the Gibbs rule, labels English private international law in this regard as 'xenophobic' and accuses it of 'maintaining dual standards with regard to the principle of universality of bankruptcy'.[312] He also points out the inconsistency that English law, while acknowledging the title of the foreign trustee to the debtor's assets in England (subject to the respective rules of English private international law), fails to apply 'the usual corollary that, in return for surrendering his available property to the trustee in bankruptcy for distribution among his creditors, the bankrupt becomes dis-

308 Nadelmann, 'Compositions: Reorganizations and Arrangements' (n 305) 822; 'Bankruptcy in English Private International Law' (n 305) 21.

309 Nadelmann, 'Compositions: Reorganizations and Arrangements' (n 305) 822-23; 'Bankruptcy in English Private International Law' (n 305) 21, 25.

310 Nadelmann, 'Compositions: Reorganizations and Arrangements' (n 305) 822-26, 'Bankruptcy in English Private International Law' 21-25.

311 *New Zealand Loan & Mercantile Agency Co. v. Morrison* [1898] AC 349 (PC); *Re Nelson, ex p. Dare and Dolphin* [1918] 1 KB 459. For a brief summary of these cases, see Nadelmann, 'Compositions: Reorganizations and Arrangements' (n 305) 824-26; 'Bankruptcy in English Private International Law' (n 305) 22-24.

312 Fletcher (n 27) para 29-067. See also Mokal, 'the Rule in Gibbs' (n 274) 59-60. Jay Westbrook also made a similar statement (albeit not in the context of the criticism of the rule in Gibbs): 'If we claim a certain global effect for our discharges, we should presumably feel a bit awkward in denying those effects to discharges granted by other legal systems, if those systems meet our usual standards of fairness' See Jay Lawrence Westbrook, 'Chapter 15 and Discharge' (2005) 13 Am Bankr Inst L Rev 503, 512.

charged from all his provable debts'.[313] English law's denial of support for foreign restructuring proceedings while maintaining a supportive approach for foreign insolvency proceedings has also been highlighted by others in academia.[314]

Look Chan Ho believes that the Gibbs rule and the CBIR are mutually exclusive, arguing that 'they are philosophically incompatible and practically irreconcilable'.[315] Like most other critics, he highlights the rule's territorialism underpinning while the CBIR being based on modified universalism.[316] He also suggests that the traditional common law rule that a discharge of an obligation is governed by its proper law should be discarded in relation to bankruptcy discharge, *inter alia*, for the following reasons. Firstly, he questions the pure contractual approach to bankruptcy discharge by underscoring that such discharge is not a consensual matter.[317] It shall rather be characterised as an *in rem* matter, according to him.[318] Additionally, a foreign bankruptcy discharge is likely to be within the expectation of a person who contracts with a foreign counterparty, even if the respective foreign law does not govern their relationship, says Look Chan Ho.[319]

Kannan Ramesh is another vocal critic of the Gibbs rule. He scrutinises Lord Esher's implied reasoning that the matter of discharge in foreign insolvency proceedings is a contractual matter rather than an insolvency issue.[320] He argues that a creditor's (dis)agreement to be bound by the law of a specific country is not a relevant issue in characterising a bankruptcy discharge due to the policy considerations underpinning such a discharge.[321] He, as a logical conclusion of this argument, indirectly answers the rhetorical question posed by Lord Esher[322] with a counter (rhetorical) question:

313 Fletcher (n 27) para 29-064.
314 See, eg, van Zwieten (ed), *Principles of Corporate Insolvency Law* (n 29) para 16-62, where both (insolvency and restructuring) proceedings are referred to as a type of sale: sale to third parties and *hypothetical* sale to creditors, respectively.
315 Ho (n 297), para 4-028.
316 ibid paras 4-029-30.
317 ibid paras 4-095-101.
318 ibid paras 4-102-03.
319 ibid paras 4-103-05. See also Ramesh (n 48) para 25; McCormack 'UK Contracts and Modification under Foreign Law' (n 166) pt 2.
320 Ramesh (n 48) para 21ff.
321 ibid paras 22-24.
322 See text to n 271.

> Once a court has properly taken subject matter jurisdiction over the distressed debtor enabling it to initiate insolvency or restructuring procedures, why should there be a lacuna in its power to discharge certain contractual debts which form part of the debtor's overall liabilities, simply because those debts are not governed by its law?[323]

Martin Glenn assesses the Gibbs rule from the perspective of the *(modified) universalism versus territorialism* debate and describes its essence as territorialism.[324] Jay Westbrook also criticises the approach taken by the EWCA in *IBA*,[325] describing it as 'pure territorialism' which might 'destroy the unity of bankruptcy law and render global management of a global insolvency nearly impossible'.[326]

The Gibbs rule has also been criticised for incentivising holdout behaviour and, thus, creating 'unfair, value-reducing outcomes'.[327]

(2) Arguments in Favour of the Gibbs Rule

The Gibbs rule also has its defenders. Sarah Paterson advances arguments in defence of the Gibbs rule in the context of restructuring proceedings, while acknowledging the strength of arguments against its application in insolvency proceedings.[328] Building on her distinction between insolvency and restructuring, where the former is defined as 'a unitary proceeding in which all creditors are subject to the same mandatory regime to determine their rights and interests' and the latter is characterised as 'renegotiation in distress with different treatment of different, affected creditors', she argues that the governing law of the contract, originally chosen by the

---

323 Ramesh (n 48) para 26.

324 Agrokor (n 52) 192. For a different view, see generally Louis Noirault, 'Rule in Gibbs: The Continuation of Territorialism by Other Means?' (2025) 15 Harv Bus L Rev 325.

325 *IBA* (n 245).

326 Westbrook, 'Comity and Choice of Law' (n 12) 262.

327 Varoon Sachdev, 'Choice of Law in Insolvency Proceedings: How English Courts' Continued Reliance on the Gibbs Principle Threatens Universalism' (2019) 93 Am Bankr LJ 343, 350.

328 See generally Paterson, 'A Qualified Defence of the Rule in Gibbs' (n 74).

parties, should govern such renegotiation.[329] In most cases, the choice of a specific law to govern a contract reflects important legal and non-legal considerations, and may influence the parties' decision whether to enter into the contract or the terms (e.g. price) upon which they do so, says Sarah Paterson.[330] In her view, therefore, it is legitimate to expect that the same law should also govern any renegotiation of the contract.[331]

The other main argument supporting the rule is legal predictability and certainty for participants of a transaction, particularly a creditor.[332] That is to say, no law other than the governing law of the contract may discharge the substantive rights of a creditor in the eyes of that law, even in the case of the debtor's insolvency or restructuring.[333] Advocates argue that this factor is of crucial importance for institutionalised lenders.[334] The absence of such certainty would have adverse practical effects on debt financing (unavailability or higher costs), say proponents.[335]

It has also been argued that the rule makes English law attractive on a global scale and is a key factor for market participants choosing English law to govern cross-border debt instruments.[336] Another related argument is that the Gibbs rule provides for good forum shopping and brings debt-restructurings to financial hubs (whose laws typically govern high-value cross-border transactions) with flexible restructuring mechanisms for the advantage of creditors.[337]

329 ibid pt IV. For Sarah Paterson's characterisation of restructuring proceedings, see also n 74 and accompanying text.
330 Paterson, 'A Qualified Defence of the Rule in Gibbs' (n 74) pt IV.
331 ibid.
332 See, eg, generally Financial Markets Law Committee (FMLC), 'The Rule in Gibbs: Exploring its Value and Practical Use in the Financial Markets as a Guarantor of Legal Predictability' (29 February 2024) <https://fmlc.org/wp-content/uploads/2024/02/Paper-The-Rule-in-Gibbs-Exploring-its-value-and-practical-use-in-the-financial-markets-as-a-guarantor-of-legal-predictability-29-February-2024.pdf)> accessed 21 October 2025.
333 ibid para 4.10.
334 ibid paras 4.8-9.
335 ibid para 4.31. See also Paterson, 'A Qualified Defence of the Rule in Gibbs' (n 74) pt IV.
336 See the discussion in James Brady, 'Investor Protections in England: The Non-Recognition of the Foreign Discharge of English Law-Governed Debt' (2019) 15 Pratt's J Bankr L 22, 27
337 See the discussion in McCormack 'UK Contracts and Modification under Foreign Law' (n 166) s 3.b.

c) *Rubin* and *New Cap*

Another significant aspect of the narrow interpretation of the British version of article 21 of the MLCBI is that foreign insolvency-related judgments, including those confirming restructuring plans, are not eligible for recognition and enforcement under this article. This is due to the authority of the decision of the UK Supreme Court ("UKSC") in *Rubin v Eurofinance SA* and *New Cap Reinsurance Corporation (In Liquidation) v A E Grant,* handed down by Lord Collins.[338] Below, this landmark decision will be briefly discussed.

aa) Background: *Cambridge Gas*

In those cases, the UKSC considered two appeals involving the issue of the recognition and enforcement of a foreign judgment in bankruptcy avoidance proceedings: one delivered by a US bankruptcy court *(Rubin)* and the other by an Australian court *(New Cap).*[339] In *Rubin v Eurofinance SA*[340] and later in *New Cap Reinsurance Corporation Limited (In Liquidation) v A E Grant*[341] (following, *inter alia,* its decision in the former case), the EWCA allowed the enforcement of the respective foreign bankruptcy judgments in England and Wales. This approach was taken under the influence of Lord Hoffmann's *dicta* in the Privy Council's decision in *Cambridge Gas Transport Corporation v Official Committee of Unsecured Creditors of Navigator Holdings plc.*[342] In *Cambridge Gas,* the Privy Council categorised bankruptcy judgments as neither *in rem,* nor *in personam* but rather *sui generis* for the purposes of the private international law rules on the recognition and enforcement of foreign judgments.[343] The main idea behind Lord Hoffmann's reasoning was that 'bankruptcy, whether

338 *Rubin v Eurofinance SA (Rubin) & New Cap Reinsurance Corporation v A E Grant (New Cap)* [2012] UKSC 46. For a more detailed summary of the decision and further developments, see Fletcher (n 27) paras 28-025-34; Walters, 'Modified Universalisms' (n 17) 95-101.

339 *Rubin & New Cap* (n 338) [1].

340 *Rubin v Eurofinance SA* [2010] EWCA Civ 895.

341 *New Cap Reinsurance Corporation Limited (In Liquidation) v A E Grant* [2011] EWCA Civ 971.

342 *Cambridge Gas Transport Corporation v Official Committee of Unsecured Creditors of Navigator Holdings plc* [2006] UKPC 26.

343 ibid [13]-[14].

personal or corporate, is a collective proceeding to enforce rights and not to establish them'.[344] With respect to the recognition and enforcement of foreign bankruptcy judgments, Lord Hoffman underscored the importance of the traditional view taken by the English common law that 'bankruptcy proceedings should have universal application', according to which a single bankruptcy case deals with the claims of all creditors.[345]

bb) Legal Issues

The UKSC considered several important matters in its decision. Below, this work will touch on three of them that are relevant to its topic.

(1) Disapproval of *Cambridge Gas* and Adherence to the Traditional Rule

A part of the decision was dedicated to *Cambridge Gas* and its analysis.[346] The UKSC disagreed with the classification of bankruptcy judgments as *sui generis*, stating that it would result in 'a radical departure from substantially settled law' and that the matter, therefore, should be addressed by the legislature, not the judiciary.[347] In his reasoning, Lord Collins described the argument that a person doing business with a foreign party impliedly submits to the insolvency legislation of the respective foreign country as 'wholly unrealistic'.[348] Hence, he posed a rhetorical question similar to one asked by Lord Esher in *Antony Gibbs*[349]: 'why should the seller/creditor be in a worse position than a buyer/debtor?'.[350] Consequently, the UKSC decided against abandoning, with respect to judgments in foreign insolvency avoidance proceedings, the traditional common law rule on the recognition and enforcement of foreign judgments *in personam*, which requires, *inter alia*, the judgment debtor to have been present in or submitted to the jurisdiction of the respective foreign country.[351]

344 ibid [15].
345 ibid [16].
346 See *Rubin* & *New Cap* (n 338) s V.
347 ibid [128]-[129].
348 ibid [116]. This argument constitutes one of the main arguments of critics of the Gibbs rule. See n 319 (and accompanying text) and text thereto.
349 See text to n 271.
350 See *Rubin* & *New Cap* (n 338) [116].
351 ibid [7].

(2) Enforcement of Foreign Insolvency-Related Judgments under the CBIR

In *Rubin*, the UKSC also considered whether foreign insolvency-related judgments could be enforced through the CBIR.[352] Lord Collins responded in the negative on that issue, firmly stating that foreign judgments in insolvency matters are not capable of recognition and enforcement under the CBIR:

> But the CBIR (and the Model Law) say nothing about the enforcement of foreign judgments against third parties. ... Recognition and enforcement of judgments in civil and commercial matters (but not in insolvency matters) have been the subject of intense international negotiations at the Hague Conference on Private International Law, which ultimately failed because of inability to agree on recognised international bases of jurisdiction.
>
> It would be surprising if the Model Law was intended to deal with judgments in insolvency matters by implication. Articles 21, 25 and 27 are concerned with procedural matters. No doubt they should be given a purposive interpretation and should be widely construed in the light of the objects of the Model Law, but there is nothing to suggest that they apply to the recognition and enforcement of foreign judgments against third parties.[353]

(3) Submission to Foreign Proceedings

Another relevant issue was submission to foreign proceedings.[354] As already noted, such submission constitutes an exception to the Gibbs rule and a creditor who does so consequently loses the protection under the rule.[355] The UKSC determined that non-appearance before the court in avoidance proceedings is not the only factor to consider, and all other relevant facts should be taken into account.[356] By submitting to the insolvency proceed-

352 ibid s VI.
353 ibid [142]-[143].
354 ibid s VIII.
355 See n 276 (and accompanying text) and text thereto.
356 *Rubin* & *New Cap* (n 338) [164]-[165].

ings (e.g. submitting proofs of debts, participating in creditors' meetings, and voting there) generally, according to Lord Collins, the judgment debtor in *New Cap* had indeed submitted to the jurisdiction of the foreign court overseeing the proceedings.[357]

cc) Reception

The approach taken by the UKSC in those landmark cases can be considered a setback to the universalist convention and, therefore, received harsh criticism from the universalist front. It was described as 'a serious reverse to the cause of international cooperation in insolvency matters'[358] or as reflecting 'a profoundly negative approach to international cooperation' under the MLCBI.[359]

The uncertainty caused by *Rubin* with respect to the nature of post-recognition relief under article 21 of the MLCBI, more specifically as to the recognition of insolvency-related judgments thereunder, prompted UNCITRAL to introduce the MLIJ.[360] In addition to a stand-alone framework for recognising foreign insolvency-related judgments, MLIJ contains a separate article (Article X) directly addressing *Rubin,* which states that foreign insolvency-related judgments can be recognised under article 21 of the MLCBI.

The UK Government also responded to the developments following *Rubin* by launching a consultation in 2022, *inter alia,* on the implementation of MLIJ.[361] That said, the Government intended to implement only Article X of the MLIJ to set aside *Rubin* instead of adopting it in full.[362]

357 ibid [157]-[158], [167].

358 Fletcher (n 27) para 28-026.

359 Westbrook, 'Interpretation Internationale' (n 43) 739.

360 Guide to the MLIJ (n 130) para 2. For a more detailed discussion, see McCormack and Wan (n 155) 298; Mevorach, 'Overlapping International Instruments' (n 166) 293.

361 n 304 and accompanying text.

362 ibid.

2. The US

a) Introduction to Chapter 15

As already identified, the MLCBI was implemented also in the US, as Chapter 15 of the BC in 2005.[363] In most parts, the text is similar or identical to that of the CBIR. That said, there are some material differences between these texts. For example, unlike the British text, the automatic effects of recognition are not limited to foreign liquidation proceedings in the American version.[364] An even more significant difference arises in the interpretation of the MLCBI in these jurisdictions with respect to the recognition of restructuring plans. To begin with, US courts are not bound by the Gibbs rule.[365] Accordingly, courts in the US attach a much broader interpretation to their discretionary powers under the American versions of articles 7 and 21 of the MLCBI (sections 1507 and 1521 of the BC, respectively). That is to say, the recognition and enforcement of foreign restructuring plans and a discharge of a debt (whether or not governed by US law) thereunder and granting a permanent moratorium fall within the scope of sections 1507 and 1521 of the BC,[366] the matters that this work will examine in-depth as subsection C.II.2 progresses.

b) Historical Background: *Gebhard*

It should be noted that the recognition and enforcement of foreign insolvency-related judgments (including those confirming foreign restructuring plans) in the US is not a new concept introduced by Chapter 15. That is to say, US courts have a long history of collaborating with foreign jurisdic-

---

363 Bankruptcy Abuse Prevention and Consumer Protection Act of 2005, Pub L No 109-8, 119 Stat 23 (2005). For a more detailed discussion of Chapter 15 and the changes it brought to US law, see generally Jay Lawrence Westbrook, 'Chapter 15 at Last' (2005) 79 Am Bankr LJ 713.

364 BC (n 37) s 1520.

365 *Agrokor* (n 52) 193-96.

366 The relation (overlap, dominance) between these two sections is not completely clear. For a more detailed discussion, see *Vitro* (87) 1054-57. See also Bruce A. Markell, 'The International Two-Step: Recognizing Domestic Chapter 15 Reorganizations' (2024) 98 Am Bankr LJ 1, 39-40. Further discussion of this matter is outside the scope of this work.

tions in cross-border insolvency cases under the doctrine of comity.[367] For example, in the 19th-century case of *Canada Southern R.Co. v. Gebhard*, a Canadian arrangement contemplating the exchange of New York law-governed bonds was recognised by the USSC and, consequently, constituted a bar to individual actions under the original bonds in the US.[368] The *Gebhard* court, emphasising that contracting with a foreign company entails an implied submission to a foreign jurisdiction, noted that 'anything done at the legal home of the corporation, under the authority of such laws, which discharges it from liability there, discharges it everywhere'.[369] The court, thus, concluded that 'true spirit of international comity requires that schemes of this character, legalized at home, should be recognized in other countries'.[370]

c) Recognition Requirements

aa) General Requirements for Recognising Foreign Judgments

In *Hilton*, the USSC summarised minimum requirements for the recognition of foreign judgments, such as: 'opportunity for a full and fair trial abroad before a court of competent jurisdiction', 'due citation or voluntary appearance of the defendant', and ' a system of jurisprudence likely to secure an impartial administration of justice between the citizens of its own country and those of other countries'.[371] Additionally, a judgment should not be tainted by 'prejudice in the court, or in the system of laws' or 'fraud in procuring the judgment', and no other special ground to deny recognition should be present.[372]

---

367 Westbrook, 'Chapter 15 at Last' (n 363) 718-19. See also Elizabeth Buckel, 'Curbing Comity: The Increasingly Expansive Public Policy Exception of Chapter 15'(2013) 44 Geo J Intl L 1281, 1287-88.

368 *Canada Southern R. Co. v. Gebhard*, 109 US 527 (1883).

369 ibid 537-38. As it can be seen, this perspective, which constitutes one of the primary arguments of critics of the Gibbs rule (see n 319 (and accompanying text) and text thereto) fully contradicts the position of Lord Esher in *Antony Gibbs* (see text to n 271) and, more recently, that of Lord Collins in *Rubin* & *New Cap* (see text to n 348).

370 *Gebhard* (368) 539.

371 *Hilton* (n 86) 202-03. See also Buckel (n 367) 1285-87.

372 ibid.

bb) Recognition Requirements under Chapter 15

With respect to the recognition of foreign restructuring proceedings and related judgments, Chapter 15 and case law thereunder specify different criteria for recognising foreign proceedings under section 1517 and for granting post-recognition relief under sections 1507 or 1521. This relief may include, *inter alia*, recognising and enforcing foreign restructuring plans (foreign court orders confirming such plans), as will be evident while exploring Chapter 15 case law.

(1) Recognition of Foreign Proceedings

The recognition of foreign restructuring proceedings is based on objective criteria under section 1517.[373] Put another way, such recognition is non-discretionary and the court must grant it once all the requirements set out in section 1517 are met, provided that the exception under section 1506 (public policy) does not apply. Even in some cases where the US courts subsequently refused to extend comity and enforce foreign restructuring plans in the US under sections 1507 and 1521, the respective foreign restructuring proceedings were initially recognised under section 1517.[374] This is due to the fact that the respective applications met the requirements of section 1517 and the public policy exception did not apply. Accordingly, the recognition of foreign proceedings under section 1517 is a relatively straightforward matter. That said, such recognition 'is not a rubber stamp exercise', and the foreign representative bears the burden of proof for each requirement of section 1517.[375]

(2) Post-Recognition Relief

As to granting post-recognition relief under sections 1507 or 1521, which also includes the recognition and enforcement of foreign restructuring plans, it shall be first stated that additional assistance under section 1507 is

373 *In re Bear Stearns High-Grade Structured Credit*, 389 BR 325, 333 (SDNY 2008).
374 See, for example, the cases discussed in sub-ss C.II.2.d)dd) and C.II.2.d)ee).
375 *In re PT Bakrie Telecom Tbk*, 628 BR 859, 870 (Bankr SDNY 2021) (*Bakrie*).

conditioned upon the requirements set out in section 1507 (b) (1) – (5)[376] and any relief under section 1521 may be granted 'only if the interests of the creditors and other interested entities, including the debtor, are sufficiently protected'.[377] Besides, unlike the recognition of foreign proceedings, granting post-recognition relief under sections 1507 or 1521 is discretionary[378] and requires the application of the subjective criteria 'that embody principle of comity'.[379] In *Bakrie*, the court summarised the main factors that courts in the US examine in deciding to extend comity: procedural fairness, public policy, and fraud.[380]

d) Case Law under Chapter 15

This work will now turn to an analysis of the case law under Chapter 15 concerning the recognition and enforcement of restructuring plans in the US. It will discuss five notable Chapter 15 cases in that respect. In the first three cases, presented chronologically *inter se,* comity was granted to the respective foreign plans. In the last two cases, presented in the same order, the recognition of foreign plans was denied by the US courts. The examination of the cases will be followed by a brief summary.

aa) *Metcalfe*

In *Metcalfe,* Judge Martin Glenn of the US Bankruptcy Court for the SDNY considered the recognition of Canadian restructuring proceedings as a foreign main proceeding and the enforcement of the Canadian court

376 These requirements do not appear in the MLCBI (or the CBIR) and have been borrowed from Chapter 15's predecessor (section 304 of the BC [repealed]) and case law. More on this, see Kristin van Zwieten, 'Article 7: Additional Assistance under Other Laws' in Reinhard Bork and Michael Veder (eds), *The UNCITRAL Model Laws on Cross-Border Insolvency and on the Recognition and Enforcement of Insolvency-Related Judgments: An Article-by-Article Commentary* (Edward Elgar 2025) para 1.7.7.

377 BC (n 37) s 1522 (a). This section corresponds to art 22 (1) of the MLCBI. For a more detailed discussion, see sub-s F.I.2.b).

378 That is because these sections use the verb *may* as opposed to *shall* used in section 1517.

379 *Bear Stearns* (n 373) 333.

380 *Bakrie* (n 375) 878.

orders sanctioning and implementing a Canadian restructuring plan in the US.[381] These orders included, *inter alia*, third-party non-debtor release and injunction.[382] The enforcement of the Canadian court orders was sought as additional assistance under section 1507 of the BC.[383] There was no controversy concerning the recognition of the Canadian proceedings as a foreign main proceeding under Chapter 15.[384] The central point of the judge's opinion, therefore, was a discussion around the post-recognition relief on the enforcement of the Canadian court orders in the US.[385] Despite 'significant limitations on bankruptcy courts ordering non-debtor releases and injunctions in confirmed chapter 11 plans' imposed by the Second Circuit,[386] the central issue was whether the Canadian orders should be enforced in the US in that Chapter 15 case rather than reassessing the merits of the respective release and injunction provisions in light of those limitations.[387] Stating that a 'U.S. bankruptcy court is not required to make an independent determination about the propriety of individual acts of a foreign court',[388] the judge concluded as follows:

> There is no basis for this Court to second-guess the decisions of the Canadian courts. Principles of comity in chapter 15

381 *In re Metcalfe Mansfield Alternative Investments*, 421 BR 685 (Bankr SDNY 2010) (*Metcalfe*).
382 ibid 688.
383 ibid 696.
384 ibid 688.
385 ibid 694-700.
386 ibid 694-95. The respective bankruptcy court hearing the case falls within the jurisdiction of the Second Circuit.
387 ibid 696. As already mentioned in s A.III, the examination of third-party releases in restructuring proceedings, including those in Chapter 11 plans, falls outside the scope of this work. However, it should be briefly noted that third-party releases constitute one of the controversial issues under Chapter 11. For years, varying approaches have prevailed among the Circuits regarding such releases. For a summary of the differing Circuit-level approaches to the matter, see *Avanti* (n 291) 606; generally Dorothy Coco, 'Third-Party Bankruptcy Releases: An Analysis of Consent Through the Lenses of Due Process and Contract Law' (2019) 88 Fordham L Rev 231. For a more detailed discussion and critical analysis, see generally Ralph Brubaker, 'Bankruptcy Injunctions and Complex Litigation: A Critical Reappraisal of Non-Debtor Releases in Chapter 11 Reorganizations' [1997] U Ill L Rev 959. It is also important to note that, in 2024, the USSC addressed the availability of *non-consensual* third-party releases under Chapter 11, more specifically, under s 1123 (b) (6) of the BC and categorically denied such availability as a matter of law. See *Harrington v. Purdue Pharma LP*, 603 US 204 (2024) (*Purdue*).
388 *Metcalfe* (n 381) 697.

> cases support enforcement of the Canadian Orders in the United States whether or not the same relief could be ordered in a plenary case under chapter 11. Therefore, the Court will enter an order recognizing this case as a foreign main proceeding and enforcing the Canadian Orders.[389]

bb) *Avanti*

In *Avanti,* the same judge considered the enforcement of a scheme of arrangement sanctioned by the EWHC and the respective court order in the US under sections 1507 and 1521 of the BC.[390] The scheme provided for a debt-for-equity exchange of the notes issued under a New York law-governed indenture.[391] Emphasising that 'in the exercise of comity that appropriate relief under section 1521 or additional assistance under section 1507 may include recognizing and enforcing a foreign plan confirmation order',[392] the judge granted the discretionary relief sought.[393]

cc) *Agrokor*

In *Agrokor*, the same judge was asked to recognise and enforce a settlement agreement approved by a Croatian court following the recognition of the respective Croatian proceedings as a foreign main proceeding under Chapter 15.[394] This settlement agreement involved the discharge of debts governed by English and New York laws (including the release of third-party guarantees).[395] The judge not only granted the relief requested [396] but also took the opportunity to examine and, consequently, criticise the Gibbs rule in detail as part of his opinion.[397]

---

389 ibid 700.
390 *Avanti* (n 291).
391 ibid 609-611.
392 ibid 616
393 ibid 619.
394 *Agrokor* (n 52).
395 ibid 169, 171-75.
396 ibid 196-97.
397 ibid 192-96.

dd) *Vitro*

Vitro was a case before the Fifth Circuit, where the court considered, *inter alia*, two appeals from a bankruptcy court decision denying the enforcement of a Mexican reorganisation plan and a permanent injunction sought under sections 1507 and 1521.[398] The bankruptcy court, whose decision was appealed, had refused, based on several provisions of Chapter 15, to enforce the Mexican reorganisation plan providing for the release of third-party non-debtor guaranties governed by New York law and to grant a permanent injunction.[399]

As to the availability of the relief requested under section 1507, the bankruptcy court referred to section 1507 (b) (4) in denying the relief.[400] According to the court, the distribution of the debtor's assets under the Mexican court order in question had substantially deviated from the order of distribution under Chapter 11,[401] which is an analogous US framework. As far as section 1521 was concerned, the bankruptcy court grounded its decision to reject the respective application on section 1522 (a), as, in the court's view, the Mexican court order had not provided sufficient protection to US creditors, nor had it maintained an adequate balance between the interests of creditors on one side and the debtor and its subsidiaries on the other.[402] The bankruptcy court also referred to section 1506 (the public policy exception) by holding that the protection of third-party claims in insolvency cases constitutes the public policy of the US, which the Mexican plan in question had failed to ensure.[403]

The debtor in the Mexican proceedings and one of its largest creditors appealed the bankruptcy court's decision.[404] The appellate court held that the respective relief falls outside section 1521 because the specific provisions under section 1521 (a) (1) – (7) and (b), as well as *any appropriate relief*

398 *Vitro* (n 87). The court also addressed a consolidated appeal by a group of creditors from the district court's decision on the recognition of the Mexican reorganisation proceedings and the appointment of the foreign representatives under Chapter 15. The respective appeal, however, will not be discussed further in this work.

399 *Vitro, S.A.B. de C.V. v. ACP Master, Ltd. (In re Vitro, S.A.B. de C.V.)*, 473 BR 117, 133 (Bankr ND Tex 2012) (*Vitro II*).

400 ibid 132.

401 ibid.

402 ibid.

403 ibid. This aspect of the bankruptcy court's decision will be separately discussed in sub-s D.I.3.a)cc).

404 *Vitro* (n 87) 1041.

under section 1521 (a) apply to the debtor only, thus, does not provide for discharge of non-debtor third-party obligations.[405] The appellate court further noted that even if the relief requested 'were theoretically available' under section 1521, the bankruptcy court had not exceeded its discretion under section 1522 in denying the relief for substantially the same reasons as under section 1507,[406] which will be summarised below.

The appellate court also ruled on the denial of the relief under section 1507, stating that although the relief sought could theoretically be available, the bankruptcy court had not been wrong in denying the relief based on section 1507 (b) (4).[407] The court found that the debtor had failed to demonstrate extraordinary factors supporting the third-party releases.[408] In addition, the court emphasised that there had been a significant retention of equity value while the distribution to the creditors had not come close to their original entitlements.[409] The court also underscored that the debtor had only reached the requisite majority because of insider voters and the majority of the affected non-insider creditors had not voted for the plan.[410] The court, thus, distinguished the facts of *Metcalfe,*[411] where a Canadian restructuring plan contemplating third-party non-debtor release had been recognised under section 1507.[412]

The appellate court did not specifically address whether the public policy exception under section 1506 should apply since the relief sought had been properly denied under both sections 1507 and 1521.[413]

ee) *Bakrie*

In *Bakrie,* a US bankruptcy court considered recognising Indonesian restructuring proceedings under section 1517 and granting additional relief on the enforcement of the Indonesian restructuring plan under sections 1507

405 ibid 1058-60.
406 ibid 1060.
407 ibid 1060-61.
408 ibid.
409 ibid 1067.
410 ibid.
411 *Metcalfe* (n 381).
412 *Vitro* (n 87) 1068.
413 ibid 1069-70.

and 1521.[414] The brief facts of the case were as follows.[415] The recognition and the additional relief sought was objected to by a group of holders of notes issued under a New York law-governed indenture. The notes (totalling 380 million US Dollars) were issued not by the debtor in the Indonesian proceedings but rather by its wholly owned subsidiary. The issuer, however, loaned the proceeds from the issuance of the notes to the debtor and subsequently assigned its rights under the respective loan arrangements to the trustee under the indenture. Besides, the repayment of the notes was separately guaranteed by the debtor under a New York law-governed parent guarantee, which provided direct recourse from the debtor for noteholders and the indenture trustee. One notable feature of this case is that, despite the assignment and the parental guarantee, neither noteholders nor the indenture trustee, instead the issuer (the wholly owned subsidiary of the debtor), had been listed as creditor and permitted to vote on the Indonesian restructuring plan for the 380 million US Dollars notes. The respective claim of the issuer had been approved by the court-appointed administrator and subsequently verified by the Indonesian courts despite the objections of the indenture trustee and an ad hoc committee of noteholders.

The bankruptcy court rejected the objecting noteholders' arguments opposing the recognition of the Indonesian restructuring proceedings as a foreign main proceeding and granted recognition under section 1517.[416] These noteholders also objected to the additional relief on enforcing the Indonesian restructuring plan in the US under sections 1507 and 1521 based on the arguments that the Indonesian restructuring plan had not properly contained the third-party releases and they had not received fair treatment during the Indonesian restructuring proceedings, underscoring their exclusion from voting.[417]

Given the discretionary nature of relief under either section 1507 or section 1521 and its dependency upon the principle of comity, the bankruptcy court decided not to enforce the Indonesian restructuring plan after conducting its comity analysis.[418] The reason for that was the lack of 'a clear and formal record' in the Indonesian court order on whether the affected

414 *Bakrie* (n 375).

415 For the facts of the case, see ibid 864-70.

416 The respective arguments of the objecting noteholders and the court's reasoning on those arguments (ibid 871-875) will not be discussed further in this work.

417 ibid 876.

418 ibid 877ff.

creditors had received adequate procedural protections in the Indonesian proceedings as to the third-party release issue and on the substantive justification or explanation for any third-party release.[419] The court, thus, distinguished previous cases where third-party releases had been enforced in the US in a Chapter 15 case.[420]

As to the voting issue raised by the objecting noteholders, the court acknowledged that the record is 'not particularly fulsome' on the issue, highlighting the importance of the factor of insider voting under US law.[421] Despite that, the court chose not to reach whether or not the matter of the exclusion of the objecting noteholders from voting would constitute a bar to extend comity to the Indonesian restructuring plan, as the relief requested had already been denied due to the matter of third-party release.[422]

ff) Summary

The cases examined above illustrated that foreign restructuring plans may be recognised and enforced in the US as discretionary post-recognition relief under the American version of the MLCBI, namely, under sections 1507 or 1521 of the BC. However, US courts do not blindly defer to foreign restructuring proceedings. Instead, they conduct their comity analysis and examine these proceedings first, but primarily in a procedural fairness context.

3. Comparative Summary

Thus far, section C.II has analysed the implementation of the MLCBI in England (the CBIR) and in the US (Chapter 15) with respect to the recognition of restructuring plans. This subsection will provide a brief comparative overview.

To begin with, the automatic effects of recognition under the CBIR only apply to foreign main proceedings that aim to liquidate (wind up) the debtor. Therefore, they do not take effect with respect to foreign restructuring proceedings. By contrast, Chapter 15 does not draw such a distinction

419 ibid 884-85.
420 ibid 885-86.
421 ibid 887-89
422 ibid 890.

and provides for those effects in relation to all foreign main proceedings upon recognition.

Furthermore, a discharge in foreign restructuring proceedings is not recognised in the eyes of English law unless it is valid under the governing law of the contract or the creditor has submitted to the foreign proceedings in question. The implementation of the MLCBI in England has not altered this position. On the other hand, such a discharge of a debt, including one governed by US law, may be recognised in ancillary Chapter 15 proceedings.

In addition, foreign insolvency-related judgments (including foreign court orders confirming restructuring plans) are not capable of recognition and enforcement under the CBIR. Instead, general rules of English private international law on the recognition and enforcement of foreign judgments apply. By contrast, such judgments may be recognised and enforced under Chapter 15 (sections 1507 or 1521 of the BC).

Finally, upon recognition of foreign restructuring proceedings as a foreign main proceeding under the CBIR, English courts lack jurisdiction to grant a moratorium that would permanently prevent creditors (whose substantive rights have not been discharged as a matter of English law) from enforcing their substantive rights. This is because it would effectively discharge those rights, which is not allowed under the Gibbs rule. However, US courts do have such jurisdiction. In exercising their discretion in this matter, as well as when recognising foreign restructuring plans and any debt discharge thereunder, US courts base their decision on the comity analysis. Hence, they primarily assess whether or not the public policy of the US is violated and the respective foreign proceedings satisfy the fundamental standards of procedural fairness.

III. Assessment of the Approaches Adopted in England and in the US

Having discussed the implementation of the MLCBI in England and in the US with respect to the recognition of restructuring plans, this work now turns to the assessment of the approaches adopted in these jurisdictions. They will be referred to as the *English* and *American* approaches, respectively. To begin with, this work argues that neither approach, taken in its entirety, strikes a fair balance between the interests of the debtor and dissenting foreign creditors in the recognition of restructuring plans. Nonetheless, each approach, particularly the American one, possesses certain advantageous features that can be functional and effective for this purpose. Below, this work will examine the advantages and disadvantages of each approach separately.

1. The English Approach

a) Advantages

The English approach offers only a few advantages. The main benefit is certainty to creditors: once a law governing a debt instrument has been selected, substantive rights and protections thereunder will remain unchanged in the eyes of this law, even if restructuring proceedings in other jurisdictions discharge the debt.[423] From a creditor's perspective, such certainty is crucial, particularly when the debtor is from a jurisdiction whose law is not well-equipped to ensure a fair outcome in the event of the debtor's restructuring. As proponents argue, this holds particularly true for institutionalised market participants lending to debtors from across the globe.[424] If the fact that the country having jurisdiction over a potential restructuring of the debtor can be changed *ex post* (e.g. due to a COMI shift) is added to the picture,[425] the importance of such certainty is hard to overstate. Providing certain safeguards for the protection of creditors' substantive rights, therefore, is not only understandable but also of necessity. However, this should not be done according to the formula of the Gibbs rule since the rule does not implement the idea in the right way.

Another advantage, albeit from a policy perspective, is that the English approach can make a significant contribution to the development of the restructuring market in jurisdictions that adopt it. That is to say, this approach effectively requires the debtor to initiate restructuring proceedings (either as parallel or main proceedings) in the jurisdiction whose law governs the debt in order to achieve its discharge.[426] Under this approach, restructurings of debtors from across the globe will be channelled to jurisdictions whose laws are typically chosen to govern cross-border transactions,

423 See text to nn 332, 333.

424 See text to n 334.

425 For a more detailed discussion, see sub-s F.II.2.b)bb).

426 In theory, it does not directly require such proceedings. Nonetheless, as Stephan Madaus puts it, most restructuring frameworks require the involvement of local courts. See Madaus, 'The Cross-border Effects of Restructurings' (n 3) 484-85.

such as England. It is not surprising that practitioners in England generally support the Gibbs rule.[427]

b) Disadvantages

The English approach, shaped by the Gibbs rule, presents several drawbacks, primarily arising from the manner of its implementation. However, this work will first focus on its doctrinal aspects. As noted earlier, this work does not agree with the pure contractual classification of restructuring proceedings.[428] It agrees with the argument of critics that the Gibbs rule treats discharge in restructuring proceedings as a purely contractual matter between the debtor and a single creditor without taking into account a background context (such as the debtor's distress) and overlooks broader policy objectives.[429]

In addition, the English approach is not principle-based. The universal effect of an English bankruptcy discharge of a debt, whether or not governed by English law, as opposed to the territorial effect of a foreign bankruptcy discharge in the eyes of English law, a paradox often highlighted by critics,[430] is noteworthy at this point.[431]

As to the implementation, as already stated, the English approach effectively requires the debtor to initiate restructuring proceedings (either as parallel or main proceedings) under the governing law of the contract.[432] This approach has certain drawbacks.[433] First and foremost, if the confirmed plan under the *lex fori concursus* treats a foreign creditor no less favourably than the treatment what the governing law of the contract would provide, there seems to be no justifiable reason for initiating costly and time-consuming parallel proceedings. Second, it is worth reiterating that discharge in this context is not merely a matter between the debtor and a single creditor. Rather, it generally affects the majority of creditors, if not all

427 See, eg, FMLC (n 332).
428 See sub-s B.I.3.a).
429 See, eg, a summary of Look Chan Ho's and Kannan Ramesh's criticism of the rule (text to nn 315-323). See also McCormack 'UK Contracts and Modification under Foreign Law' (n 166) pt 2.
430 n 312 (and accompanying text) and text thereto.
431 n 290 (and accompanying text) and text thereto.
432 n 426 (and accompanying text) and text thereto.
433 For a criticism of that aspect of the Gibbs rule by the author of this work, see also Abbasov (n 188) pt II.

of them. It is not uncommon for various foreign laws to govern the debts affected by a restructuring plan. Were all these foreign laws to adopt a similar approach, the debtor would be required to initiate several concurrent proceedings in the respective foreign jurisdictions. Such multiple parallel proceedings could have detrimental effects on costs and efficiency and might even obstruct an otherwise viable plan.[434]

Furthermore, this work also agrees with critics on the point that the Gibbs rule is inconsistent with the principle of modified universalism,[435] which is based on the concept of a single set of proceedings with universal effect. This work has already touched on the advantages of administering cross-border insolvency and restructuring cases under the respective concept.[436]

Finally, this work agrees with the arguments that the Gibbs rule effectively incentivises holdout behaviour and may lead to unfair and value-destructive outcomes.[437] That is to say, the rule encourages foreign creditors not to cooperate in restructuring proceedings in the debtor's home jurisdiction from the outset, since it might amount to submission to those proceedings.[438]

2. The American Approach

a) Advantages

To begin with, the American approach does not pose any of the problems associated with the English approach, as discussed above. That is to say, a discharge of a debt (including one governed by US law) in foreign restructuring proceedings may theoretically be recognised in the US. Furthermore, foreign court orders confirming restructuring plans may be recognised and

434 For similar arguments, see Westbrook 'Internationalist Principle' (n 43) 570. For a different view, see Paterson, 'A Qualified Defence of the Rule in Gibbs' (n 74) s VII.B.

435 See, eg, text to nn 316, 324, 326.

436 See sub-s B.II.3.a).

437 See, eg, nn 309, 310, 327 (and accompanying text) and text thereto. For criticism of such holdout behavior, see Westbrook 'Internationalist Principle' (n 43) 568-69. For a different view, see Paterson, 'A Qualified Defence of the Rule in Gibbs' (n 74) ss VII.B, VII.C, VII.D.

438 Submission to foreign proceedings is an exception to the Gibbs rule. A creditor submitting to the foreign proceedings in question loses the protection of the rule. See text to nn 276, 277.

given full force (combined with a permanent moratorium) under Chapter 15. All those matters can be resolved in an ancillary Chapter 15 proceeding. Consequently, no main or parallel restructuring proceedings in the US are required. To sum up, the American approach is, on its surface, a notable example of how modified universalism can function in practice.

b) Disadvantages

There is little room for criticism of the American approach, given all the advantages mentioned above. Nonetheless, this work argues that the American approach is not without shortcomings either. As already identified (B.II.4), the principle of modified universalism contemplates an evaluation of the fairness of foreign proceedings before recognising their cross-border effects. As noted earlier, US courts primarily evaluate foreign proceedings based on procedural fairness and public policy considerations, which are important safeguards in this context. That said, equally important is a safeguard for ensuring that foreign creditors' substantive rights have been adequately protected in a restructuring in the debtor's home jurisdiction (substantive fairness review), as already highlighted in this work.[439] Put another way, 'foreign creditors are entitled to more than just the right to be heard and voted down in a foreign proceeding'.[440] It should also be noted that US courts' review of the fairness of foreign proceedings is not purely procedural in nature and also encompasses some substantive aspects without expressly referring to substantive fairness. However, they conduct their analysis on substantive matters mainly within a procedural framework, as generally observed in the cases examined in this work. For example, in *Bakrie,* the court denied the recognition of an Indonesian plan containing third-party release due to a lack of a formal court record on the issue.[441] In *Vitro*, the court's decision to deny comity to a Mexican plan (again, on the issue of third-party releases) was significantly influenced by the fact that the plan had been adopted only with the support of insiders.[442] However,

439 See sub-s C.III.1.a). See also Abbasov (n 188) pt II.

440 Stephan Madaus, 'The Rule in Gibbs, or How to Protect Local Debt from a Foreign Discharge' (OBLB 19 December 2018) <https://blogs.law.ox.ac.uk/business-law-blog/blog/2018/12/rule-gibbs-or-how-protect-local-debt-foreign-discharge> accessed 21 October 2025.

441 *Bakrie* (n 375). For a more detailed discussion of this case, see sub-s C.II.2.d)ee).

442 *Vitro* (n 87). For a more detailed discussion of this case, see sub-s C.II.2.d)dd).

in *Metcalfe*, where no such kind of procedural irregularities were present, a Canadian plan contemplating third-party release was granted comity in the US.[443] This work argues that such an approach is not entirely preferable since it may not guarantee substantive fairness in all cases and may lead to inconsistent outcomes.[444]

Another noteworthy issue is that the American approach is primarily designed to protect US creditors. That is to say, in assessing the outcome of foreign proceedings, similarity to US law is required under this approach.[445] Hence, the American approach focuses not on the governing law of the contract but rather on the law of the forum (US law) for this purpose. In cases where US law (e.g. New York law) is also the governing law of the contract (perhaps in most cases), this issue does not arise. However, there may be cases where the governing law of the contract is the law of a state other than the state in which recognition is sought (in most cases, due to the location of assets in the latter state) and opposed by the respective creditor. The legal order and public policy of the receiving state should undoubtedly be taken into account, but not within the framework of a substantial fairness review. These are the subject matters of procedural fairness review and the public policy exception. This is one of the occasions where the distinction between asset-oriented insolvency proceedings and debt-oriented restructuring proceedings becomes significant.[446] That is to say, restructuring proceedings primarily focus on the claims against the debtor rather than the debtor's assets and generally do not involve the marshalling or sale of the debtor's entire asset pool. Therefore, in the context of a substantive fairness review invoked by the opposing creditor, similarity should be required with the governing law of the contract. Accordingly, this work advocates developing a more principled approach to the matter, which will be elaborated in greater detail later.

IV. Towards a Balanced Model

Section C.III illustrated that both the English and American approaches have their advantages and disadvantages, with the latter ultimately being preferable. Hence, this work suggests a middle-ground model between the

443 *Metcalfe* (n 381). For a more detailed discussion of this case, see sub-s C.II.2.d)aa).
444 This point will be revisited in sub-s F.II.2.a)dd).
445 BC (n 37) s 1507 (b) (4). See, eg, the case discussed in sub-s C.II.2.d)dd).
446 See sub-s B.I.3.a).

English and American approaches, leaning more closely towards the latter. This model attempts, to the extent possible, to combine the fairly advantageous features of both approaches and eliminate their one-sided, unfairly disadvantageous aspects.

Hence, the model suggested in this work aims to prevent parallel proceedings in multiple jurisdictions, while ensuring robust procedural and substantive protections for foreign creditors affected by a restructuring in the debtor's home country.[447] This model draws on the American approach, as it is more consistent with the current best practices in cross-border insolvency law, including the adherence to the principles of comity and modified universalism. Furthermore, the American approach provides well-established criteria for evaluating procedural fairness in foreign proceedings. With these considerations in mind, there is a solid foundation (the American approach) on which to develop the intended model. That said, the American approach should raise the bar for fairness review to expressly encompass the substantive fairness of foreign restructuring plans in contested cases.

In the framework of the respective model, this work will first analyse the traditional safeguards in recognising foreign judgments, such as public policy and procedural fairness, which are also relevant under the MLCBI (Part D). As mentioned earlier, the American approach offers a well-established framework in this regard. Therefore, Chapter 15 case law will be closely examined. Then, this work will turn to substantive fairness in restructuring. It will discuss this concept in a domestic context (Part E), before delving into a thorough analysis of ensuring substantive fairness in considering the recognition of restructuring plans under the MLCBI and developing a framework for this purpose (Part F). This work will particularly seek to find a solution that balances the interests of the debtor and dissenting foreign creditors.

V. Summary

In Part C, this work analysed the recognition of restructuring plans under the MLCBI, focusing on the different approaches to the matter under the adopted versions in England and in the US. It first illustrated the

447 See Abbasov (n 188) pt III, where the author of this work underscored a need for such an approach and outlined his initial general ideas regarding a substantive fairness review in the framework of the mentioned approach.

differences using the example of the IBA restructuring proceedings (C.I) and then separately examined each jurisdiction (C.II). This was followed by an assessment of the approaches adopted in the respective jurisdictions (C.III). The assessment identified that neither the English approach nor the American one is entirely preferable. That is to say, certain aspects of the English and American approaches can unfairly disadvantage the debtor and dissenting foreign creditors, respectively. More to the point, the English approach views discharge in restructuring proceedings as a purely contractual matter and, thus, requires proceedings under the governing law of the contract to bind dissenting foreign creditors. While this approach offers certainty to creditors, it is not in line with modified universalism, thus, denying the advantages that a modified universalism-based system offers. Nor does it align with the spirit of the MLCBI specifically. As to the American approach, it generally is in conformity with modified universalism but evaluates substantive aspects of foreign restructuring proceedings primarily within a procedural context, which may lead to inconsistency regarding substantive fairness. In addition, the American approach prioritises US law (over the governing law of the contract) when comparing the substantive outcome of foreign restructuring proceedings.

Hence, this work suggested a model, to the extent possible, combining the fairly advantageous aspects of the respective approaches while eliminating their unfairly disadvantageous features (C.IV). This model is primarily based on the American approach but includes a substantive fairness review in contested cases.

D. Traditional Safeguards in the Recognition of Foreign Judgments: Public Policy and Procedural Fairness

As the title suggests, Part D will focus on the traditional safeguards in recognising foreign judgments, namely, public policy and procedural fairness. This work refers to these safeguards as *traditional* and brings them together in Part D because they are not specific to cross-border restructuring or insolvency cases. Instead, they have long been in place as general safeguards in the context of the recognition of foreign judgments in civil and commercial matters and form part of most cross-border instruments in that area.[448] Another reason they are grouped in this Part is that these safeguards are mainly in place to protect, in a broad sense, the legal order of the forum. Hence, these safeguards serve as a shield against the recognition and enforcement of foreign judgments that either conflict with the public policy of the forum or are tainted by procedural irregularities. Part D will provide a detailed analysis of the safeguards mentioned above, with a focus on their position under the MLCBI. Section D.I will examine public policy. Section D.II will analyse procedural fairness, followed by a summary in section D.III.

I. Public Policy

1. Introduction to the Public Policy Doctrine

Public policy is a legal doctrine that monitors private law arrangements, foreign laws, or foreign judgments to ensure that they align with the public policy (public interests, public morality, public security) of the forum.[449] The required degree of the alignment varies depending on the subject being

448 See, eg, Brussels I bis Regulation (n 135) art 45 (1) (a)-(b). See also sub-s C.II.2.c)aa).

449 Farshad Ghodoosi, 'The Concept of Public Policy in Law: Revisiting the Role of the Public Policy Doctrine in the Enforcement of Private Legal Arrangements' (2016) 94 Neb L Rev 685, 689-90.

monitored. In the literature, two main concepts of public policy have been identified in this context: domestic and international public policy.[450]

Domestic, national, or internal public policy is a part of domestic (substantive) law and focuses on domestic private law arrangements.[451] In most jurisdictions, the legislation includes express norms against private law arrangements that are contrary to good morals.[452] The principal application of domestic public policy is in contract law, where it sets the boundaries for the cornerstone principle of party autonomy.[453] The focus of domestic public policy, however, is not the formation of a contract but rather its effects.[454] Accordingly, contracts that are properly formed in the eyes of contract law and are not illegal may still fall within the scope of domestic public policy.[455] The consequence of a successful invocation of the public policy defence can be the voidness or unenforceability of a contract, depending on the jurisdiction.[456]

International or external public policy is also a part of domestic law, specifically its private international law branch. When successfully invoked, it leads to the outcome that otherwise applicable foreign law is not applied, or a foreign judgment or award that is otherwise eligible for recognition

450 In the literature, transnational or truly international public policy is also distinguished. Unlike domestic or international public policy, here, the policy sought to be protected is based not on domestic law or values but rather on the fundamental principles and values under public international law, such as the prohibition of slavery, child labour, corruption, and so forth. Its typical area of application is international arbitration. See Alex Mills, 'The Dimensions of Public Policy in Private International Law' (2008) 4 J Priv Intl L 201, 214-15; Olaf Meyer, 'A Flexible System in Flux: On the Realignment of Public Policy' in Olaf Meyer (ed), *Public Policy and Private International Law: A Comparative Guide* (Edward Elgar Publishing 2022) paras 1-1049-52. Not many issues arise regarding this concept of public policy for the purposes of the present work, as what constitutes public policy is of universal nature accepted by most states and confined to particularly fundamental matters. Besides, issues concerning most of the values and principles protected by transnational public policy (child labour, slavery, and so forth) generally do not arise in the context of restructuring law. Therefore, this work will not discuss transnational public policy.

451 Bram Akkermans, 'Public Policy (Orde Public): A Comparative Analysis of National, Private International Law, and EU Public Policy' (2019) 8 EPLJ 260, 266-68.

452 German Civil Code (Bürgerliches Gesetzbuch), s 138; French Civil Code (Code civil), art 6.

453 Akkermans (n 451) 268.

454 Ghodoosi (n 449) 696.

455 ibid 696-98; Akkermans (n 451) 268.

456 For a comparative analysis, see Akkermans (n 451) 268-271. For a historical analysis of common law, see Ghodoosi (n 449) 695-96.

is not recognised.[457] In most civil law jurisdictions, the legislation contains express norms dedicated to international public policy.[458] However, it may also be applied as a doctrine of private international law without any specific norm in the legislation (e.g. France).[459] It has even been argued that international public policy may be invoked as a general principle under all international instruments of private international law if the respective instrument is silent on the matter.[460]

Based on these insights, the public policy exception under the MLCBI (article 6) can easily be attributed to international public policy. Additionally, as this work will identify later (D.I.3), the Guide to the MLCB expressly recommends differentiating public policy under article 6 of the MLCBI from domestic public policy.[461] Hence, this work will briefly explore the concept of international public policy in general (D.I.2) before examining the public policy exception under the MLCBI (D.I.3).

2. International Public Policy

a) Introduction to International Public Policy

aa) Role of Public Policy

Even though states are free to design their own private international law rules or to be part of international or regional private international law instruments, rules of private international law are traditionally based on objective criteria.[462] These rules aim to determine the best law or forum for each case and generally do not consider subjective criteria like the

---

457 P.B. Carter, 'The Role of Public Policy in English Private International Law' (1993) 42 Intl & Comp LQ 1, 1; Mills (n 450) 201.

458 See, eg, Germany: Introductory Act to the Civil Code (Einführungsgesetz zum Bürgerlichen Gesetzbuche ["EGBGB"]), art 6; Code of Civil Procedure (Zivilprozessordnung), s 328 (1) (4).

459 Akkermans (n 451) 279.

460 Mills (n 450) 201 (fn 5 therein and accompanying text).

461 Therefore, hereinafter, the analysis of public policy will mostly be confined to international public policy. Accordingly, hereinafter, the reference to *public policy* should be understood as the reference to *international public policy* only, unless an express indication to the contrary (such as the usage of adjectives *domestic* or *transnational*).

462 Meyer, 'A Flexible System in Flux' (n 450) para 1-001.

quality, modernity, or fairness of a legal system in specific states.[463] That said, underlying legal principles and societal values that form the basis of legal systems vary globally, logically leading to differences in the substantive content of laws in different states. While some differences are (and should be) acceptable when considering deference to foreign laws, the variation may be so substantial that it conflicts with the fundamental principles of law or morality of the *lex fori*.[464] This is the point at which the public policy exception intervenes, preventing the application of a foreign law or the recognition of a foreign judgment violating these fundamental principles.[465]

The exception is often described through metaphoric expressions such as *escape route*,[466] *last bastion of defence*,[467] *life vest*,[468] and *safety net*[469] due to its crucial role against foreign laws or judgments that are irreconcilable with the fundamental principles of the legal system of the *lex fori*. Therefore, the importance of the public policy exception in private international law is widely acknowledged in scholarship despite the problematic issues associated with it, which this work will discuss later. Even in the context of EU law, where a significant number of areas of law are harmonised and the principle of mutual trust reigns among Member States regarding one another's legal system, the public policy exception retains its place in almost all EU private international law instruments.[470] Thus far, most proposals to exclude the public policy exception have not succeeded.[471]

bb) Public Policy and Overriding Mandatory Provisions

The modern concept of public policy has a negative function, as it does not specify which law should be applied to the matter but rather prevents

463 ibid paras 1-001-02.
464 ibid paras 1-002-3.
465 ibid paras 1-003.
466 Carter (n 457) 1; Meyer, 'A Flexible System in Flux' (n 450) para 1-005.
467 Meyer, 'A Flexible System in Flux' (n 450) para 1-003.
468 Peter Mankowski and Svenja Langenhagen, 'Germany' in Olaf Meyer (ed), *Public Policy and Private International Law: A Comparative Guide* (Edward Elgar Publishing 2022) para 8-001.
469 Mills (n 450) 202; Meyer, 'A Flexible System in Flux' (n 450) para 1-005.
470 Meyer, 'A Flexible System in Flux' (n 450) 1-006 (fn 7 therein and accompanying text); Wolfgang Wurmnest, 'Public Policy in European Private International Law' in Olaf Meyer (ed), *Public Policy and Private International Law: A Comparative Guide* (Edward Elgar Publishing 2022) para 2-004 (fn 10 therein and accompanying text).
471 Meyer, 'A Flexible System in Flux' (n 450) para 1-026.

the application of foreign laws that would otherwise be applicable (or the recognition of foreign judgments and awards that would otherwise be eligible for recognition).[472] A positive function in this context is fulfilled by another concept of private international law, namely, *overriding mandatory provisions*,[473] which dictates the application of certain mandatory norms of the *lex fori* to the relationship of the parties, regardless of the applicable law under private international law.[474]

cc) Public Policy and Procedural Fairness

When discussing the public policy exception in the context of the recognition of foreign judgments, one may ask whether the public policy exception should also encompass the procedural fairness of the respective foreign proceedings or be confined to the substantive content only. In some jurisdictions, due process (in foreign proceedings) constitutes a sub-branch (procedural public policy) of public policy along with substantive public policy.[475] This view is also supported by the language used in article 7 of the MLIJ, which expressly states that public policy includes 'the fundamental principles of procedural fairness' of the receiving state.[476] Besides, many cross-border private international law instruments, such as the EIR, do not expressly refer to procedural fairness, which is presumed to fall within the scope of the general public policy exception under these instruments. For example, In *Eurofood IFSC Ltd*, the Court of Justice of the European Union ("CJEU") acknowledged that the right to be heard may constitute the fundamental public policy of Member States and fall within the scope of the public policy exception under the EIR's predecessor.[477] An alternative view is that procedural fairness falls outside the scope of public policy

472 Akkermans (n 451) 273-74; Wurmnest (n 470) para 2-009.

473 The concept of *overriding mandatory provisions* will not be discussed further in s D.I of this work, but will be revisited in a different context in sub-s F.II.3.b).

474 Akkermans (n 451) 273-74; Meyer, 'A Flexible System in Flux' (n 450) para 1-011; Wurmnest (n 470) para 2-009.

475 eg, Dutch law. See Akkermans (n 451) 276.

476 Guide to the MLIJ (n 130) para 74. See also Wan Wai Yee, 'Article 7: Public Policy Exception' in Reinhard Bork and Michael Veder (eds), *The UNCITRAL Model Laws on Cross-Border Insolvency and on the Recognition and Enforcement of Insolvency-Related Judgments: An Article-by-Article Commentary* (Edward Elgar 2025) para 2.7.1.

477 Case C-341/04 *Eurofood IFSC Ltd* [2006] ECR I/3813, [60]-[68].

and should be assessed under the framework of *natural justice*.[478] Both perspectives, however, agree that a judgment should not be recognised if the respective foreign proceedings lack due process. Therefore, the distinction between these two perspectives is not relevant for the purposes of the present work. That said, section D.I will discuss public policy solely in a substantive context. That is primarily because procedural fairness, which will be a matter for section D.II of this work, may be assessed even without invoking the public policy exception under the MLCBI.[479]

b) Problematic Aspects of Public Policy

This work has already highlighted the importance of the role that the public policy exception plays under private international law. However, it is essential to note that the exception is not without shortcomings. In that sense, there are two notable aspects related to the public policy exception.

One of the issues involves the ambiguity surrounding the definition of public policy.[480] In many jurisdictions, public policy is either not defined or defined in vague or general terms. For example, Dutch law simply refers to *public policy (order)*,[481] while under German law it is defined as *fundamental principles of German law* with a specific focus on *civil rights*.[482] As one commentator aptly puts it, 'Usually public policy is defined through examples of its application, or by what it is not'.[483] Even international or regional instruments on the harmonisation of different areas of private international law do not attempt to define public policy, leaving the matter to national laws.[484] One commentator points out in the general EU law context that the exception 'is the unharmonized part of private international law'.[485] Despite all undesired consequences that will be outlined below, this seems to be

478 Carter (n 457) 1; John Briggs, 'Bars to Common Law Recognition' in Richard Sheldon (ed) *Cross-Border Insolvency* (4th edn, Bloomsbury Professional 2015), para 11.10.
479 See n 570 (and accompanying text) and text thereto.
480 Mills (n 450) 202; Akkermans (n 451) 262-63; Meyer, 'A Flexible System in Flux' (n 450) para 1-007.
481 Dutch Civil Code (Burgerlijk Wetboek), art 10:6.
482 n 458 and accompanying text.
483 Akkermans (n 451) 262-63.
484 See, eg, Guide to the MLCBI (n 17) para 101.
485 Meyer, 'A Flexible System in Flux' (n 450) para 1-006.

a rather deliberate approach.[486] One reason for such an approach might be that even a carefully designed, all-encompassing definition of public policy bears the risk of omitting some important policies worth protecting. Second, public policy is a dynamic notion as the society's values upon which it is based are constantly changing.[487] Therefore, the policies deemed worthy of protection under the public policy exception today may not be considered so in the near future, and vice versa. Hence, avoiding clearly defining public policy, despite all the difficulties arising out of it, may be seen as a solution.

Another noteworthy problematic aspect concerns the application process, specifically the judiciary's broad or even unfettered discretion in considering the application of the public policy exception.[488] In some, if not many, jurisdictions, there are no guidelines for judges at all in this regard.[489] English judges are not even bound by the doctrine of precedent when applying the public policy exception, which is not the case with the application of domestic public policy.[490] Such broad discretion may be a result of a deliberate approach not to limit the power of judges for largely the same reasons behind the lack of a clear definition, as discussed above. Second, the absence of a clear definition of public policy itself may make it difficult to frame judges' discretion, even if the rationale behind it is set aside.

Those problematic aspects of the public policy exception, despite having some rationale behind them, result in unpredictability and uncertainty surrounding the notion.[491] The oft-quoted remark by an English judge describing the public policy exception as 'a very unruly horse, and when once you get astride it you never know where it will carry you' is fitting in this context.[492]

486 See, eg, Akkermans (n 451) 277 arguing it for Dutch law.

487 Akkermans (n 451) 277; Meyer, 'A Flexible System in Flux' (n 450) para 1-013.

488 For arguments against the judiciary's unfettered discretion, see Mills (n 450) 202, Meyer, 'A Flexible System in Flux' (n 450) para 1-028.

489 See, eg, Mills (n 450) 203 arguing it for English law.

490 Akkermans (n 451) 279-280. See also, Mills (n 450) 206 (fn 34 therein and accompanying text).

491 Mills (n 450) 202.

492 *Richardson v Mellish* [1824] 2 Bing 229, 252.

c) Limited Application of Public Policy: Key Dimensions

After touching on the problematic aspects of public policy and their implications, this work will below explore the considerations to minimise them. Specifically, it will join the arguments supporting the limited use of public policy and outline the dimensions developed in the literature to frame the application of the exception.

aa) Limited Application

To begin with, scholarship generally agrees that international public policy should be used more sparingly than domestic public policy and should be limited to the most fundamental policies of the *lex fori*.[493] Under most cross-border legal instruments that aim to harmonise different areas of private international law and contain the public policy exception, the sparing application of the exception is implied by the usage of the qualifying language, such as *manifestly*.[494] Hence, not every mandatory norm or every policy of the *lex fori* that is important in a domestic context should constitute a bar to the application of a foreign law or the recognition of a foreign judgment. The logic of private international law itself is based on the idea that applying a foreign law may lead to an outcome different from the one that might be achieved as a result of the application of the *lex fori*.[495]

In addition, as correctly stated by Alex Mills, private international law rules also constitute public policies of states.[496] Hence, the overuse of the public policy exception with respect to a certain rule of private international law could undermine the public policy behind the establishment of the respective rule.[497] Furthermore, systematic unsparing use of the public policy exception in one state may have negative consequences for that state and its citizens. That is to say, it could potentially lead to other states reciprocating, particularly in terms of recognising judgments issued in that

493 See, eg, Carter (n 457) 2; Akkermans (n 451) 272-73; Meyer, 'A Flexible System in Flux' (n 450) paras 1-010 (and cited literature in fn 12 therein), 1-039; Wurmnest (n 470) paras 2-016-18.

494 Meyer, 'A Flexible System in Flux' (n 450) paras 1-054-56, Carter (n 457) 2 (the author, however, prefers *strongly* over *manifestly*).

495 Meyer, 'A Flexible System in Flux' (n 450) para 1-002.

496 Mills (n 450) 206.

497 ibid.

state. Although reciprocity is not always necessary for the operation of private international law rules, it is generally assumed that other states will follow similar rules.[498] In addition, the economic interests of that state and its nationals may be adversely affected over time, as fewer international actors may be willing to engage with that jurisdiction due to the unsparing application of the public policy exception.[499]

There are also strong arguments favouring the view that the assessment under the public policy exception should primarily focus on the result of the application of the foreign law in question rather than the content of that law.[500] That said, the mere content of a foreign law may also be a ground for the invocation of the public policy exception if it is 'unacceptably repugnant'.[501]

bb) Dimensions

As previously discussed, in most jurisdictions, public policy is not clearly defined and its application is at the judiciary's wide discretion. Hence, and also given the need to use the public policy exception sparingly, the establishment of certain principles or criteria to frame its application is of utmost necessity. In the literature, three main dimensions of the application of public policy have been developed for this purpose, which, according to the prevailing opinion,[502] should not be applied separately but rather be balanced against one another. Below, this work will summarise these dimensions.

(1) Proximity to the Forum

The fact that the respective rules of private international law point to a foreign legal system (applicable law and/or competent forum) does not mean that there is no domestic interest in the dispute in question at all.[503] The stronger such domestic interest is, the more justified the application of the

498 Akkermans (n 451) 273.
499 ibid (quoted text from the case cited in fn 62 therein).
500 Wurmnest (n 470) para 2-019; Mankowski and Langenhagen (n 468) para 8-021.
501 Carter (n 457) 3. See also Mills (n 450) 209.
502 Mills (n 450) 218ff; Meyer, 'A Flexible System in Flux' (n 450) para 1-035.
503 Mills (n 450) 211.

public policy exception.[504] Conversely, tolerance of a foreign legal concept is greater when it has only limited domestic effect.[505] Under German law, for example, specific relation to Germany (*Inlandsbezug*) is also necessary for successfully invoking the exception, even though article 6 of the EGBGB does not expressly contain such a requirement.[506]

(2) Worthiness of Protection

This dimension focuses on the importance of a policy being safeguarded by the public policy exception. According to Alex Mills, the more such a policy is shared universally or considered absolute, the stronger the argument for protecting it and invoking the public policy exception.[507] That said, this perspective is not fully shared in the literature.[508]

(3) Seriousness of the Breach

Not every violation of a policy that is worth protecting warrants invoking the exception. That is to say, a rule worth protecting may only be violated in a technical manner and that alone may not be sufficient grounds for applying the public policy exception.[509] As a result, the more significant the violation, the more likely the public policy exception will be invoked.[510]

---

504 ibid 211-12.

505 Meyer, 'A Flexible System in Flux' (n 450) para 1-068.

506 Mankowski and Langenhagen (n 468) para 8-032.

507 See Mills (n 450) 216. For a more detailed discussion, see ibid 212-18.

508 See, eg, Kenny Chng, 'A Theoretical Perspective of the Public Policy Doctrine in the Conflict of Laws' (2018) 14 J Priv Intl L 130, 157, where it is argued that international consensus is only a reflection of the fundamental and universal character of a policy, not vice versa. See also Meyer, 'A Flexible System in Flux' (n 450), where it is argued (paras 1-034, 1-039) that the importance of a policy depends on its position within the domestic system as a whole (eg comparing constitutional rights to the mere technical provisions), but also admitted (para 1-044) that when the respective policy is of significant importance also in other states, the arguments in favour of the application of the exception gain additional weigh.

509 Mills (n 450) 218.

510 ibid; Meyer, 'A Flexible System in Flux' (n 450) para 1-034.

3. The Public Policy Exception under the MLCBI

As noted earlier, the public exception is not unique to cross-border insolvency and restructuring law instruments. Most, if not all, international, regional, and national frameworks contemplating, in one form or another, deference to a foreign jurisdiction include the public policy exception.[511] That said, the exception is of particular importance under the reign of modified universalism, where insolvency or restructuring of the debtor with worldwide effect is conducted in its home jurisdiction, and all other affected states are expected to defer to that particular jurisdiction. Even the EIR, which expressly refers to the universal scope of insolvency proceedings within the EU and mutual trust among Member States,[512] contains the public policy exception.[513] The MLCBI is no different in that regard. Article 6 provides for the general exception of public policy, which applies to recognition under article 17, as well as granting any additional relief or assistance, e.g. under articles 7 or 21:

> Article 6. Public policy exception
> Nothing in this Law prevents the court from refusing to take an action governed by this Law if the action would be manifestly contrary to the public policy of this State.

Neither the instrument itself nor the Guide to the MLCBI attempts to define *public policy*, deliberately leaving the matter to national laws.[514] Notwithstanding, the Guide to the MLCBI highlights the dichotomy between 'domestic public policy' and 'public policy as it is used in matters of international cooperation and the question of recognition of effects of foreign laws'.[515] Accordingly, the Guide to the MLCBI emphasises the need for a restrictive interpretation of the exception and its application 'under exceptional circumstances' by referring to the word *manifestly* in the text of article 6.[516] It is worth noting that some jurisdictions (e.g. Canada, Serbia, Singapore, and South Korea) enacted article 6 without the word

511 See, eg, nn 448, 458 and accompanying text.
512 EIR (n 13) recs 23, 65.
513 ibid art 33.
514 Guide to the MLCBI (n 17) para 101.
515 ibid para 103.
516 ibid para 104. For a more detailed discussion of the (narrow) interpretation, see Kristin van Zwieten, 'Article 6: Public Policy Exception' in Reinhard Bork and Michael Veder (eds), *The UNCITRAL Model Laws on Cross-Border Insolvency and*

manifestly.[517] However, it has been argued that this omission should not necessarily be interpreted as an indicator of the legislative intent in those jurisdictions to construct the public policy exception broadly.[518]

a) The Public Policy Exception under Chapter 15

Below, this work will separately discuss Chapter 15 with respect to the public policy exception. This is because this issue has been extensively litigated in Chapter 15 cases, and the difference with other jurisdictions implementing the MLCBI is significant in that regard.[519]

To begin with, the US adopted article 6 of the MLCBI almost verbatim (section 1506 of the BC). Therefore, by keeping the phrase *manifestly contrary* unchanged during the adoption, the US legislature adhered to the approach favouring the limited use of the exception.[520] US courts, too, hold the view that the public policy exception should be construed restrictively and applied only when the fundamental policies of the US are at stake.[521]

---

on the Recognition and Enforcement of Insolvency-Related Judgments: An Article-by-Article Commentary (Edward Elgar 2025) paras 1.6.11-18.

517 van Zwieten, 'Article 6: Public Policy Exception' (n 516) para 1.16.19. See also Michael A. Garza, 'When Is Cross-Border Insolvency Recognition Manifestly Contrary to Public Policy' (2015) 38 Fordham Intl LJ 1587, 1596; UNCITRAL, 'Digest of Case Law on the Model Law on Cross-Border Insolvency' (UN 2021) <https://uncitral.un.org/sites/uncitral.un.org/files/media-documents/uncitral/en/20-06293_uncitral_mlcbi_digest_e.pdf> accessed 21 October 2025 (Digest of Case Law), 22 (Note 3 therein and accompanying text); Kristy Zander, 'Application of the Public Policy Exception in the UNCITRAL Model Law on Cross Border Insolvency: Issues and Challenges' (December 2022) INSOL International, Technical Paper Series 54 <https://insol.azureedge.net/cmsstorage/insol/media/document-library/technical%20paper%20series/application-of-the-public-policy-exception-in-the-uncitral-model-law-on-cross-border-insolvency.pdf> accessed 21 October 2025, s 2.2 (fn 7 therein and accompanying text).

518 Garza (n 517) 1596-97. For a more detailed discussion, see van Zwieten, 'Article 6: Public Policy Exception' (n 516) para 1.6.19.

519 Buckel (n 367) 95 (fn 91 therein and accompanying text). See also Digest of Case Law (n 517) 22-23, where it can be observed that a vast majority of the cited cases are Chapter 15 cases.

520 Garza (n 517) 1604, 1627-28. See also. Omer Shahid, 'The Public Policy Exception: Has Sec. 1506 been a Significant Obstacle in Aiding Foreign Bankruptcy Proceedings' (2010) 9 J Intl Bus & L 175, 181-182; Markell, 'The International Two-Step' (n 366) 42.

521 *In re Ephedra Products Liability Litigation,* 349 BR 333, 336 (SDNY 2006).

Merely having a foreign law different from US law, without other considerations, does not justify applying the exception.[522]

As to the scope of the application of the exception, US courts have developed certain principles that distinguish between two categories of cases. One category concerns cases in which foreign proceedings have not been procedurally fair.[523] As mentioned earlier, the matters related to procedural fairness will be discussed separately in section D.II of this work. Below, this work, therefore, will explore only the other category of cases in which the action sought under Chapter 15 'would frustrate a U.S. court's ability to administer the Chapter 15 proceeding and/or would impinge severely a U.S. constitutional or statutory right, particularly if a party continues to enjoy the benefits of the Chapter 15 proceeding'.[524]

In most Chapter 15 cases, when the issue of public policy had been raised, the courts decided against applying the exception.[525] Nonetheless, these cases are of significance, as they provide some guidelines as to what constitutes, or to be more precise, what does not constitute the public policy of the US. For example, it was stated that the relief granted in foreign proceedings does not have to be identical to that available under US law.[526] Additionally, it was held that the fact that US creditors may receive less than they would in similar US proceedings, without other considerations, does not justify invoking the public policy exception.[527]

As to the cases where the exception was applied, this work will below briefly discuss three of them in chronological order.

aa) *Toft*

In re Toft, a US bankruptcy court considered issuing *ex parte* relief, under sections 1507, 1519, and 1521 of the BC, recognising and enforcing a mail interception order that had been granted by a German court.[528] The court highlighted the significance of the protection of privacy rights as a matter of policy under US law:

522 *Micron Technology, Inc. v. Qimonda AG (In re Qimonda AG Bankruptcy Litigation)*, 433 BR 547, 570 (ED Va 2010).

523 ibid.

524 ibid.

525 Digest of Case Law (n 517) 21 (para 8 and cited US cases therein).

526 *Metcalfe* (n 381) 697.

527 *In re Ernst Young, Inc.*, 383 BR 773, 781 (Bankr D Colo 2008).

528 *In re Toft*, 453 BR 186 (Bankr SDNY 2011).

> The relief sought would directly compromise privacy rights subject to a comprehensive scheme of statutory protection, available to aliens, built on constitutional safeguards incorporated in the Fourth Amendment as well as the constitutions of many States. Such relief would impinge severely a U.S. constitutional or statutory right.[529]

The court, therefore, concluded that the public policy exception should be applied.[530]

bb) *Qimonda*

In re Qimonda AG, a US bankruptcy court addressed, *inter alia,* the issue of whether the termination (non-continuation) of US patent cross-licences by an insolvency administrator under German insolvency law[531] was manifestly contrary to the public policy of the US.[532] The issue was considered in light of the fact that the BC would protect the licensees in a similar scenario.[533] Stating that 'Although innovation would obviously not come to a grinding halt if licenses to U.S. patents could be cancelled in a foreign insolvency proceeding, ... the resulting uncertainty would nevertheless slow the pace of innovation', the court decided in favour of the application of the exception to protect 'U.S. public policy promoting technological innovation'.[534]

The decision of the bankruptcy court has received controversial commentaries. Some critics argue that there was no need for the court to address public policy issues after denying the relief under section 1522 of the BC,[535] endorsing the approach taken by the appellate court in reviewing the case.[536] Others additionally point out that the court's interpretation of what constitutes public policy (i.e. technological innovation) was too broad

529 ibid 198 (footnotes and citations omitted).
530 ibid 201.
531 InsO (n 35) s 103.
532 *In re Qimonda AG*, Case No 09-14766-SSM (Bankr ED Va 2011).
533 BC (n 37) s 365 (n).
534 *Qimonda* (n 532) 33-34.
535 See, eg, Garza (n 517) 1590 (fns 9-11 therein and text thereto).
536 *Jaffé v Samsung Elecs Co*, 737 F3d 14, 32 (4th Cir 2013).

and, thus, not in line with the objectives of Chapter 15.[537] The bankruptcy court's reasoning has also been endorsed in the literature.[538]

cc) *Vitro II*

In *Vitro II,* a US bankruptcy court reached the conclusion that the protection of third-party claims constitutes a fundamental policy of the US and the enforcement of a foreign plan (in that case, a Mexican plan) non-consensually extinguishing such claims would be manifestly contrary to the public policy of the US.[539] In this case, too, the appellate court did not address the issue because the release sought had already been denied under other provisions of Chapter 15.[540] However, the appellate court's reasoning on the matter suggests that it was leaning against the application of the public policy exception in that particular case.[541] The bankruptcy court's position on applying the public policy exception with respect to third-party releases has not been shared by several other courts[542] and has been criticised by some commentators.[543]

537 Buckel (n 367) 1304-06. See also Lia Metreveli, 'Toward Standardized Enforcement of Cross-Border Insolvency Decisions: Encouraging the United States to Adopt UNCITRAL's Recent Amendment to Its Model Law on Cross-Border Insolvency' (2017) 51 Colum JL & Soc Probs 315, 338.

538 See, eg, generally John J. Chung, 'In Re Qimonda AG: The Conflict between Comity and the Public Policy Exception in Chapter 15 of the Bankruptcy Code' (2014) 32 BU Intl LJ 89.

539 *Vitro II* (n 399) 132.

540 *Vitro* (n 87) 1070. For a more detailed discussion of the case, see sub-s C.II.2.d)dd).

541 *Vitro* (n 87) 1069-70.

542 See, eg, *Bakrie* (n 375) 890-91. It is open to question, however, whether this trend will continue following the recent USSC decision in *Purdue* (n 387), which categorically denied non-consensual third-party releases under Chapter 11 as a matter of law (see n 387 and accompanying text). That said, it has been suggested that the USSC's position in that case should not affect Chapter 15 proceedings, as nothing in the court's opinion indicates that non-consensual third-party releases violate the public policy of the US. See Anthony J. Casey and Joshua C. Macey, 'Purdue Pharma and the New Bankruptcy Exceptionalism' (2025) [2024] Sup C Rev 365, 397. The present work supports this view.

543 See, eg, Buckel (n 367) 1306-07.

b) The Public Policy Exception in Other Jurisdictions Implementing the MLCBI

As already noted, the public policy exception under the MLCBI has not been litigated in other jurisdictions implementing the MLCBI as extensively as in the US.[544] That said, in several other jurisdictions (such as Australia, Canada, and England), too, courts tend to interpret the exception narrowly.[545] For example, in *Akers v Deputy Commissioner of Taxation*, an Australian court concluded that remitting assets of the debtor to the foreign jurisdiction where the debtor was being wound up without paying local taxes would not violate the Australian public policy.[546] In a recent Australian case, it was held that 'The public policy exception is to be construed restrictively and only invoked in exceptional circumstances in relation to matters of fundamental importance for Australia'.[547] In *Hartford Computer Hardware,* a Canadian court interpreted the exception restrictively and granted the recognition and implementation (in Canada) of a US court order (issued in a Chapter 11 proceeding) containing a provision (*roll up*) that would not be available under Canadian law.[548] In *Agrokor DD,* in considering the recognition of Croatian proceedings as a foreign main proceeding under the CBIR, the EWHC refused to apply the public policy exception on the grounds of, *inter alia,* the possible non-compliance with the *pari passu* principle[549] in the Croatian proceedings.[550] The court stated that the priorities of foreign law in restructuring or liquidation of companies being different from those of English law does not justify the application of the exception.[551]

544 See n 519 (accompanying text) and text thereto.

545 See Zander (n 517) sub-ss 2.3.2-3, where its restrictive application in Australia and Great Britain is highlighted. See also Briggs (n 478) para 11.5, where it is stated that public policy is rarely applied in cross-border insolvency cases in England.

546 *Akers as a joint foreign representative of Saad Investments Company Limited (in Official Liquidation) v Deputy Commissioner of Taxation* [2014] FCAFC 57 [144]-[148].

547 *PricewaterhouseCoopers Inc in its Capacity as Foreign Representative of IE CA 3 Holdings Ltd v IE CA Holdings Ltd* [2024] FCA 1208 [131].

548 *Hartford Computer Hardware, Inc. (Re),* 2012 ONSC 964, [17]-[18].

549 For a more detailed discussion of the *pari passu* principle, see sub-s E.I.1.

550 *In the matter of Agrokor DD* [2017] EWHC 2791 (Ch) [109]-[131].

551 ibid [131].

c) Analysis of the Main Issues

aa) Limited Application

This work has already highlighted the problematic aspects of public policy in a general private international law setting, namely, the lack of a clear definition and the judiciary's broad discretion in the application process. The public policy exception under the MLCBI is no exception in this regard. Those aspects eventually result in inconsistency in the application of the public policy exception under the MLCBI.[552] Such inconsistency, in turn, leads to uncertainty and unpredictability,[553] contradicting one of the core objectives of the MLCBI.[554] The overuse of the exception under the MLCBI framework, whether consistently or inconsistently, is even more problematic since it may undermine the entire framework. This work has already discussed the importance of using the exception sparingly in a general private international law context. The same applies to the MLCBI. The exception should be limited to essential policies, such as constitutional guarantees or fundamental values on which the legal system of the receiving state is built. In addition, restricting the application of the exception to genuinely exceptional cases would promote consistency and increase legal certainty and predictability.

More to the point, article 6 of the MLCBI sets out not a general rule but rather an exception. In addition, as previously noted, international public policy should be applied more restrictively compared to its domestic counterpart. Hence, not every deviation from domestic law justifies the application of the exception. The public policy exception should be interpreted even more restrictively in commercial matters, including restructuring of corporate debtors, compared to other areas, such as family law. This is because the affected parties may require greater protection, and moral and social considerations may play a significantly larger role in the latter. The argument supporting a more restrictive application of the exception in commercial matters is particularly relevant for cross-border insolvency and restructuring cases under the MLCBI, which is underpinned by modified universalism. As already noted, under this principle, a single main forum

552 Zander (n 517) s 3.3.

553 ibid s 3.4. For a discussion of the significance of the predictability and legal certainty, albeit mostly in a procedural context, in cross-border insolvency, see Bork, *Principles of Cross-Border Insolvency Law* (n 93) para 3.30ff.

554 MLCBI (n 17) Preamble (b).

(in the debtor's home jurisdiction) oversees the liquidation or restructuring of the debtor, to which all other affected states are expected to defer. Therefore, the tolerance towards foreign jurisdictions should be much greater under frameworks like the MLCBI, despite the important role of the exception in such frameworks, as highlighted earlier.

Furthermore, as Alex Mills correctly notes, main private international law rules, with public policy as an exception, also represent public policies of states.[555] Therefore, protecting one public policy of a state should not come at the expense of another public policy of that state. That is to say, extensively using the public policy exception would weaken the public policy of the state on which the respective rule of private international law is based.[556] This raises the question of why the main rule was necessary in the first instance.

More specifically, by implementing the MLCBI, the enacting states make it part of their public policy, *inter alia*, to participate in an international framework based on modified universalism. This involves cooperating with and deferring to insolvency or restructuring proceedings in the debtor's home jurisdiction. This public policy has its own rationale that is worth protecting. That is to say, a system based on modified universalism (a single set of proceedings in the debtors' home jurisdiction with universal effect through the cooperation of the courts of all other affected states) offers several advantages such as value maximisation, efficiency, and just treatment of all creditors.[557] Consequently, each state would naturally desire this framework to function properly for the debtors who have their COMI within its territory. However, this framework works in both directions.[558] That is to say, what Ian Fletcher and other scholars argue about double standards in the treatment of bankruptcy discharge under English law holds true, *mutatis mutandis*, also in this context.[559]

Hence, being part of an international framework based on modified universalism is a significant policy objective that should not be undermined by a broad construction and the extensive application of the public policy

---

555 See text to n 496.

556 See text to n 497.

557 See sub-s B.II.3.a).

558 It is worth reiterating that the MLCBI does not require reciprocity. However, the existence of the exception under the MLCBI is often linked to the absence of a reciprocity requirement within the instrument. See van Zwieten, 'Article 6: Public Policy Exception' (n 516) para 1.6.06.

559 n 312 (and accompanying text) and text thereto.

exception under the MLCBI.[560] This policy objective is likely one of the main reasons why many developed jurisdictions, such as the US, Great Britain, Australia, Canada, Japan, and the Republic of Korea, which host multi-billion dollar transnational companies with business operations and assets around the world, have implemented the MLCBI. Once again, the extensive use of the public policy exception would significantly undermine the respective policy objective.

To summarise the current point, once a main rule, whatever it may be, is put into effect, the public policy exception should only be applied in cases where fundamental policies, such as constitutional guarantees, are being violated, and such violation cannot be justified by the policy objectives of the state behind the main rule. That holds also for the policy objectives behind the implementation of the MLCBI in a particular jurisdiction.

bb) Premature Consideration and Misinterpretation of the Purpose

Another set of issues worth discussing concerns the premature consideration and the misinterpretation of the purpose of the public policy exception under the MLCBI, particularly when it is invoked to protect local interests. This work supports the arguments against prematurely considering the exception.[561] That is to say, article 6 is placed in Chapter I (General provisions) of the MLCBI. Accordingly, the public policy exception is an exception of a general nature and should be considered only after all specific defences have been exhausted.[562] For example, when relief is sought under article 21, the requirements of article 22 should be examined first.[563] If those requirements are met, then the public policy exception may be considered, but it does not necessarily need to be applied.

In addition, the primary purpose of public policy exception is not to secure the interests of local creditors or other local interests,[564] but rather

560 See Scott C. Mund, '11 U.S.C. 1506: U.S. Courts Keep a Tight Rein on the Public Policy Exception, but the Potential to Undermine Internationals Cooperation in Insolvency Proceedings Remains' (2010) 28 Wis Intl LJ 325, 334, where it is correctly argued that a broad interpretation of the exception would undermine the advantages of the MLCBI.

561 See, eg, Garza (n 517) 1623.

562 *Toft* (n 528) 195-96; Garza (n 517) 1625-27.

563 ibid.

564 For similar concerns, see Bork, *Principles of Cross-Border Insolvency Law* (n 93) para 2.29. For a different view, see Chung (n 538) 116. For a discussion of the

to safeguard the most fundamental policies of the receiving state.[565] When, for example, the recognition of a foreign restructuring plan is sought under article 21, again, article 22 is the appropriate provision for assessing whether the interests of the creditors (including local ones) have been adequately protected in the respective foreign restructuring proceedings.[566] It is also noteworthy to reiterate that under US case law, the mere fact that foreign law is not identical to US law[567] or that the treatment of US creditors in foreign proceedings is worse than it would be in similar US proceedings[568] is not sufficient for the application of the public policy exception.

II. Procedural Fairness

As already identified in this work, deference to foreign insolvency (restructuring) proceedings has its limitations under the principle of modified universalism. The procedural unfairness of the foreign proceedings in question is one of the most notable limitations, not only in this context but also generally in the recognition of foreign judgments. For example, it has been long established under US case law that comity can be granted to foreign court judgments if, *inter alia*, due process has been followed in the respective foreign proceedings.[569]

For determining the place of procedural fairness review within the ML-CBI framework, the model developed under Chapter 15 case law provides a suitable reference. Specifically, when considering the recognition of foreign restructuring proceedings under section 1517 of the BC, any issue regarding the non-compliance with due process in foreign proceedings should be addressed as part of the public policy analysis under section 1506, which is the only possible basis for denying recognition. When deciding on discretionary post-recognition relief under sections 1507 or 1521 of the

---

problem of local interests in cross-border insolvency in general, see generally John A. E. Pottow, 'Greed and Pride in International Bankruptcy: The Problems of and Proposed Solutions to Local Interests' (2006) 104 Mich L Rev 1899.

565 Nonetheless, it should be noted that the interests of certain local parties may be safeguarded by the most fundamental policies of the receiving state and, thus, protected by the public policy exception.

566 Buckel (n 367) 1307-11. The respective point will be revisited later in sub-s F.I.1.c) of this work.

567 See text to n 522.

568 See text to n 527.

569 See text to n 371.

BC, procedural fairness may be evaluated within the comity analysis even without resorting to the public policy exception under section 1506 of the BC.[570]

As to the notion itself, as Riz Mokal puts it, fairness in a procedural context is not a substantive goal of insolvency (restructuring) law.[571] It rather focuses on the fairness of process that enables the realisation of substantive goals (one of which is fairness in a substantive context)[572] of that law.[573] Guaranteeing procedural fairness is primarily the responsibility of the national law of the state where the process takes place.[574] The respective rules need not be identical to those of the receiving state and the difference can be tolerated to some extent.[575] Nonetheless, a review of the procedural fairness of foreign proceedings in granting comity is mainly based on the fundamental procedural fairness standards of the receiving state.[576] Article 7 of the MLIJ also expressly refers to 'the fundamental principles of procedural fairness' of the receiving state. For example, US courts have developed a non-exhaustive list of factors to consider when evaluating the procedural fairness of foreign proceedings in Chapter 15 cases:

> (1) whether creditors of the same class are treated equally in the distribution of assets; (2) whether the liquidators are considered fiduciaries and are held accountable to the court; (3) whether creditors have the right to submit claims which, if denied, can be submitted to a bankruptcy court for adjudica-

570 See, eg, *Bakrie* (n 375). However, several courts assessed the procedural fairness of foreign proceedings within public policy analysis when considering granting relief under section 1521. See, eg, *Ephedra* (n 521); *In re Sivec SRL*, Case No 11-80799-TRC (Bankr ED Okla 2011).

571 Riz Mokal, 'Fairness' in Lorenzo Stanghellini and others (eds), *Best Practices in European Restructuring: Contractualised Distress Resolution in the Shadow of the Law* (Wolters Kluwer 2018) sub-ss 1.1, 1.3.

572 Rizwaan Jameel Mokal, 'On Fairness and Efficiency' (2003) 66 MLR 452, 457, 462-63.

573 Mokal, 'Fairness' (n 571) sub-s 1.3.

574 Bork, *Principles of Cross-Border Insolvency Law* (n 93) para 3.53.

575 See, eg, *Ephedra* (n 521) 337, where a US District Court held that the absence of jury trial alone, which would have been the case under US law, does not suffice to conclude on the procedural unfairness of foreign proceedings. See also *In re OAS S.A.*, 533 BR 83, 104-5 (Bankr SDNY 2015), where a US bankruptcy court stated with respect to *ex parte* orders of a foreign court that 'even the absence of certain procedural or constitutional rights will not itself be a bar under § 1506' (citations omitted).

576 *In re Hourani*, 180 BR 58, 64 (Bankr SDNY 1995).

> tion; (4) whether the liquidators are required to give notice to the debtors' potential claimants; (5) whether there are provisions for creditors' meetings; (6) whether a foreign country's insolvency laws favor its own citizens; (7) whether all assets are marshalled before one body for centralized distribution; and (8) whether there are provisions for an automatic stay and for the lifting of such stays to facilitate the centralization of claims.[577]

The right to a fair trial, which encompasses most of the factors listed above, undoubtedly constitutes the core of procedural fairness. It is one of the universally accepted fundamental human rights enshrined in international treaties.[578] A fair and full opportunity to make their case for affected parties is also a recognised right in most soft and hard law sources of cross-border insolvency (restructuring) law.[579] Below, this work will examine several elements of the right to a fair trial, particularly those that are relevant in a restructuring context.

1. Right to Be Heard

a) Due Notice

Due notice serves as both a minimum requirement and an outer limit for the right to a fair trial in general and the right to be heard in particular. It is considered a minimum requirement because if an affected party has not been properly notified, it can be assumed that due process has not been adhered to in the proceedings in which that party was absent.[580] It also serves as an outer limit because the absence or inaction of a party who has been duly notified is generally irrelevant in assessing procedural fairness.[581] This holds true even when a party leaves the jurisdiction to avoid being served with notice.[582]

577 *Finanz Ag Zurich v. Banco Economico S.A.*, 192 F3d 240, 249 (2d Cir 1999).
578 See, eg, Convention for the Protection of Human Rights and Fundamental Freedoms (Rome 1950), art 6. See also *Eurofood* (n 477) [65].
579 Bork, *Principles of Cross-Border Insolvency Law* (n 93) paras 3.54-55.
580 *Hourani* (n 576) 67-68; *Sivec* (n 570).
581 Briggs (n 478) para 11.11.
582 ibid.

The notice requirement in restructuring proceedings primarily involves notifying all affected parties and stakeholders about the start of the proceedings so that they can adjust their legal positions accordingly.[583] In addition, affected parties, particularly creditors, should be informed of all procedural actions that can impact their legal positions.[584] This includes (but is not limited to) being notified about court hearings, creditors' meetings (time, location, and agenda), and procedural documents.

aa) Means of Notice

One of the important issues related to the due notice requirement is the method of giving notice. This work supports the argument that all affected known and traceable creditors should be individually notified in order to fully comply with due process.[585] In restructuring proceedings, it is extremely important to send individual notices for creditors' meetings, especially the one where the proposed plan will be voted on,[586] and for court hearings, particularly the one where the court will consider the confirmation of the adopted plan. The requirement for individual notice is essential for foreign creditors with no other business in the jurisdiction where the proceedings take place.[587] It should also be noted that providing actual notice to the specific creditor should meet the due process requirement, even if foreign law does not mandate individualised notice to known creditors.[588]

Collective announcements via publication in official newspapers, public registries, and/or on the website of the debtor or the designated authority also play an important role in insolvency and restructuring proceedings,

---

583 Bork, *Principles of Cross-Border Insolvency Law* (n 93) para 3.23.

584 Mokal, 'Fairness' (n 571) s 3 (and Policy Recommendation #2.2).

585 *Hourani* (n 576) 68; Mokal, 'Fairness' (n 571) s 3 (and Policy Recommendation #2.4). For a discussion of the international instruments of insolvency law that provide for individual notice, see Bork, *Principles of Cross-Border Insolvency Law* (n 93) para 3.26.

586 Mokal, 'Fairness' (n 571) s 3.

587 See *Hourani* (n 576) 68, where the court stated that it is unreasonable to expect a known foreign creditor to check local media in the debtor's home country on a routine basis when an option of individual notice to that creditor is possible.

588 *Finanz* (n 577) 249. That said, not all US courts share this view. See, eg, *Hourani* (n 576) 68, where the court stated in this context that 'It is the integrity of the liquidation process being reviewed ... not the happenstance of a particular incident'.

given the risk of exclusion of unknown and untraceable creditors (e.g. tort creditors) from distribution.[589] That said, such collective announcements generally should not replace individual notices for known and traceable creditors but rather supplement them.[590]

bb) Adequacy of Notice

Another important issue regarding the requirement for providing due notice is adequacy. Merely being notified, even individually, is not sufficient. The recipient of the notice should also have enough time to prepare for the notified action.[591] This includes having sufficient time to review the relevant documents (such as a draft plan or a court decision), prepare a legal position (for example, by hiring a lawyer and preparing a defence), and make any necessary travel arrangements. Under the MLIJ, failing to give notice of proceedings 'in sufficient time and in such a manner as to enable a defence to be arranged' constitutes a ground to deny the recognition and enforcement of an insolvency-related judgment.[592] In *Eurofood*, the CJEU stated that any urgent measures that restrict the right to be heard must be justified and procedural guarantees must be in place to ensure that affected persons can challenge such urgent measures.[593] Again, the sufficient time requirement is particularly important for foreign creditors. This is because there may be additional issues, such as translation, complexity of the local legal system, representation in a foreign country, legalisation of documents, and travel restrictions.[594]

589 Bork, *Principles of Cross-Border Insolvency Law* (n 93) para 3.26.

590 See *Hourani* (n 576) 68.

591 Riz Mokal suggests a range of two to four weeks in the plan confirmation process. See, Mokal, 'Fairness' (n 571) s 3 (and Policy Recommendation #2.2).

592 MLIJ (n 130) art 14 *(a)* (i).

593 *Eurofood* (n 477) [66]. One of the issues raised before the court concerned sufficient notice, as the provisional liquidator appointed in the Irish proceedings had been notified of a court hearing in Italy only a few days before the date of the hearing (see ibid [22]).

594 For a similar discussion, see Rodrigo Rodriguez, 'Article 14: Grounds to Refuse Recognition and Enforcement of an Insolvency-related Judgment' in Reinhard Bork and Michael Veder (eds), *The UNCITRAL Model Laws on Cross-Border Insolvency and on the Recognition and Enforcement of Insolvency-Related Judgments: An Article-by-Article Commentary* (Edward Elgar 2025) para 2.14.13. For a discussion of the potentially unfavourable position of foreign creditors, see McCormack and Wan (n 155) 292.

b) Participation in Proceedings

aa) Lodging Claims

Since restructuring proceedings generally result in the collective modification of the claims of all or some of the debtor's creditors, affected creditors should play a central role in these proceedings. First and foremost, all affected creditors must have an opportunity to file their claims when such filing is a prerequisite for participation.[595] As already noted, creditors, particularly foreign creditors, should be duly notified and given sufficient time to lodge their claims.

bb) Right to Information

Additionally, creditors must have the right to information.[596] In order to make an informed decision before taking a stance on the proposed plan, affected creditors must have the opportunity to access all relevant information about the actual financial situation of the debtor, measures to ensure the continued operation of the debtor's business, and the position of all affected parties under the plan as well as in the alternative scenario.[597] In most jurisdictions, similar information is required by law to be included in the plan, with which the affected creditors must have an opportunity to get familiar before voting.[598] Even in such a case, a creditor's request for additional information should be respected, provided that this information is relevant for the purpose mentioned above.

---

595 Bork, *Principles of Cross-Border Insolvency Law* (n 93) para 3.58. That said, most stand-alone restructuring frameworks do not require creditors to lodge their claims. See, eg, the frameworks examined in sub-ss C.I.1, E.II.1, E.II.2.a), E.II.2.b), E.II.2.c).

596 For a discussion of the right to information in a general insolvency law context, see Bork, *Principles of Cross-Border Insolvency Law* (n 93) paras 3.27-29. See also *Hourani* (n 576) 66-67.

597 Jay Lawrence Westbrook and others, *A Global View of Business Insolvency Systems* (World Bank and Brill 2010) s 4.4; Mokal, 'Fairness' (n 571) ss 3-4 (and Policy Recommendations #2.5-6); Bob Wessels and Stephan Madaus, *Rescue of Business in Europe: A European Law Institute Instrument* (OUP 2020) s 8.8 (Recommendation 8.03 therein).

598 See, eg, InsO (n 35) s 220.

cc) Participation and Voting in Creditors' Meeting

Finally, all affected creditors should have the opportunity to participate in creditors' meetings and vote on the issues on the agenda.[599] Again, they should be duly notified of such a meeting. Of utmost importance is, undoubtedly, a meeting convened to vote on the proposed restructuring plan. All affected creditors must be duly notified and have the opportunity to participate in this meeting, propose amendments, and vote on the plan.

dd) Illustrative Example: *Bakrie*

As already noted, nearly all of the issues discussed above concerning creditor participation in foreign proceedings were raised in *Bakrie.* [600] In the Indonesian proceedings, an ad hoc committee of a group of affected creditors claimed that the Indonesian plan had not provided sufficient information to make an informed decision. In addition, the case allegedly involved the exclusion of some creditors from participating in the creditors' meeting and voting on the plan. The Indonesian courts approved the administrators' decision to exclude these creditors because the debtor's record and report did not contain the respective claims. The US court, however, did not decide on the alleged voting irregularities while considering the recognition of the Indonesian plan since it had already denied recognition on another ground.[601]

c) Right to Contest

The judicial oversight of the plan confirmation process is of particular significance, since a successfully confirmed plan can modify substantive rights against the will of their holders.[602] The process is susceptible to abuse and, therefore, requires external supervision, which is most appropriately

599 Wessels and Madaus (n 597) s 8.8 (Recommendation 8.06 therein).

600 *Bakrie* (n 375). For a more detailed discussion of the facts of the case, see sub-s C.II.2.d)ee).

601 See text to n 422.

602 For a discussion of the central role of the court in restructuring proceedings, see generally Payne, 'The Role of the Court' (n 2). See also Westbrook and others (n 597) sub-s 4.2.5.

provided by the court.[603] Binding effect on holdouts is the main feature that sets formal restructuring proceedings apart from out-of-court workouts, in which substantive rights can be modified only with the consent of their holders.[604] Hence, courts play a central role in protecting creditors' substantive rights and ensuring the fairness of outcome in restructuring proceedings, particularly with respect to holdouts. It is commonly accepted that an administrative body designated by law can also take on this role.[605] Nonetheless, the court is considered a better option for this task,[606] and the confirmation decision made by an administrative body (as the case may be) should be subject to a court review (again, due to the non-consensual alteration of substantive rights).[607]

The court's intervention may be necessary at various stages of restructuring proceedings, such as classifying claims and convening meetings of creditors.[608] However, the most significant role is the fairness assessment, which determines whether the adopted plan should bind the dissent.[609] The extent and manner of the court's intervention at this stage, nonetheless, may vary depending on the restructuring mechanism being used.[610] Most mechanisms require court confirmation once the requisite majority has approved the plan and the plan only becomes binding if the court confirms it in a so-called *confirmation* or *sanctioning* hearing.[611] Under some mechanisms, however, the plan becomes final once it has been approved by the requisite majority without any court involvement.[612] Nonetheless, an affect-

---

603 Payne, 'The Role of the Court' (n 2) 130-33. For an analysis from a constitutional law perspective, see Madaus, 'A Proposal to Divide the Realms of Insolvency and Restructuring Law' (n 4) 638-39. For a discussion of the advantages (and disadvantages) of judicial (or administrative) supervision over the plan confirmation, see Ignacio Tirado, 'Examining and Confirming Plans' in Lorenzo Stanghellini and others (eds), *Best Practices in European Restructuring: Contractualised Distress Resolution in the Shadow of the Law* (Wolters Kluwer 2018) sub-s 4.2.

604 Payne, 'The Role of the Court' (n 2) 127.

605 See, eg, Tirado (n 603) sub-s 4.3.

606 ibid. See also Payne, 'The Role of the Court' (n 2) 133.

607 See, eg, PRD (n 15) rec 65; Tirado (n 603) sub-s 4.3.

608 For a discussion of the court's role at this stage (in the example of the English scheme of arrangement), see Payne, 'The Role of the Court' (n 2) 135-137.

609 For a discussion of the court's role at this stage (in the example of the English scheme of arrangement), see ibid 137-140.

610 For a discussion of different options, see Tirado (n 603) sub-s 4.4. See also Payne, 'The Role of the Court' (n 2) 133.

611 See, eg, the mechanisms examined in sub-ss C.I.1, E.II.1, E.II.2.b), E.II.2.c).

612 See, eg, the mechanism examined in sub-s E.II.2.a).

ed party can still challenge the plan on fairness or other grounds before the court and, if successful, have it suspended or revoked.[613] Although there are some differences in the respective types of court involvement,[614] they are not of great significance for the purpose of the right to be heard before the court. Ultimately, a dissatisfied party has the opportunity to challenge a plan that modifies the party's rights without consent. The main focus here is the dissatisfied party's ability to present its case and respond to the opposing party's arguments before the court.

That said, the court is by no means bound by the evidence and arguments of the contesting party. When reviewing the procedural fairness of foreign proceedings in this context, the focus is not on the merits of the final decision but on ensuring that all affected parties had had the opportunity to express their views to the decision-maker before the decision was made. One detail, however, should be clarified in this context. The fact that the merits of the respective decision cannot be reassessed through a procedural fairness review at the recognition stage should not lead to the conclusion that the decision on the respective substantive matter should not be justified at all. Mere granting access to the courtroom and hearing the arguments of the dissatisfied party do not suffice. The decision should contain a 'clear and formal record' of how the contesting party's right to be heard has been ensured as well as the justification of the respective decision, whatever it may be, on the substantive matter in question.[615]

2. Right of Appeal

Whether the affected parties should have the right of appeal in restructuring proceedings remains open for debate.[616] Best practices recommend granting affected parties the right to appeal in a general insolvency law

613 See, eg, the *unfair prejudice* challenge in sub-s E.II.2.a)bb).

614 For a more detailed discussion, see Tirado (n 603) sub-s 4.4. See also Payne, 'The Role of the Court' (n 2) 133.

615 See *Bakrie* (n 375) 887, where the court refused to recognise and enforce an Indonesian plan in the US not merely because of third-party releases under the plan but rather due to the absence of 'at least a rudimentary record in the foreign proceeding as to the basis for such releases and procedural fairness of the underlying process'. For a more detailed discussion of the case, see sub-s C.II.2.d)ee).

616 See, eg, Bob Wessels, 'Should Parties Have the Right to Appeal a Restructuring Plan?' (7 August 2023) Bob Wessels Blog (2023-08-doc1) <https://bobwessels.nl/blog/2023-08-doc1-should-parties-have-the-right-to-appeal-a-restructuring-p

context.[617] When it comes to restructuring proceedings, the respective right is often discussed in the context of appealing the court order confirming or rejecting the plan and is generally recommended.[618] It is also recommended that an appeal from the decision on confirmation, if permitted, should generally not prevent the plan from taking effect.[619]

In restructuring proceedings, where time and certainty are crucial, a lengthy process of appeal, particularly one delaying the implementation of the plan, can potentially undermine the chance of a successful outcome.[620] Perhaps this explains why some modern restructuring tools do not include a second court review of plan confirmation.[621] On the other hand, no court decision is immune to judicial errors. Recent cases decided by the EWCA have indeed illustrated how a second court review could reinstate substantive justice, particularly in the context of newly implemented restructuring frameworks.[622]

The question of whether foreign proceedings should be considered unfair in the absence of the right of appeal is not easy to answer. This work argues in favour of the right of appeal in restructuring proceedings without an automatic stay of the implementation of the plan, as noted above. However, it argues that the lack of the right of appeal by itself should not result in denying recognition of foreign plans due to procedural unfairness. Instead, this aspect should be assessed in the overall context of the procedural fairness of the proceedings in question. In this context, it

---

lan/> accessed 21 October 2025. For a comparative summary of jurisdictions across Europe, see Wessels and Madaus (n 597) s 8.5.4.

617 See, eg, UNCITRAL, *Legislative Guide on Insolvency Law, Parts One and Two* (UN 2005) <https://uncitral.un.org/sites/uncitral.un.org/files/media-documents/uncitral/en/05-80722_ebook.pdf> accessed 21 October 2025, pt 2, ch III, para 120 (and Recommendation 138); World Bank, 'Principles for Effective Insolvency and Creditor/Debtor Regimes' (World Bank 2021) <https://documents1.worldbank.org/curated/en/391341619072648570/pdf/Principles-for-Effective-Insolvency-and-Creditor-and-Debtor-Regimes.pdf)> accessed 21 October 2025, pt C2.1.

618 See, eg, PRD (n 15) rec 65; Tirado (n 603) sub-s 4.5 (and Policy Recommendation #6.4).

619 See, eg, PRD (n 15) art 16 (3); Tirado (n 603) sub-s 4.5 (and Policy Recommendation #6.4); Wessels and Madaus (n 597) s 8.8 (Recommendation 8.10 therein).

620 Tirado (n 603) sub-s 4.5.

621 See, eg, Dutch Act on the Confirmation of Extrajudicial Restructuring Plans (Wet Homologatie Onderhands Akkoord), art 1 (F) (thereby introduced art 369 (10) to the Dutch Bankruptcy Act (Faillissementswet).

622 *Strategic Value Capital Solutions Master Fund LP & Ors v AGPS BondCo PLC (Re AGPS BondCo PLC)* [2024] EWCA Civ 24 (*Adler*); *Saipem SPA & Ors v Petrofac Ltd & Anor* [2025] EWCA Civ 821 (*Petrofac*).

is crucial to consider, *inter alia*, the following factors: (i) whether the plan was initially confirmed by an administrative agency or a court; (ii) if by a court, whether by a general civil or administrative court or a specialised bankruptcy (commercial) court; (iii) whether the confirmation hearing was a mere formality or genuinely addressed fairness concerns; and (iv) whether affected parties had had the opportunity to object to the plan and present their case before the decision was made.[623]

3. Non-Discrimination of Foreign Creditors

The equal treatment of similarly situated creditors is one of the main substantive objectives of insolvency law.[624] This substantive principle is also central to the concept of universalism, which aims to distribute the debtor's assets to all creditors in a single proceeding, regardless of their location.[625] The principle is relevant in a procedural context, too, as all creditors, irrespective of their domicile, nationality, place of business, and so forth, should have the same procedural rights in restructuring proceedings.[626] Several cross-border insolvency and restructuring instruments contain express provisions on equal procedural rights of foreign and local creditors.[627] As noted earlier, foreign creditors should be given additional consideration as far as matters such as individualised notices or the adequacy of notice are concerned. Positive discrimination of foreign creditors in this context, therefore, should be allowed and encouraged.

As stated above, the issue of discrimination against foreign creditors extends beyond a procedural setting. Such discrimination, if present, is not easily identifiable through a procedural fairness review alone. Therefore, the matter will be revisited later in this work when arguing for the necessity of a substantive fairness review at the recognition stage.

623 See, Tirado (n 603) sub-s 4.5, where most of those aspects are highlighted in the context of whether an appeal should be heard by a court of first instance or a higher court. The same arguments are also relevant in this context.

624 For a more detailed discussion, see sub-s E.I.1.

625 van Zwieten (ed), *Principles of Corporate Insolvency Law* (n 29) para 16-09.

626 Bork, *Principles of Cross-Border Insolvency Law* (n 93) paras 2.62, 3.56.

627 See, eg, MLCBI (n 17) art 13 (1). For a more detailed discussion, see McCormack and Wan (n 155) 291-93.

4. Absence of Arbitrariness

The absence of arbitrariness is one of the core pillars of procedural justice. Procedural safeguards, some of which have been discussed in this work, should not be granted arbitrarily on an ad hoc basis. Instead, they should be based on clear norms and principles of law.[628] Even when discretion is given in granting certain safeguards (e.g. permitting an appeal and ordering disclosure), the decision-maker should not act arbitrarily but instead follow the respective principles of law.[629] The need to avoid arbitrariness applies not only in relation to procedural safeguards but is also true when deciding on substantive matters. This is particularly crucial in restructuring proceedings where several substantive matters are at the discretion of the court, as will be elaborated on in subsection E.I.2.

5. Absence of Fraud

The fact that a foreign judgment has been obtained by fraud constitutes a general defence to its recognition and enforcement.[630] This applies to orders of foreign courts in insolvency or restructuring proceedings as well.[631] Below, this work will touch on some important aspects of the fraud defence generally.

What constitutes fraud in foreign proceedings can be given a broad construction. It has been argued that fraud in foreign proceedings '"*includes every variety of mala fides and mala praxis whereby one of the parties misleads and deceives a judicial tribunal*"'.[632] Two main types of fraud have been distinguished. One common type involves unlawfully influencing the foreign court, for example, through corruption or bribery, to reach a decision in favour of the winning party (*fraud by the court*).[633] The other type involves deceiving the court by the winning party, for example, through

628 *Hourani* (n 576) 67

629 Bork, *Principles of Cross-Border Insolvency Law* (n 93) para 3.1.

630 See, eg, *Hilton* (n 86) 202-03, Pippa Rogerson, *Colliers's Conflict of Laws* (4th edn, CUP 2013) 254; Briggs (n 478) para 11.6.

631 See, eg, MLIJ (n 130) art 14 *(b)*.

632 See Rogerson (n 630) 254 quoting *Jet Holdings Inc v Patel* [1990] 1 QB 335.

633 See Rogerson (n 630) 254 and cited cases therein. See also Timothy G. Nelson, 'Down in Flames: Three U.S. Courts Decline Recognition to Judgments from Mexico, Citing Corruption' (2010) 44 Intl L 897, 90, classifying it as *extrinsic fraud*.

bribed witnesses or forged evidence (*fraud on the court*)[634]. There are other patterns of fraud as well, such as *fraud on the merits* and *collateral fraud*.[635]

The fact that the alleged fraud has been raised before the foreign court and been rejected does not generally preclude the application of the fraud exception at the recognition stage under English law,[636] subject to a few exceptions.[637] Nor does the fact that the party invoking the fraud defence could have done (but did not do) so in the foreign proceedings in question.[638] Such a broad approach, however, has been questioned.[639] This work agrees with the criticism of the respective broad approach and also considers that invocation of the fraud defence at the recognition stage should be primarily limited to the *fraud by the court* cases. Other types of fraud should generally be invoked and litigated in the respective foreign jurisdiction.[640]

That said, it can be challenging to prove fraud in foreign proceedings, particularly *fraud by the court*. The party claiming fraud during the recognition stage is generally required to provide at least *prima facie* evidence to support the respective claim.[641] General arguments and evidence are typically deemed insufficient by US courts in Chapter 15 cases. For example, objections to the recognition and enforcement of a foreign plan based on expert testimony on the corruption generally in the respective foreign (Mexican) judicial system were overruled in *Vitro II*.[642] Similarly, objections to recognising and enforcing an Indonesian plan based on the corruption of the Indonesian proceedings, citing country reports on human rights by the US Department of State, were not upheld in *Bakrie*.[643]

---

634 See Rogerson (n 630) 254 and cited cases therein. See also Nelson (n 633) 901, classifying it as *intrinsic fraud*.

635 For a more detailed discussion, see Rogerson (n 630) 254 and cited cases therein.

636 Rogerson (n 630) 255; Briggs (n 478) para 11.7.

637 One main exception to the mentioned approach is when the fraud issue has been separately litigated in the foreign jurisdiction. See Rogerson (n 630) 256.

638 ibid 255.

639 See *Bakrie* (n 375) 879, where it was held that the fraud defence should be invoked in cases where 'there was no adequate opportunity for correction of the fraud in the foreign proceeding, including a timely appeal' and 'Alleged fraud must relate to matters other than issues that could have been litigated'. See also Rogerson (n 630) 255-56.

640 Nelson (n 633) 902.

641 Rogerson (n 630) 256.

642 *Vitro II* (n 399) 130.

643 *Bakrie* (n 375) 890.

The difficulty of proving fraud in foreign proceedings, too, justifies the need for a substantive fairness review at the recognition stage, as suggested by this work. Therefore, the respective aspect will be revisited later in this work.

III. Summary

In Part D, this work discussed two main general safeguards in the context of recognising foreign court judgments, both of which are also relevant under the MLCBI framework: public policy (D.I) and procedural fairness (D.II). This work examined key aspects of these safeguards, particularly those relevant to restructuring proceedings and the position of foreign creditors in these proceedings. Despite acknowledging the importance of applying the standards of the receiving state when considering the invocation of those safeguards, this work underscored the need to exercise caution in considering their application. That holds particularly true for the public policy exception. This work underscored the importance of its restrictive application and that the main purpose of the exception is to protect the fundamental policies of the receiving state rather than the interests of local creditors.

E. Restructuring Proceedings and Substantive Fairness

Before delving into the matter of ensuring substantive fairness under the MLCBI, it is essential to discuss the concept of substantive fairness in a domestic restructuring context. Hence, Part E of this work will lay the groundwork for Part F. Below, this work will analyse the importance and complexity of ensuring substantive fairness in restructuring proceedings, highlighting the difference with insolvency proceedings in that regard (E.I). It will then examine the implementation of the concept, focusing on two jurisdictions as well as the PRD and provide their comparative analysis (E.II). A summary of the main points discussed will conclude this Part (E.III).

I. Importance and Complexity of Ensuring Substantive Fairness in Restructuring Proceedings

In a restructuring context, substantive fairness (fairness of outcome) refers to the fairness of the distribution under the plan.[644] In insolvency proceedings, too, fairness, as a substantive goal, concerns the distribution of the debtor's asset pool.[645] However, substantive fairness is achieved in substantially different ways in these two proceedings. Below, this work will elaborate on this difference to highlight the complexity and importance of ensuring substantive fairness in restructuring proceedings.

---

644 Sarah Paterson associates substantive fairness with 'some sort of imbalance', giving some examples, such as a comparison of the treatment of different parties and the balance between efforts (or expectations) and actual gain. It is noteworthy that all the examples mentioned point to the outcome of the distribution. See Paterson, 'Notions of Fairness' (n 6) 600. For a discussion of procedural and substantive goals of law regarding debt-restructuring as well as the fairness of process and outcome, see Mokal, 'Fairness' (n 571) sub-ss 1.1, 1.3.

645 See the discussion in Mokal, 'On Fairness and Efficiency' (n 572) 457-59, 462ff.

1. Substantive Fairness in Insolvency Proceedings

The fair distribution of the proceeds from the realisation of the remaining assets of an insolvent debtor is one of the principal substantive goals of insolvency law.[646] That is to say, in the case of the individual enforcement of claims against a non-performing solvent debtor, the issue of substantive fairness does not arise in a distribution context. All creditors can theoretically be fully satisfied without adversely affecting the possibility of full satisfaction of others, thus, avoiding any unfair outcomes in distribution. However, with an insolvent debtor, the situation differs significantly. For various reasons,[647] some creditors are likely to be paid in full, while others may receive less than they are owed or even nothing at all because the debtor's assets are not enough to fully satisfy all creditors.[648] To prevent such unfair outcomes, separate rules are in place that prohibit individual acts of enforcement and provide a framework for the collective satisfaction of all claims against an insolvent debtor, known as insolvency law.[649]

In traditional insolvency proceedings, which involve the realisation of the entire asset pool of the debtor, whether through piecemeal or going concern sale, and the distribution of the proceeds among the creditors, the fairness of outcome is mainly achieved during the norm-making process. There is minimal discretion when applying the law, as most insolvency laws establish strict and inflexible but relatively straightforward (to implement) distribution and priority rules.[650] That is to say, insolvency laws are typically based on the idea of treating similar claims equally, which is achieved through the *pari passu* rule, i.e. *pro rata* satisfaction of all admitted claims.[651] This default rule, however, is not absolute and comes with several

646 Bork, *Principles of Cross-Border Insolvency Law* (n 93) para 4.5.

647 The reasons may be, *inter alia*, the debtor's preference, certain creditors' (eg, banks and tax authorities) faster access to the debtor's assets, and variations in the duration of the enforcement process.

648 Bork, *Principles of Cross-Border Insolvency Law* (n 93) para 4.6.

649 ibid.

650 Baird, 'The Uneasy Case' (41) 139; Westbrook, 'A Global Solution' (n 100) 2301-02; van Zwieten (ed), *Principles of Corporate Insolvency Law* (n 29) para 16-62.

651 For a more detailed discussion of the *pari passu* rule, see van Zwieten (ed), *Principles of Corporate Insolvency Law* (n 29) paras 8-02-06. See also Bork, *Principles of Cross-Border Insolvency Law* (n 93) para 4.6. For a critical analysis, see Rizwaan Jameel Mokal, *Corporate Insolvency Law: Theory and Application* (OUP 2005) 92ff.

limitations and exceptions.[652] To begin with, secured claims are generally fully paid up to the total value of the collateral.[653] The costs of insolvency proceedings are typically prioritised for payment as well.[654] Certain claims, such as those of employees and tax authorities, may also receive preferential treatment in some jurisdictions.[655] Creditors may also have the right to set off their claims against what they owe.[656] Some creditors, on the other hand, may have a lower priority for payment, either by operation of law or through private agreements.[657]

The design of distribution rules involving all or some of the aspects mentioned above is a policy matter for each state. The fairness of various aspects of the distribution order specified in the law (e.g. the preferential treatment of tax claims) can be scrutinised or questioned by scholars but certainly not by judges during the application. That is to say, judges, insolvency practitioners, and other participants in the process are obligated to adhere to those rules once they are given legal force by legislators. This leaves little room, if any, for discretion in this context.

2. Substantive Fairness in Restructuring Proceedings

The same does not hold for restructuring proceedings, where most matters are open.[658] Setting aside the academic debate on the underpinning of restructuring proceedings (B.I), there are fundamental differences in how substantive fairness is achieved in those two proceedings. As already noted above, insolvency proceedings are relatively straightforward proceedings that lead to the distribution of the proceeds from the realisation of the debtor's asset pool. The fairness of outcome is determined during the norm-making process through the adoption of a certain distribution order, which is applied in a similar manner in each proceeding.

To begin with, the norm-maker plays an important role in restructuring proceedings, too. Most restructuring laws set certain frameworks for distri-

---

652 For a more detailed discussion, see van Zwieten (ed), *Principles of Corporate Insolvency Law* (n 29) para 8-07ff. See also Bork, *Principles of Cross-Border Insolvency Law* (n 93) paras 4.20-26.

653 See, eg, InsO (n 35) s 49ff.

654 See, eg, ibid ss 53, 54.

655 See, eg, LIB (n 191) art 53.

656 See, eg, InsO (n 35) s 94.

657 See, eg, ibid s 39.

658 Baird, 'The Uneasy Case' (41) 139.

bution, such as establishing a certain priority rule or a fairness test, as this work will observe later (E.II). However, due to the inherent uncertainty involved in various aspects of restructuring proceedings, which this work will analyse below, it is impossible to strictly regulate every aspect of the fairness of outcome in these proceedings. Some matters are intentionally left to be determined during the application process, considering the circumstances of each case. Compared to insolvency proceedings, therefore, much more is required during the application process to guarantee the fairness of outcome in restructuring proceedings.[659] The fairness of outcome can be scrutinised, evaluated, and eventually determined on a case-by-case basis, as long as all those occur within the framework provided by law. Accordingly, judges play a crucial role in ensuring that the outcome of restructuring proceedings is fair.[660] The respective difference in how substantive fairness is achieved in these two proceedings is mainly because of the inherent uncertainties associated with certain aspects of restructuring proceedings as well as their ability to modify substantive rights. That said, this work in no way argues that every aspect of insolvency proceedings is certain and predictable. Indeed, certain matters affecting outcomes are subject to participants' judgment and may be questioned or contested in insolvency proceedings, too. For example, it may be asked whether the insolvency practitioner obtained the best possible price in the sale of assets. What is argued is the existence of fundamental differences in how these two proceedings function and, as a result, substantive fairness is achieved in them. Put another way, ensuring substantive fairness in restructuring proceedings is a much more complex and important matter. This work identifies at least five key distinctive aspects of restructuring proceedings in that respect.

a) Value Available for Distribution

One aspect concerns the value available for distribution. In insolvency proceedings, this value mirrors the debtor's current liquidation value, which is relatively easy to calculate. In most cases, there is even no need for calculation. Generally, not the assets, but rather the proceeds generated

659 For a more detailed discussion of the challenges associated with ensuring fairness in restructuring of different types of companies, see generally Paterson, 'Notions of Fairness' (n 6).

660 For a more detailed discussion of the role of the court in restructuring proceedings, see generally Payne, 'The Role of the Court' (n 2).

from the actual sale of assets, whether a piecemeal or going concern, are distributed among creditors pursuant to the distribution order provided by law.[661] Accordingly, the exact value of the distribution is generally known before the distribution takes place. The matter is not that straightforward in restructuring proceedings. Here, what is distributed is not the actual liquidation value of the debtor or the proceeds from the actual sale but rather the *reorganisation (restructuring) surplus*,[662] which may be challenging to predict or calculate. As Stephan Madaus puts it, 'Any restructuring plan is a *bet* on the debtor's future returns, i.e. the value of its assets and of its future income'.[663] This value is distributed before implementing the plan, thus, before it is certain that it will be fully achieved or achieved at all.

b) Restructuring Measures

To maintain the flexibility of restructuring mechanisms, it is generally recommended not to prescribe an exhaustive list of specific restructuring measures of a mandatory nature in the law.[664] Most laws allow the plan proponent to select the measures that are necessary for the debtor's successful restructuring.[665] The measures to be implemented, thus, depend on the circumstances of the case and can include reducing principal amounts,

661 See, eg, InsO (n 35) s 187ff.

662 Stephan Madaus defines the *reorganisation surplus* as 'the value which can only be realised in a restructuring of the debtor'. See Stephan Madaus, 'Is the Relative Priority Rule Right for Your Jurisdiction? A Simple Guide to RPR' (18 January 2020) <https://papers.ssrn.com/sol3/papers.cfm?abstract_id=3827696> accessed 21 October 2025, pt 1. According to Riz Mokal, the *restructuring surplus* is 'the value sought to be preserved and perhaps created by the implementation of the plan itself'. See Riz Mokal, 'The Two Conditions for the Pt 26A Cram Down' (2020) 11 JIBFL 730, 730. In a recent case, the EWCA preferred the term 'benefits preserved or generated by the restructuring' (as a substitute for the term *restructuring surplus*). *Kington SARL & Ors v Thames Water Utilities Holdings Ltd & Anor* [2025] EWCA Civ 475 (*Thames Water*), [117]. See also Axel Krohn, 'Rethinking Priority: The Dawn of the Relative Priority Rule and the New "Best Interests of Creditors" Test in the European Union' (2021) 30 Intl Ins Rev 75, 83, where the author defines the *reorganisation surplus* as 'the difference in value between the value recoverable in a liquidation of the debtor's assets and the assumed value of the reorganized firm'.

663 Madaus, 'Relative Priority Rule' (n 662) pt 2 (emphasis added).

664 Wessels and Madaus (n 597) s 8.8 (Recommendation 8.04 therein).

665 See, eg, BC (n 37) s 1123.

extending maturity dates, and debt-equity swaps.[666] This leads directly to the next aspect.

c) Non-Consensual Alteration of Substantive Rights

Another key distinctive aspect of restructuring proceedings is their ability to alter the substantive rights of involved parties, e.g. creditors and shareholders, against their will. As already discussed in this work, insolvency proceedings are asset-oriented and do not directly discharge the substantive rights of participants.[667] The primary goal of these proceedings is to efficiently realise the remaining assets of the debtor and fairly distribute the proceeds from the sale without affecting the substantive claims against the debtor. If, for example, additional assets of the liquidated debtor are discovered, creditors are entitled to enforce the unsatisfied part of their claims against those assets.[668] Restructuring proceedings are significantly different also in this aspect. As already mentioned several times in this work, restructuring proceedings can, and most often do, modify substantive rights.[669] On top of that, it can be done against the will of the holders of those rights and has a binding effect on them.[670] The extent and way those rights will be altered are to be determined in each case, as elaborated above regarding the previous aspect. The possibility of the non-consensual alteration of substantive rights alone underscores the importance of ensuring substantive fairness in the application process.

d) Post-Restructuring Contributions

Insolvency proceedings typically end with the debtor being liquidated, and the fairness of outcome in these proceedings does not consider any further role of one or another stakeholder in the debtor's business. The distribution rules are designed accordingly. In restructuring proceedings, on the contrary, the debtor continues to exist and, more importantly, to trade. Some stakeholders, such as a shareholder providing new funds, a family business

666 See n 1 (and accompanying text) and text thereto.
667 See text to n 35. See also the discussion in sub-ss B.I.3.a), E.I.1.
668 See n 35 and accompanying text.
669 See, eg, text to nn 36, 38.
670 See text to n 5.

owner, an employee, an essential supplier, or the debtor's bank, may have a more crucial role in the debtor's business continuation regardless of the type or amount of their claims. The fairness of outcome would require that those stakeholders are rewarded in proportion to their post-restructuring contributions. Again, many factors in this context depend on the specific circumstances of each proceeding. It is practically impossible to formulate detailed rules that encompass all such scenarios. As will be revealed later (E.II), general fairness frameworks provided by law often struggle to fully address the issue and this is one of the main factors in evaluating the suitability of a certain fairness framework in comparison with another.

e) Classification

Most laws require some creditor support behind the plan, the level of which may differ depending on the framework.[671] Therefore, creditors should vote on the plan. Most restructuring mechanisms involve placing creditors with different positions (such as varying pre-restructuring ranks or legal nature of claims) into different classes in order to ensure fairness. Most laws require such separate classification to be proper and justified.[672] It is essential to thoroughly evaluate whether the classes have been properly constituted in each case, as the process may be vulnerable to manipulation by plan proponents to achieve the desired outcome.[673]

3. Summary

To sum up, ensuring substantive fairness in restructuring proceedings is an important and complex matter which should take into account the peculiarities of the case at hand, as compared to insolvency proceedings. The courts, therefore, play a central role in this process. A restructuring case may involve a thorough judicial assessment of various matters that affect the fairness of outcome in that case, such as proper classification, justification for discrimination, and adherence to the established priority rule.

---

671 See, eg, InsO (n 35) s 244; BC (n 37) s 1126 (c).

672 InsO (n 35) s 222 (2).

673 For a more detailed discussion, see Mokal, 'The Two Conditions' (n 662) 732-33.

II. Substantive Fairness Frameworks

After discussing the importance and complexity of ensuring substantive fairness in restructuring proceedings, this work will now explore how the concept is implemented in different jurisdictions.[674] Specifically, this work will focus on two jurisdictions, the US and England, as well as the fairness frameworks under the PRD. Both the US and England are selected for this purpose because of their status as *restructuring hubs*. Both jurisdictions possess well-developed principles and frameworks in this area, established under statutory and case law dating back to the 19th century. Besides, these jurisdictions were also compared in this work in a cross-border context,[675] so it is important to explore how restructuring operates domestically in the same jurisdictions. The influence of US law in this field on other jurisdictions across the globe also has a significant impact on the selection.[676] The PRD will be closely examined as it significantly reshaped the laws of almost all Member States in this area and introduced a new concept of fairness that sparked heated debate in academic circles.

Examining fairness frameworks in different jurisdictions is of particular importance for the purposes of this work. It is crucial to understand how substantive fairness is ensured in a domestic context before delving into whether there is a need for a separate substantive fairness review in considering the recognition and enforcement of foreign restructuring plans. Thus, this work will set the scene for Part F, which will analyse, *inter alia*, the necessity for a substantive fairness review during the recognition stage.

The fairness frameworks in both jurisdictions and under the PRD will be examined regarding the position of individual dissenting creditors within an assenting class of creditors and that of dissenting classes of creditors.

---

674 That said, this work acknowledges that the depiction of the jurisdictions examined in the present section may be somewhat academic, ie reflective of how the system is designed to operate in law. As Christoph Paulus notes 'the law in action' may be different from 'the written law' even in jurisdictions equipped with modern insolvency instruments. Christoph G. Paulus, 'Global Insolvency Law and the Role of Multinational Institutions' (2007) 32 Brook J Intl L 755, 760.

675 See s C.II.

676 See Madaus, 'A Proposal to Divide the Realms of Insolvency and Restructuring Law' (n 4) 628-29. See also Mevorach and Walters (n 34) 858 (fn 13 therein and accompanying text).

1. The US (Chapter 11)

In the US, Chapter 11 provides for a court-supervised debtor-in-possession reorganisation regime. A single corporate reorganisation regime resulted from bankruptcy reforms in the 1970s.[677] A plan under Chapter 11 should be confirmed by the court[678] and section 1129 of the BC sets forth the requirements for confirmation, such as good faith[679] and feasibility.[680] Once the plan has been duly confirmed and become final, all original obligations of the debtor are discharged and creditors can sue the debtor only with respect to the obligations under the plan.[681]

a) Impairment, Class Composition, and Voting Thresholds

Another confirmation requirement is that the plan should be accepted by at least one class of impaired claims, excluding any 'acceptance of the plan by any insider'.[682] A claim is unimpaired if the plan leaves the (legal, equitable, and contractual) rights of its holder unaltered or cures any default and compensates for any damages, and so forth.[683] Courts should and, often

677 For a discussion of the historical background of reorganisation regimes and fairness tests, see Jonathan Hicks, 'Foxes Guarding the Henhouse: The Modern Best Interests of Creditors Test in Chapter 11 Reorganizations' (2005) 5 Nev LJ 820, 822ff.

678 BC (n 37) s 1128.

679 ibid s 1129 (a) (3). S 1129 does not set forth any material (imminent) insolvency requirement.

680 ibid s 1129 (a) (11): 'Confirmation of the plan is not likely to be followed by the liquidation, or the need for further financial reorganization…'. For a discussion of the standard of the burden of proof of the feasibility test, see Olivares-Caminal and others (n 38) paras 3.150-51.

681 Olivares-Caminal and others (n 38) para 3.130. For the effects of the confirmation of a Chapter 11 plan and other post-confirmation matters, see BC (n 37) ch 11, sub-ch III.

682 BC (n 37) s 1129 (a) (10). For a critical analysis, see Mokal, 'The Two Conditions' (n 662) 731-32.

683 For the full definition, see BC (n 37) s 1124; For a more detailed discussion of the definition of *impairment*, see Kenneth N. Klee, 'All You Ever Wanted to Know about Cram Down under the New Bankruptcy Code' (1979) 53 Am Bankr LJ 133, 138-39; Denise R. Polivy, 'Unfair Discrimination in Chapter 11: A Comprehensive Compilation of Current Case Law' (1998) 72 Am Bankr LJ 191, 193; Mokal, 'The Two Conditions' (n 662) 731.

do, look at whether the class has been formed to create an 'artificial impairment'.[684]

The BC allows a separate classification of claims and interests, provided that a claim or an interest is substantially similar to those in the same class.[685] However, it does not expressly mandate that all similar claims must be placed in a single class.[686] Nonetheless, most courts do not approve of a separate classification of claims of the same rank unless there is legitimate (business) justification behind it.[687] It should also be noted that all creditors within a particular class should be treated equally under the plan unless a less favourably treated creditor provides consent.[688]

As to the requisite majority for the acceptance of the plan in each class of claims, the approval of at least two-thirds of creditors in value and a simple majority of creditors in number is required.[689] An unimpaired class (each member of it) is deemed to have accepted the plan.[690]

b) Fairness Assessment with Respect to Dissenting Creditors

Chapter 11, namely, section 1129 of the BC, also sets forth several standards regarding the (substantive) fairness of the distribution, to which courts should adhere before confirming the plan. Below, this work will examine these standards first in relation to dissenting individual creditors and then dissenting classes of creditors.

684 Polivy (n 683) 193.
685 BC (n 37) s 1122.
686 G. Eric Brunstad Jr. and Mike Sigal, 'Competitive Choice Theory and the Unresolved Doctrines of Classification and Unfair Discrimination in Business Reorganizations under the Bankruptcy Code' (1999) 55 Bus Law 1, 3
687 Bruce A. Markell, 'A New Perspective on Unfair Discrimination in Chapter 11' (1998) 72 Am Bankr LJ 227, 243; Polivy (n 683) 194. It is noteworthy that case law is inconsistent with respect to the classification issue. For a discussion of the proper classification standards under case law, see Brunstad and Sigal (n 686) 32-37.
688 BC (n 37) s 1123 (a) (4).
689 ibid s 1126 (c).
690 ibid s 1126 (f).

aa) Dissenting Individual Creditors

Section 1129 (a) (7) (A) (ii) of the BC, known as the *best interests test* ("BIT"), is designed to safeguard the interests of individual dissenting creditors whose claims are impaired by the plan.[691] According to the BIT, each impaired dissenting creditor should get under the plan at least the value that the creditor would receive if the company were liquidated under Chapter 7 of the BC on the effective date of the plan.[692] The rationale behind the BIT is that, while the consent of every impaired individual creditor is not required to confirm a Chapter 11 plan, the reorganisation of the debtor may not result in worsening the position of dissenting creditors. That is to say, dissenting creditors should get under the plan at least the value that they would obtain in a liquidation of the debtor. Anything exceeding this minimum guaranteed amount, however, is 'subject to group vote rather than individual demand'.[693] In order to demonstrate that the BIT is satisfied, the plan proponent is expected to present evidence, typically in the form of expert testimony, regarding the hypothetical liquidation analysis of the debtor.[694] That said, it is not always clear what the liquidation value of the debtor is and the process may be subject to speculation.[695]

bb) Dissenting Classes of Creditors

If a Chapter 11 plan is consensual, i.e. adopted by all impaired classes (but not necessarily by all creditors within those classes), section 1129 (a) of the BC applies, and the only requirement regarding the fairness of the distribution under the plan is the satisfaction of the BIT, as discussed above. If the BIT is met, dissenting creditors may not challenge the plan on fairness grounds.

When, however, a plan is non-consensual or *cramdown*, meaning it is not adopted by at least one impaired class of creditors, the situation

691 Olivares-Caminal and others (n 38) para 3.131.
692 ibid. For a discussion of the respective (present) values, see Timothy C. G. Fisher and Jocelyn Martel, 'Does It Matter How Bankruptcy Judges Evaluate the Creditors' Best-Interests Test' (2007) 81 Am Bankr LJ 497.
693 Hicks (n 677) 831.
694 Olivares-Caminal and others (n 38) para 3.132.
695 ibid para 3.132 (fn 208 therein and accompanying text). See also Hicks (n 677) 832ff.

changes.[696] In this case, the confirmation of the plan is subject to section 1129 (b) (1) of the BC, which sets forth two additional requirements with respect to each dissenting class.[697] Below, this work will examine the respective requirements:

(1) The *Fair and Equitable* Requirement

One of these requirements states that the plan should be fair and equitable in relation to dissenting impaired classes.

(a) Class of Secured Claims

With respect to a class of secured claims, the plan is fair and equitable when each secured creditor under the plan: (i) retains its security interest in the collateral and receives deferred cash payments equal to at least the amount of its claim; (ii) in the event of the collateral being sold, receives a security interest in the proceeds of the sale; or (iii) can realise 'indubitable equivalent' of its claim.[698]

(b) Class of Unsecured Claims: The Absolute Priority Rule

The *fair and equitable* requirement with respect to a class of unsecured creditors states that, *inter alia*, dissenting classes of senior claimants should be paid in full before any more junior claimant receives anything under the plan.[699] Put another way, old shareholders cannot retain any equity interest in the reorganised company unless all dissenting classes of creditors are paid in full and junior creditors cannot receive anything unless all dissenting classes of senior creditors are fully satisfied.[700] This requirement

696 For a more detailed discussion of cramdown plans, see generally Klee (n 683).

697 It is noteworthy that the confirmation requirements of s 1129 (a) should be fulfilled also in this scenario, except that of paragraph (8) which provides that a plan should be adopted by all affected classes. This means that, *inter alia*, a plan should be adopted at least by one class of impaired claims.

698 BC (n 37) s 1129 (b) (2) (A).

699 ibid s 1129 (b) (2) (B).

700 Stephen J. Lubben, 'The Overstated Absolute Priority Rule' (2016) 21 Fordham J Corp & Fin L 581, 581.

is known as the *absolute priority rule* ("APR").[701] The APR does not create the priority of claims but rather honours those set outside bankruptcy.[702] The APR applies to dissenting classes only and, therefore, even in the case of a non-consensual plan, dissenting creditors in assenting classes may not challenge the fairness of the distribution under the plan by referring to the APR.[703] The only available route for this purpose is, again, the BIT.

(aa) Historical Background

The APR existed before it was officially included in the BC in its current form and originated from the era of equity receiverships of railroad companies.[704] Its initial purpose was to prevent abusive scenarios under that mechanism, i.e. where old equity-holders, in collision with secured creditors, retained equity interests in the reorganised company, while junior creditors received little or nothing.[705] It was, however, in *Case v Los Angeles Lumber Products Co,* where the USSC, for the first time, defined the statutory *fair and equitable* requirement under 1930 bankruptcy reforms as a 'fixed principle' that had been developed in case law: 'rule of full or absolute priority'.[706] It is also noteworthy that, unlike the BC, under its predecessors, the *fair and equitable* requirement, and accordingly, the APR applied to all dissenting creditors irrespective of whether or not the plan was consensual.[707]

701 Klee (n 683) 143.

702 Jonathan M. Seymour and Steven L. Schwarcz, 'Corporate Restructuring under Relative and Absolute Priority Default Rules: A Comparative Assessment' [2021] U Ill L Rev 1, 3.

703 Klee (n 683) 141 (fn 67 therein and accompanying text).

704 For a historical analysis, see Edward S. Adams, 'Toward a New Conceptualization of the Absolute Priority Rule and Its New Value Exception [1993] Det C L Rev 1445, s I.A; Lubben (n 700) pt I; Bruce Grohsgal, 'How Absolute Is the Absolute Priority Rule in Bankruptcy: The Case for Structured Dismissals' (2017) 8 Wm & Mary Bus L Rev 439, pt II.

705 For initially decided cases, see *Louisville Trust Co v Louisville, New Albany. & Chicago Railway Co,* 174 US 674 (1899); *Northern Pacific Railway Co v Boyd,* 228 US 482 (1913); *Kansas City Terminal Railway Co v Central Union Trust Co,* 271 US 445 (1926).

706 *Case v Los Angeles Lumber Products Co,* Ltd., 308 US 106 (1939) 116-17.

707 Klee (n 683) 141 (fn 67 therein and accompanying text); Lubben (n 700) 594-95.

(bb) Consensual Deviations from the APR: Valuation of the Debtor

Despite its title, the absolute nature and fundamental role of the APR have been roundly questioned in the literature.[708] In practice, too, the APR is often disregarded. One case study from 1990 illustrated that in twenty-three out of the thirty sample cases under the BC, the APR had been consensually deviated from, i.e. shareholders had been paid excessive amounts, which would not have been the case in a cramdown plan scenario under the APR.[709] The authors of the study suggest that one reason for these deviations could be to avoid expensive and time-consuming valuations in a cramdown plan scenario.[710] It should be noted that a valuation of the debtor is a crucial part of the process where APR applies since the courts should also be mindful to ensure that senior creditors are not overcompensated in a cramdown scenario.[711] Other reasons include, in the authors' view, the leverage of the debtor's management against creditors at earlier stages of Chapter 11 proceedings under the BC, such as the exclusive right to file a plan, discretion in setting priority levels, and power in relation to the suspension of post-petition interests as well as the leverage associated with their 'natural information advantage'.[712]

Douglas Baird and Donald Bernstein underscore another aspect of the debtor's valuation in an APR-adhered cramdown scenario where equity is transferred to creditors, namely, the inherent uncertainty associated with judicial valuations.[713] According to them, that is one of the main factors encouraging negotiated deviations from the APR.[714] Douglas Baird argues in favour of the relative priority model over the APR, which eliminates the need to value the debtor at the confirmation stage.[715] Instead, it provides

708 See, eg, Lubben (n 700) pt III; Grohsgal (n 704) s III.C; Riz Mokal, 'The Court's Discretion in Relation to the Pt 26A Cram Down' (2021) 1 JIBFL 12, 13ff.

709 Allan C. Eberhart, William T. Moore, and Rodney L. Roenfeldt, 'Security Pricing and Deviations from the Absolute Priority Rule in Bankruptcy Proceedings' (1990) 45 J Fin 1457, 1458. For a summary of the outcomes of several other studies (illustrating the proportion of deviations from the rule in these studies and noting the declining trend in recent years), see Mokal, 'The Court's Discretion' (n 708) 16 (en 9 therein).

710 Eberhart, Moore, and Roenfeldt (n 709) 1459.

711 Olivares-Caminal and others (n 38) para 3.139.

712 Eberhart, Moore, and Roenfeldt (n 709) 1459.

713 Douglas G. Baird and Donald S. Bernstein, 'Absolute Priority, Valuation Uncertainty, and the Reorganization Bargain' (2006) 115 Yale LJ 1930, 1941-43.

714 ibid 1966.

715 See generally Baird, 'Priority Matters' (n 30).

out of the money junior creditors with a call option, allowing them to exercise this option later if the reorganised company ends up being worth more than the total owed to senior creditors.[716] He describes this model as the 'postponing the day of reckoning' from the confirmation stage until a certain later point when affected parties will have a clearer picture of the value of the reorganised company.[717]

(cc) The New Value Exception to the APR

Apart from the possibility of negotiated deviations discussed above, the APR also includes an exception known as the *new value exception*.[718] This exception allows old shareholders to maintain an equity interest in the reorganised company, even if not all creditors have been fully paid, provided that the former provides new value to the company.[719] The exception, like the APR itself, antedates the BC and was developed by courts.[720] In *Los Angeles Lumber*, the USSC recognised the possibility of retaining equity interests by old equity holders as long as the following three requirements are met: (i) the necessity of the infusion of the new value; (ii) 'contribution in money or in money's worth'; and (iii) reasonable equivalence to the retained interest.[721]. The *Los Angeles Lumber* court further clarified that old shareholders' 'financial standing and influence in the community' and role in 'continuity of management' do not fulfil the *money's worth* requirement.[722] In *Norwest Bank Worthington v Ahlers,* the USSC held that 'a promise to contribute future labor, management, or expertise' does not meet this requirement either.[723]

Unlike the APR, the exception has never been codified. As a result, there had been a lot of discussion in the literature and case law about the survival

716 According to Douglas Baird, such a call option should have two components: 'exercise date' and 'strike price' the latter being the total amount of the debt owed to senior creditors. See ibid 796.

717 ibid 815.

718 Adams (n 704) 1448; Olivares-Caminal and others (n 38) para 3.141.

719 ibid.

720 For a historical analysis, see Adams (n 704) s I.B; Douglas S. Neville, 'The New Value Exception to the Chapter 11 Absolute Priority Rule' (1995) 60 Mo L Rev 465, s III.B.

721 *Los Angeles Lumber* (706) 121-22. For a more detailed discussion of those requirements, see Adams (n 704) pt II.

722 *Los Angeles Lumber* (706) 122.

723 *Norwest Bank Worthington v Ahlers,* 485 US 197 (1988) 204-05.

of the exception after the BC codified the APR but did not mention the exception.[724] In *Bank of American National Trust and Savings Association v 203 North LaSalle Street Partnership,* the USSC acknowledged, albeit not stating expressly, the survival of the exception but limited its application with a non-exclusivity requirement.[725] Edward Adams had also previously argued, as part of his new economic approach, against the exclusivity in a cramdown scenario and for giving third parties the right to outbid the debtor's self-appraisal of the going-concern value of the company.[726]

(dd) Attempts at Non-Consensual Deviations from the APR

Several attempts have been made, both in theory and in practice, to non-consensually deviate from the APR. The *gifting* doctrine, according to which senior creditors can gift part of their entitlements under the plan to junior creditors or shareholders by bypassing intermediary classes, constitutes one of them.[727] The doctrine has been applied by several bankruptcy courts,[728] while being subsequently disapproved by some circuit courts.[729]

Another attempt for a non-consensual deviation from the APR involved structured dismissals, i.e. the dismissal of a Chapter 11 case without confirmation of a plan but with the court's approval of a priority-violating settlement of certain claims.[730] This approach, however, was expressly rejected by the USSC in *Czyzewski v. Jevic Holding Corp.*[731] Nevertheless, the USSC, *in*

724 For a summary of the arguments in favour and against the survival of the exception, see Adams (n 704) s I.C.

725 *Bank of American National Trust and Savings Association v 203 North LaSalle Street Partnership,* 526 US 434 (1999) 449ff.

726 See Adams (n 704) pt IV.

727 See generally Michael Carnevale, 'Is Gifting Dead in Chapter 11 Reorganizations? Examining Absolute Priority in the Wake of the Second Circuit's No-Gift Rule in re DBSD' (2012) 15 U Pa J Bus L 225; Olivares-Caminal and others (n 38) paras 3.145-48. See also generally Amy Timm, 'The Gift That Gives Too Much: Invalidating a Gifting Exception to the Absolute Priority Rule' [2013] U Ill L Rev 1649.

728 See Carnevale (n 727) 231-32 and cited cases therein.

729 See *In re Armstrong World Industries, Inc,* 432 F3d 507 (3d Cir 2005); *DISH Network Corp. v. DBSD North America Inc.,* 634 F3d 79 (2d Cir 2010).

730 For a more detailed discussion of structured dismissals and arguments favouring deviations from the rule in the case of structured dismissals, see Grohsgal (n 704) pts I, V-VII.

731 *Czyzewski v. Jevic Holding Corp.,*137 S Ct 973 (2017). For a brief summary of the case, see Grohsgal (n 704) 534ff.

dicta, left open the possibility of a non-consensual deviation from the APR for interim distributions.[732]

(2) The *Unfair Discrimination* Requirement

A further requirement for confirming a non-consensual plan is the absence of *unfair discrimination.*[733] This requirement, too, applies only to dissenting classes and not to dissenting individual creditors within an assenting class.[734] The *unfair discrimination* requirement represents the horizontal dimension of fairness of the distribution under a non-consensual plan, whereas the *fair and equitable* requirement constitutes its vertical pillar.[735] The *unfair discrimination* requirement, thus, focuses on the distributions to the classes of creditors of the same rank as those of the dissenting class.[736] Accordingly, there should be at least two classes of creditors with the same rank for it to apply. That said, the issue of proper classification[737] is not the subject matter of the *unfair discrimination* requirement since placing similar claims in different classes does not automatically result in discrimination between these classes.[738]

Unlike the *fair and equitable* requirement, the BC is completely silent on what constitutes unfair discrimination. One scholar, therefore, described it as 'an orphan in Chapter 11 reorganization practice'.[739] One detail is,

732 *Jevic* (n 731) 985. For the arguments in favour of the strict application of the rule at all stages, including interim settlements, of Chapter 11 proceedings, see generally Maxx M. Johnson, 'The Not-So-Settled Absolute Priority Rule: The Continued Threat of Priority-Deviation Through Interim Distributions of Assets in Chapter 11 Bankruptcy' (2017) 13 Seton Hall Cir Rev 291.

733 BC (n 37) s 1129 (b) (1).

734 Klee (n 683) 141 (fn 67 therein and accompanying text).

735 Markell, 'A New Perspective on Unfair Discrimination' (n 687) 227-28, 247.

736 It should be noted that, as already mentioned in this work, intra-class discrimination is not allowed unless the less favourably treated creditor agrees to such treatment. See n 688 and text thereto.

737 See sub-s E.II.1.a).

738 See Markell, 'A New Perspective on Unfair Discrimination' (n 687) 243 (fn 75 therein and accompanying text), where the author notes that proper classification of similar claims in different classes shall be assessed under s 1129 (a) (1) rather than s 1129 (b) (1). See also Polivy (n 683) 196-99; Committee on Bankruptcy and Corporate Reorganization of the Association of the Bar of the City of New York (ABCNY), 'Making the Test for Unfair Discrimination More "Fair": A Proposal' (2002) 58 Bus Law 83, 85-86.

739 Markell, 'A New Perspective on Unfair Discrimination' (n 687) 227.

nonetheless, clear from the language of section 1129 (b) (1): not every but only *unfair* discrimination is prohibited thereunder.[740]

(a) Forms and Rationales of Discrimination

The analysis of case law illustrates that discrimination between two or more classes of creditors with the same rank may take place in various forms: variances in payment percentage and/or maturity date, conditional payments, and source of payment, to name a few.[741] Discrimination, in one form or another, may have various rationales behind it, such as differences in the legal nature or amount of claims, differences in pre-insolvency expectations, importance for the survival of the business, rewarding or punishing the plan voting behaviour, and benefiting insiders.[742]

(b) Unfairness of Discrimination: Different Approaches and Tests

As mentioned above, the text of the BC contains no criteria to assess whether the discrimination between the classes of the same rank is unfair. The uncertainty surrounding the requirement, however, does not end there. That is to say, case law is also inconsistent on the matter.[743] Different approaches have been followed by courts, such as the *restrictive*, *mechanical*, or *broad* approaches.[744] Additionally, different competing tests have been developed to assess the unfairness of the discrimination, two of which this work will summarise below.

740 Brunstad and Sigal (n 686) 37. It should be noted that this point is one of the main arguments against the *mechanical approach*, according to which every single deviation from the *pro rata* distribution constitutes unfair discrimination. See n 744 and accompanying text.

741 See Polivy (n 683) s II.D. See also Markell, 'A New Perspective on Unfair Discrimination' (n 687) 239-41.

742 See Polivy (n 683) s II.C. See also Markell, 'A New Perspective on Unfair Discrimination' (n 687) 239-41; ABCNY (n 738) 86-87.

743 See Polivy (n 683) pt II.

744 See Polivy (n 683) sub-s II.B.1 and cases cited therein. See also ABCNY (n 738) 87-92 and cases cited therein. To sum up, the *restrictive* approach confines unfair discrimination to the cases involving subordination of claims. According to the *mechanical* approach, every single deviation from *pro rata* distribution is unfair. The *broad* approach, which is widely followed by courts, looks into the specific circumstances of each case at hand to evaluate whether the discrimination between the similarly situated classes is fair. The first two approaches have been followed by only few courts.

The *Aztec* test, which originated from Chapter 13 (of the BC) case law, consists of four parts to assess the fairness of discrimination:

> (1) whether the discrimination is supported by a reasonable basis; (2) whether the debtor can confirm and consummate a plan without the discrimination; (3) whether the discrimination is proposed in good faith; and (4) the treatment of the classes discriminated against.[745]

According to an alternative test, suggested by Bruce Markell and later known also as the *Dow Corning* test, unfair discrimination is presumed in case there is:

> (1) a dissenting class; (2) another class of the same priority; and (3) a difference in the plan's treatment of the two classes that results in either (a) a materially lower percentage recovery for the dissenting class (measured in terms of the net present value of all payments), or (b) regardless of percentage recovery, an allocation under the plan of materially greater risk to the dissenting class in connection with its proposed distribution.[746]

According to the author of this test, the presumption of unfairness can be rebutted when the disparate treatment (factors (3) (a) and (3) (b) of the test) under the plan conforms to pre-insolvency status and expectation of creditors and, in the case of disparate recovery under the plan (factor (3) (a) of the test) also when an equivalent contribution is provided by the favoured class.[747] In a relatively recent case, the Third Circuit upheld the

745 *In re Aztec Co*, 107 BR 585, 590 (Bankr MD Tenn 1989); Olivares-Caminal and others (n 38) para 3.135. For a critical analysis, see Markell, 'A New Perspective on Unfair Discrimination' (n 687) s IV.A, sub-s IV.C.2 (where the author refers to the test as the *Ambanc/Aztec standard*); ABCNY (n 738) 92-94 (where the test is referred as the *Broad Test*). For a summary of its criticism and further formulations, see Polivy (n 683) sub-s II.B.2. To summarise, the test has been criticised mainly for being too subjective in nature.

746 Markell, 'A New Perspective on Unfair Discrimination' (n 687) 249. For the judicial application of the test see, eg, *In re Dow Corning Corp*, 244 BR 696, 701-5 (Bankr ED Mich 1999). For a critical analysis, see ABCNY (n 738) 98-101.

747 Markell, 'A New Perspective on Unfair Discrimination' (n 687) 250. For a proposal to replace the test for the rebuttal of the presumption under Markel's proposal with a more objective test, see ABCNY (n 738) 106-07. For Markell's counter-argu-

application by the bankruptcy court of Bruce Markell's proposal over other tests while referring to it as the *rebuttable presumption* test.[748]

c) Summary

In subsection E.II.1, this work examined Chapter 11, focusing on the fairness assessments thereunder. Although a cross-class cramdown is available under Chapter 11, the plan should be accepted by at least one class of impaired claims. As to dissenting individual creditors in assenting classes in both consensual and cramdown plan scenarios, the court should ensure that they are not in a worse position than they would be if the debtor were liquidated. The fairness assessment in relation to dissenting classes is more complex and has two prongs. The vertical aspect, the APR, looks at the treatment of classes of unsecured claims with different ranks: junior claimants cannot receive anything unless dissenting classes of more senior claimants are fully paid (subject to the new value exception). The horizontal aspect focuses on the treatment of different classes of the same rank and whether there is unfair discrimination. The BC does not provide all the details, particularly regarding the horizontal aspect. Case law is also not consistent regarding certain matters, again, particularly in relation to the *unfair discrimination* requirement.

2. England

As already discussed, Chapter 11 provides a centralised route for the rescue of distressed companies under US law. However, no single centralised gateway exists under English law to rescue financially troubled companies.[749] Instead, there are several mechanisms available under different legislative acts, which can be used stand-alone or in combination.[750] These mechanisms provide for different entry requirements, voting procedures, and fairness assessment standards.

ments regarding that proposal, see generally Bruce A. Markell, 'Slouching Toward Fairness: A Reply to the ABCNY's Proposal on Unfair Discrimination' (2002) 58 Bus Law 109.

748 *In re Tribune Co*, 972 F3d 228, 241-42 (3d Cir 2020).

749 Olivares-Caminal and others (n 38) para 3.233.

750 For a detailed overview of English restructuring instruments, see ibid pt I, ch 3, ss VIII-XIII.

Below, this work will examine three debt restructuring mechanisms under English law that can bind dissenting creditors:[751] Company Voluntary Arrangements ("CVA"),[752] Schemes of Arrangement ("Scheme"),[753] and Restructuring Plans ("Part 26A Plan").[754] This work will mainly examine fairness standards with respect to dissenting creditors and classes (as the case may be) as well as related issues (e.g. class composition) under the restructuring mechanisms of English law mentioned above.

a) CVA

The CVA is a mechanism that allows companies to propose 'a composition in satisfaction of its debts or a scheme of arrangement of its affairs'.[755] The CVA was introduced to English law as part of the insolvency reforms of 1985-86.[756] A company does not need to be insolvent to propose a CVA.[757]

aa) Voting Thresholds and Effects of Approval

For the CVA to be approved, it requires a majority of members in value and seventy-five per cent of creditors in value to vote in favour in their respective meetings.[758] Despite the possibility of being treated differently, creditors vote in a single class.[759] The claims of preferential and secured creditors cannot be compromised without their consent.[760] Unlike secured creditors

751 Administration (another mechanism of English law), if used stand-alone, cannot bind dissenting creditors (ibid para 3.261). Therefore, this work will not separately discuss the respective mechanism.
752 Insolvency Act 1986, pt I.
753 Companies Act 2006, pt 26.
754 ibid pt 26A.
755 Insolvency Act 1986, s 1 (1)
756 Jennifer Payne, 'Debt Restructuring in English Law: Lessons from the US and the Need for Reform' (30 January 2014) Oxford Legal Studies Research Paper No 89/2013 <https://papers.ssrn.com/sol3/papers.cfm?abstract_id=2321615> accessed 21 October 2025, s 3.2.
757 ibid.
758 Insolvency (England and Wales) Rules 2016, SI 2016/1024 (Insolvency Rules), rr 2.36, 15.34 (3).
759 Payne, 'Debt Restructuring in English Law' (n 756) s 3.2; Olivares-Caminal and others (n 38) para 3.298.
760 Insolvency Act 1986, s 4 ((3)-(4)).

(with respect to the secured part of their claims), however, preferential creditors' votes are counted towards the requisite majority.[761] Once has been duly approved, the CVA becomes effective without requiring court intervention and binds, *inter alia*, dissenting unsecured creditors.[762]

bb) The *Unfair Prejudice* Challenge

A dissenting creditor can, nonetheless, challenge the CVA in court, particularly on the *unfair prejudice* grounds under the Insolvency Act 1986.[763] The statutory text, however, does not provide any guidance on what exactly constitutes *unfair prejudice* in this context.

That said, some guidelines have been established in case law. That is to say, in *Prudential Assurance Co Ltd v PRG Powerhouse Ltd*, Etherton J thoroughly examined the matter.[764] First, the judge mentioned that prejudice, although not necessarily *unfair*, can be established if a creditor is in a worse position under the CVA than before the CVA.[765] Secondly, the judge acknowledged that there is no single and universal test to assess unfairness in the respective context and all relevant circumstances, including available alternatives, should be taken into account.[766] According to the judge, a comparative analysis from different perspectives, such as vertical and horizontal comparisons, may be conducted as part of the fairness assessment.[767] In the judge's view, the vertical component of the analysis should compare the position of the creditor with the respective position that would have been in insolvent liquidation to ensure that the creditor is not worse off under the CVA.[768] However, the judge also noted that the vertical comparison alone should not be enough to establish unfair prejudice.[769]

761 Insolvency Rules (n 758) rr 15.28 (5), 15.31 ((1), (4)-(5)). Olivares-Caminal and others (n 38) para 3.298.

762 Insolvency Act 1986, s 5 (2).

763 ibid s 6 (1). The CVA may also be challenged on the *material irregularity* ground under this section. For a more detailed discussion of the challenge of CVAs, see Olivares-Caminal and others (n 38) paras 3.305ff.

764 *Prudential Assurance Co Ltd v PRG Powerhouse Ltd* [2007] EWHC 1002 (Ch). See also *Lazari Properties 2 Ltd v New Look Retailers Ltd* [2021] EWHC 1209 (Ch).

765 *Powerhouse* (n 764) [72]-[73].

766 ibid [74].

767 ibid [75].

768 ibid [77]-[82].

769 ibid [83].

That is to say, the judge emphasised the importance of considering how other creditors are treated under the CVA and whether there is a differential treatment of creditors, which involves conducting a horizontal comparison.[770] The judge noted that differential treatment does not necessarily result in unfair prejudice and may even be necessary for fairness.[771] Additionally, the judge found it helpful to compare the respective positions of the parties under a potential Scheme, while underscoring the need for caution in that context.[772]

b) Scheme

The Scheme is a mechanism under Part 26 of the Companies Act 2006 ("Part 26") that provides for a 'compromise' or an 'arrangement' between a company and its creditors and/or members or any class of them.[773] It is worth noting that a company does not have to be insolvent or in financial difficulty to be eligible under Part 26.[774] Besides, the Scheme does not have to include all creditors and members of the company.[775]

aa) Class Composition, Voting Thresholds, and Effects of Confirmation

The proper classification of creditors is governed by case law. According to the rules established under case law, a Scheme class 'must be confined to those persons whose rights are not so dissimilar as to make it impossible for them to consult together with a view to their common interest'.[776] When determining whether classes have been properly composed, it is important

770 ibid [83]-[87].
771 ibid [88]-[89].
772 ibid [95].
773 Companies Act 2006, s 895. For a discussion of the definition of *compromise* or *arrangement*, see Jennifer Payne, *Schemes of Arrangement: Theory, Structure and Operation* (2nd edn, CUP 2021), 21-27; See also Mokal, 'The Two Conditions' (n 662) 731; Sarah Paterson, 'Judicial Discretion in Part 26A Restructuring Plan Procedures' (24 January 2022) <https://papers.ssrn.com/sol3/papers.cfm?abstract_id=4016519> accessed 21 October 2025, s V.A.
774 Payne, 'Debt Restructuring in English Law' (n 756) s 3.3.
775 Olivares-Caminal and others (n 38) para 3.406.
776 *Sovereign Life Assurance v Dodd* [1892] 2 QB 573, 583 per Bowen LJ. For a detailed analysis of the class composition issue under Schemes, see Payne, *Schemes of Arrangement* (n 773) 56ff. See also Olivares-Caminal and others (n 38) paras 3-414-28.

to analyse the rights that are altered or discharged, as well as the new rights given by the Scheme.[777] If the Scheme is put forward as an alternative to the insolvent liquidation of the debtor, the rights that are altered or discharged by the Scheme are the respective rights those creditors would have in the liquidation.[778]

The Scheme shall be approved in each summoned class of creditors or members by a majority in number and seventy-five per cent majority in value present in the respective meetings.[779] The Scheme becomes binding on all affected creditors once it has been sanctioned by the court and all statutory procedural requirements have been met.[780]

bb) Fairness Assessment

Under Part 26, a stand-alone class cramdown is not possible.[781] Hence, the court has no jurisdiction to sanction the Scheme if the requisite majority in each Scheme class has not been reached.[782]

Accordingly, the fairness issue can only arise with respect to individual dissenting creditors within assenting classes. This matter is considered when the court decides whether to sanction the Scheme. That is to say, the court still has a genuine discretion not to sanction the Scheme in the sanctioning hearing, even if the requisite majority has been reached in each Scheme class.[783] When exercising their discretion, English courts apply a four-stage test originating from 19th-century cases, with the second and third stages being particularly important in safeguarding the interests of a minority within assenting scheme classes:

> ii) At the second stage, the Court must consider whether the class was fairly represented by the meeting, and whether the majority were coercing the minority in order to promote interests adverse to the class whom they purported to represent.

777 *Hawk Insurance Co Ltd* [2001] EWCA Civ 241 [30].
778 ibid [42].
779 Companies Act 2006, s 899 (1).
780 ibid s 899 ((3)-(4)).
781 Payne, 'Debt Restructuring in English Law' (n 756) s 3.3.
782 ibid.
783 *Hawk* (n 777) [33]; Payne, 'Debt Restructuring in English Law' (n 756) s 3.3. For a detailed analysis of the court's discretion, see Payne, *Schemes of Arrangement* (n 773) 84ff.

> iii) At the third stage, the Court must consider whether the scheme is a fair scheme which a creditor could reasonably approve. Importantly it must be appreciated that the Court is not concerned to decide whether the scheme is the only fair scheme or even the "best" scheme.[784]

At the second stage, when determining whether the majority fairly represents the assenting class in question, the court is likely to consider, *inter alia*, the turnout at the meeting and any collateral interests other than the interest of the class.[785] At the third stage, which involves determining whether a reasonable creditor would approve the Scheme, the court is likely to examine the position of the dissenting parties in the relevant alternative to the Scheme.[786] Additionally, the fact that the majority (both in value and in number) has supported the Scheme, as long as the requirements of the second stage have been fulfilled, is also likely to influence the court's assessment of whether a reasonable creditor would support the Scheme.[787]

c) Part 26A Plan

A new restructuring tool under Part 26A of the Companies Act 2006 ("Part 26A") for companies in financial difficulties was introduced to English law as part of the 2020 reforms.[788] In the years leading up to the reforms, numerous scholars advocated for the modernisation of English debt-restructuring law.[789] The new restructuring procedure, which reflects some

784 *Noble Group Limited* [2018] EWHC 3092 (Ch) [17] as recently paraphrased by Snowden J (as he then was). For an older version, see *Telewest Communications plc* [2004] EWHC 1466 (Ch) [20] (quoting *Re National Bank Ltd* [1966] 1 WLR 819. For a more detailed discussion, see Paterson, 'The Conceptual Foundation' (n 73) s 2.A.

785 Olivares-Caminal and others (n 38) para 3.434; See also Payne, 'The Role of the Court' (n 2) 138.

786 Olivares-Caminal and others (n 38) para 3.433.

787 Paterson, 'Judicial Discretion' (n 773) s IV.A.

788 Corporate Governance and Insolvency Act 2020, sch 9, s 1. For a critical analysis as to the implementation of the reforms, see generally Kristin van Zwieten, 'Mid-Crisis Restructuring Law Reform in the United Kingdom' (2023) 24 EBOR 287.

789 See, eg, Payne, 'Debt Restructuring in English Law' (n 756) pt 4; generally Sarah Paterson, 'Reflections on English Law Schemes of Arrangement in Distress and Proposals for Reform' (2018) 15 ECFR 472.

of these suggestions, was primarily based on the Scheme framework.[790] Despite that, Part 26A plans differ in several ways from Schemes. One major difference is the possibility of a stand-alone cross-class cramdown under section 901G of the Companies Act 2006, which will be discussed in detail below. The other differences are related to eligibility requirements,[791] voting thresholds,[792] and participants of class meetings.[793]

aa) Class Composition, Voting Thresholds, and Effects of Confirmation

Like Schemes, creditors can be placed in different classes, and the same case law principles that govern the composition of classes under Part 26 (i.e. the *similarity of rights* test)[794] also apply to Part 26A plans.[795] The Part 26A plan must be approved by at least seventy-five per cent of the majority in value present in each summoned class of creditors or members.[796] If this threshold is not met, the plan can only be confirmed under the cramdown provisions of section 901G. However, it is up to the court to decide whether to sanction the Part 26A plan in either case.[797] Once it has been sanctioned by the court and become final, the Part 26A plan binds all creditors and members, including dissenting ones.[798]

bb) Fairness Assessment

This work will now turn to the fairness framework to protect the interests of dissenting creditors under Part 26A. To begin with, the EWCA upheld the approach that the *rationality* test under Part 26 case law[799] should continue

790 Olivares-Caminal and others (n 38) para 3.472.
791 Companies Act 2006, s 901A. It is noteworthy that a company shall be or likely to be in financial difficulty to be eligible under Part 26A. For a more detailed discussion, see Olivares-Caminal and others (n 38) paras 3.475-77.
792 Companies Act 2006, s 901F. For a more detailed discussion, see Olivares-Caminal and others (n 38) para 3.488.
793 Companies Act 2006, s 901C. For a more detailed discussion, see Olivares-Caminal and others (n 38) paras 3.478-87.
794 See sub-s E.II.2.b)aa).
795 *Adler* (n 622) [114].
796 Companies Act 2006, s 901F (1)
797 ibid ss 901F (1), 901G (2).
798 ibid s 901F ((5)-(6)).
799 See sub-s E.II.2.b)bb).

to apply with respect to dissenting creditors within assenting classes of Part 26A plans irrespective of whether or not a cross-class cramdown is engaged.[800] The fairness assessment with respect to dissenting creditors within assenting classes under Part 26A, therefore, will not be addressed further in this work.

As to dissenting classes under Part 26A, the fairness assessment has two prongs. First, the court has jurisdiction to sanction the Part 26A plan only if two statutory conditions have been satisfied.[801] Second, sanctioning the plan is still at the court's discretion, even if both conditions have been fulfilled.[802] Below, this work will examine the jurisdictional requirement and the court's discretion in the respective order.

(1) Jurisdictional Requirement

If the requisite majority is not reached in at least one of the plan classes, section 901G of the Companies Act 2006 sets out two additional conditions that must be met before the court can use its discretion to sanction the Part 26A plan.

(a) Condition A

One of the conditions (Condition A) states that members of the dissenting class shall not be treated worse than they would be in case of 'the relevant alternative' that, according to the court, would 'most likely occur' if the plan were not sanctioned.[803] This condition, also referred to as the *no worse off* test, is considered a vertical limb of the fairness assessment under Part 26A.[804] That said, the test is similar in nature to the BIT under Chapter 11[805] rather than APR, which constitutes the vertical pillar of the fairness assessment with respect to dissenting classes under Chapter 11. That is to say, the statutory *no worse off* test does not take into account how the plan affects classes with lower priority but rather focuses on how the dissenting class would be treated in the relevant alternative.

800 *Adler* (n 622) [117], [128].
801 Companies Act 2006, s 901G ((2) - (5)).
802 *Adler* (n 622) [153].
803 Companies Act 2006, s 901G ((3)-(4)).
804 *Adler* (n 622) [12], [152].
805 For a more detailed discussion of the BIT, see sub-s E.II.1.b)aa).

Although Condition A and the BIT share some textual and conceptual similarities, there are two significant differences between them. First, unlike the latter, the *no worse off* test under section 901G applies only in a cramdown plan scenario and only with respect to creditors in dissenting classes[806] and, therefore, not to individual dissenting creditors in assenting classes.[807] Second, for the purpose of the statutory *no worse-off test,* the benchmark for comparison is not necessarily the liquidation or winding-up of the company (which is a low bar[808]), but rather the relevant alternative that would most likely occur without the plan. Identifying this relevant alternative and the position of the dissenting class within that alternative, therefore, is one of the central, though not always straightforward, issues under Part 26A.[809] That said, the issue is not new to English courts. Determining the relevant alternative is a familiar topic to them from the Scheme (regarding matters related to class composition or the rationality test) and CVA (regarding the unfair prejudice challenge) cases.[810]

(b) Condition B

According to the other condition (Condition B), at least one class of plan claimants who would make a recovery or have 'a genuine economic interest in the company' in the relevant alternative shall accept the plan.[811] Condition B is akin to the Chapter 11 requirement stipulating that at least one impaired class must vote for the plan.[812] However, the former does not necessitate any impairment and instead focuses on the position in the relevant alternative.[813] Nevertheless, the rationale behind these two requirements is similar, which is the indication of some actual creditor support and, thus, the reasonableness of the plan.[814]

806 Mokal, 'The Two Conditions' (n 662) 731.
807 For the avoidance of doubt, it is not argued that dissenting creditors in assenting classes can be treated worse than they would be in the relevant alternative. What is argued is that this issue is not assessed under s 901G.
808 Payne, 'The Role of the Court' (n 2) 139; Seymour and Schwarcz (n 702) 29.
809 Paterson, 'Judicial Discretion' (n 773) pt II.
810 Mokal, 'The Two Conditions' (n 662) 730. For a brief summary of the case law on the matter, see Olivares-Caminal and others (n 38) paras 3.493-95.
811 Companies Act 2006, s 901G (5).
812 See sub-s E.II.1.a).
813 Mokal, 'The Two Conditions' (n 662) 731.
814 ibid; Olivares-Caminal and others (n 38) para 3.491.

(2) Judicial Discretion

As already noted earlier in this work, Part 26A introduced a significant feature previously not found in English restructuring law: a stand-alone cross-class cramdown procedure. However, the legislation did not specify any priority rule for a cramdown scenario (such as the APR under Chapter 11), deliberately leaving the matter to be determined by courts.[815] Hence, the new restructuring tool also introduced uncertainty about how courts should exercise their discretion, particularly when sanctioning a Part 26A plan involving a cross-class cramdown.

(a) Early-Stage Academic Discussion

To that end, several initial suggestions have been made in the literature. Riz Mokal suggested that courts shall look at, as a default rule, whether the 'restructuring surplus' is distributed between different classes under the plan in a ratio that would apply to the distribution between the respective classes in the relevant alternative and deviating proportions under the plan should be justified.[816] In a paper addressing the issue, Sarah Paterson analysed several proposed frameworks, such as transplanting Part 26 or Chapter 11 frameworks and subsequently argued against both due to, *inter alia*, 'design differences'.[817] She suggested that courts should adopt a flexible approach but proposed several guidelines with a focus on whether other classes receive 'too much unfair value'.[818] In her opinion, several patterns could indicate receiving too much unfair value (such as leaving some liabilities unimpaired, retention of equity by shareholders, and so forth) and should be given special regard.[819]

---

815 van Zwieten, 'Mid-Crisis Restructuring Law Reform' (n 788) 307.

816 Mokal, 'The Court's Discretion' (n 708) 15. For Riz Mokal's definition of the *restructuring surplus,* see n 662 and accompanying text. For a discussion of the potential shortcomings of or difficulties associated with the Riz Mokal's proposal, see Paterson, 'Judicial Discretion' (n 773) s IV.C.

817 Paterson, 'Judicial Discretion' (n 773) pt IV.

818 ibid pt V. For a critical analysis, see Riz Mokal, 'Cram Dos, Don'ts, and Darn Its: The 'Too Much Unfair Value' Approach to the UK Cramdown' [2025 April] South Square Digest 36, 37-41.

819 Paterson, 'Judicial Discretion' (n 773) pt V.

(b) *Adler*

In *Adler*, the EWCA brought clarity to various matters concerning the court's discretion to sanction a cramdown Part 26A plan.[820] The facts of the case are briefly summarised as follows.[821] The restructuring plan in question provided for the winding down of the entire group by gradually realising its assets and sequentially (and fully) repaying holders of different series of notes, mainly in accordance with the original maturity dates of the respective notes. The plan received approval from the requisite majority of noteholders in all classes, except for one class of noteholders who would be repaid last after the full repayment of the holders of the notes with earlier maturity dates. The EWHC sanctioned the plan based on the expert evidence that the proceeds from the sale of the group's assets would suffice to fully pay all noteholders, including those in the dissenting class. The EWHC judgment was subsequently appealed by several noteholders in the dissenting class, and Lord Snowden handed down the judgment of the EWCA.

As noted, the EWCA examined significant matters regarding the court's discretion to sanction a cramdown Part 26A plan, which will be summarised below.

(aa) Fairness Framework with Respect to Dissenting Classes of Creditors

To begin with, the EWCA held that the mere fact that the statutory jurisdiction requirement (Conditions A and B) has been fulfilled does not presume the fairness of the plan.[822] The *Adler* court also acknowledged that the same fairness concepts developed under case law for Part 26 cases, specifically the rationality test, cannot apply to dissenting classes under Part 26A Plans.[823] In the *Adler* court's opinion, due to the dissimilarity of interests between dissenting and assenting classes, the fairness of the plan towards dissenting classes cannot be judged on the basis that other

820 *Adler* (n 622).
821 The facts stated herein are taken from the judgment of Lord Snowden (ibid). For a broader summary of the facts and procedural background of the case, see ibid [13]-[104].
822 ibid [153]-[154].
823 ibid [129].

classes have voted for the plan.[824] As mentioned earlier in this work, the EWCA stated that courts should nevertheless continue to apply the Part 26 fairness concepts with respect to holdout creditors within assenting classes of cramdown Part 26A plans.[825]

In reference to the fairness assessment with respect to a dissenting class of creditors under Part 26A plans, the *Adler* court stressed the importance of the *vertical comparison* and *horizontal comparison* concepts developed in the CVA jurisprudence.[826] According to Lord Snowden, courts should focus on the horizontal comparison while exercising their discretion to sanction cramdown Part 26A plans since the vertical comparison also constitutes a part of the jurisdictional requirement (Condition A).[827] Lord Snowden agreed with the view that, in exercising its discretion to sanction a cross-class cramdown Part 26A plan, the court should determine 'whether the plan provides for differences in treatment of the different classes of creditors *inter se* and, if so, whether those differences can be justified', with the relevant alternative serving as 'an obvious reference point for this exercise'.[828]

In the court's opinion, if the relevant alternative is the insolvency of the debtor and the creditors in all the plan classes would rank equally as unsecured creditors in that alternative (which was the case in *Adler*), the distribution under the plan should generally follow the *pari passu* principle[829] to reflect the relevant alternative.[830] According to Lord Snowden, a deviation from that principle is possible, provided that there is a proper justification behind it.[831] Nonetheless, the *Adler* court deliberately refrained from formulating a full list of criteria in that regard but gave a few examples, such as favourable treatment of a class of creditors that provide additional value or are necessary for the continuation of the business.[832] Lord Snowden also endorsed the view that courts should look at whether a fairer plan would be available as part of the horizontal comparison.[833]

824 ibid [133]-[134].
825 ibid [117], [128].
826 ibid [148]-[149].
827 ibid [152]-[156].
828 ibid [159].
829 For a more detailed discussion of the *pari passu* principle, see sub-s E.I.1.
830 *Adler* (n 622) [165].
831 ibid [166].
832 ibid [167]-[172].
833 ibid [173]-[182].

Applying this reasoning to the case at hand, Lord Snowden, with whom the other judges fully agreed, reversed the decision of the EWHC on the grounds that the plan put a greater risk to the dissenting class and, thus, deviated from the *pari passu* rule without a proper justification.[834]

(bb) Retention of Equity by Old Shareholders

Another important matter analysed by the EWCA in *Adler* is the retention of equity interests of old shareholders in the restructured company in cases where creditors are not fully paid. Two observations from Lord Snowden's analysis of the matter merit brief mention.[835] First, Lord Snowden referred to his position in *Virgin Active*[836] endorsing the *gifting* doctrine.[837] In that case, Snowden J (as he then was) concluded that it was for in the money creditors to share the value that might be generated under the plan with the existing shareholders and the objections of out of the money creditors in that regard should be given no consideration.[838] Second, according to Lord Snowden, courts are not given 'a power to extinguish claims or confiscate shares for no consideration' under Part 26A since such power is not compatible with the definition of a *compromise or arrangement*.[839]

---

834 ibid [197], [280].

835 For a full analysis of the matter, see ibid [239]-[278].

836 *Virgin Active Holdings* Ltd [2021] EWHC 1246 (Ch).

837 *Adler* (n 622) [252].

838 *Virgin Active* (n 836) [266]. For a more cautious approach to gifting against the objection of an in the money creditor, see *Great Annual Savings Company Ltd* [2023] EWHC 1141 (Ch), [123]ff.

839 *Adler* (n 622) [271]-[275]. For a more detailed discussion of the definition of a *compromise or arrangement*, see cited sources in n 773. This argument (that out of the money creditors or members should receive something under the plan) also constituted one of the guidelines (based on the Scheme jurisprudence) of the flexible framework initially suggested by Sarah Paterson, see Paterson, 'Judicial Discretion' (n 773) s V.A. That said, shareholders and out of the money creditors may still receive nothing under Part 26 if the Scheme is combined with pre-packaged administration. See *Adler* (n 622) [260]-[262]. For a more detailed discussion, see Payne, 'Debt Restructuring in English Law' (n 756) s 3.5; Olivares-Caminal and others (n 38) pt I, ch 3, s XII; Paterson, 'The Conceptual Foundation' (n 73) s 2.B.

(c) Developments in the Literature and Case Law Following *Adler*

The emerging principles surrounding the Part 26A cross-class cramdown in the initial cases, particularly *Adler,* have been closely scrutinised in the literature. Sarah Paterson raises concerns about the limited, if any, consideration given to out of the money classes and the acceptance of the gifting doctrine in the initial cases.[840] She consequently proposes a conceptual framework in which the aim of cross-class cramdown is 'not only to motivate cooperative bargaining but also to enforce a fair bargain that the dissenting creditors could reasonably approve' (*the bargaining approach*).[841]

Riz Mokal, Stephan Madaus, Irit Mevorach, and Ignacio Tirado generally endorse most of the conclusions reached in the initial cases.[842] However, they question the approach to determining 'whether the class has a real economic interest in the debtor'[843] and highlight the need to exercise caution regarding gifting.[844] This analysis of the case law was conducted against the backdrop of a conceptual framework for cross-class cramdown they advocate (*fair allocation of the restructuring surplus*), which envisages the relative priority rule[845] as a default rule and requires any departure therefrom to be 'normatively defensible'.[846]

It should be noted that some of these issues, particularly the treatment of out of the money classes, were subsequently addressed by the EWCA in two recent cases: *Thames Water*[847] and *Petrofac*.[848] That is to say, the EWCA rejected the argument, based upon earlier case law, that out of the money classes need not be offered under the plan anything more than *de minimis*, the amount sufficient only to fulfil the jurisdictional requirement regarding the definition of a *compromise* or *arrangement*.[849] Instead, the EWCA held that:

840 Paterson, 'The Conceptual Foundation' (n 73) 12-14.
841 ibid 17ff. For a critical analysis of Sarah Paterson's early formulation of this framework, see Mokal, 'The 'Too Much Unfair Value' Approach' (n 818) 42-47.
842 Riz Mokal and others, 'The Cramdown: A Conceptual Framework' in Jennifer Payne and Kristin van Zwieten (eds), *Corporate Restructuring Law in Flux* (Hart Publishing 2025) 120-31.
843 ibid 122.
844 ibid 129-31.
845 For a discussion of the relative priority rule, see sub-ss E.II.3.b), E.II.3.c).
846 Mokal and others (n 842) 116-118.
847 *Thames Water* (n 662).
848 *Petrofac* (n 622).
849 *Thames Water* (n 662) [120]-[156]; *Petrofac* (n 622) [111]-[117].

> ... the proper use of the cross-class cram down power is to enable a plan to be sanctioned against the opposition of those unreasonably holding out for a better deal, where there has been a genuine attempt to formulate and negotiate a reasonable compromise between all stakeholders.[850]

d) Summary

In subsection E.II.2, this work examined three English law restructuring frameworks that can bind holdouts: the CVA, the Scheme, and the Part 26A plan. Each of the frameworks mentioned differs in certain aspects, such as entry requirements and voting procedure.

The CVA is particularly distinctive since creditors vote in a single class and it does not require the court's sanctioning to bind holdouts. A dissenting unsecured creditor, however, can challenge a CVA on the *unfair prejudice* grounds. Courts conduct vertical (comparison with the possible position of the challenging creditor in the debtor's insolvent liquidation scenario) and horizontal (comparison with the position of other creditors under the CVA) comparisons in assessing fairness.

Under the Scheme and the Part 26A plan frameworks, creditors can be placed in different classes and the court's sanctioning is required by law. Unlike Part 26A plans, a stand-alone cross-class cramdown is not possible in Scheme cases. Hence, here, the fairness assessment concerns only dissenting individual creditors in assenting classes. In assessing fairness under the Scheme, courts mainly examine whether the assenting majority genuinely represents the class and whether a reasonable creditor would accept such a Scheme.

The same principles apply to assessing fairness in relation to dissenting creditors within assenting classes in Part 26A plan cases. Nonetheless, unlike Schemes, under the Part 26A plan framework, a cross-class cramdown is possible, subject to two statutory conditions and the court's discretion to sanction.

One of the statutory conditions (Condition A) ensures that members of the dissenting class are not worse off under the plan than they would be in the relevant alternative. The other condition (Condition B) requires that at least one class of the plan claimants who would be in the money in the relevant alternative shall accept the plan.

850 *Petrofac* (n 622) [191].

English courts are in the process of developing principles for the exercise of their discretion in sanctioning cramdown Part 26A plans on a case-by-case basis. As Condition A already encompasses the vertical comparison, in exercising their discretion to sanction, courts primarily focus on the horizontal comparison in assessing the fairness of the Part 26A plan with respect to the dissenting classes. That is to say, courts examine whether different classes are treated differently under the plan and, if so, whether such differential treatment is justified in light of the respective positions of those classes in the relevant alternative. If, for example, the relevant alternative is insolvent liquidation of the debtor, the distribution under the plan among the unsecured creditors of the same rank should comply with the *pari passu* principle and any deviation should be based on justifiable grounds. Notably, recent cases place greater emphasis than earlier ones on the position of out of the money classes in considering the fair allocation of the benefits of the restructuring.

3. The PRD

The PRD, adopted in 2019,[851] obliges Member States to adapt their national legislation accordingly by 17 July 2021, with the possibility of a one-year extension.[852] The aim of the PRD is, *inter alia*, to ensure that effective preventive restructuring mechanisms are in place in Member States in order to address the need for the rescue of viable businesses facing financial difficulties.[853] As to the fairness of these mechanisms and protection of dissenting creditors, the PRD offers various options for Member States. Below, this work will discuss the options related to dissenting individual creditors and dissenting classes of creditors, followed by a summary of academic opinions on the new fairness concept under the PRD.

851 PRD (n 15). For a discussion of the origins of the PRD, see Christoph G. Paulus, 'European and Europe's Efforts for Attractivity as a Restructuring Hub' (2021) 56 Tex Intl L J 95, 98-99.

852 PRD (n 15) art 34.

853 ibid rec 1.

a) Dissenting Individual Creditors

The PRD provides for the 'best-interest-of-creditors test' ("EU BIT") to protect dissenting individual creditors in assenting classes, whether in a consensual or cramdown plan scenario.[854] The EU BIT is satisfied when a dissenting creditor is not worse off under the proposed plan than this creditor would be in liquidation (through piecemeal or going concern sale) or in 'the next-best-alternative scenario' if the proposed plan were not sanctioned.[855] It is up to Member States to choose one of those baselines as a comparator.[856] What can be considered as the *next-best-alternative scenario* is unclear and the definition has been questioned in the literature.[857] It, however, is evident from the text of the PRD that the comparator for the purposes of the EU BIT should not necessarily be the liquidation of the debtor in formal proceedings, whether through piecemeal or going concern sale. It can also be an alternative plan, going-concern sale outside formal proceedings, or the continuation of ordinary business.[858]

b) Dissenting Classes of Creditors

In case a plan is not consensual, i.e. not approved by all classes, the PRD provides two options for Member States for assessing fairness with respect to dissenting classes. The default option ensures that dissenting classes receive at least the same treatment as other classes of the same rank (the

854 ibid arts 10 (2) (d), 11 (1) (a).

855 ibid art 2 (6).

856 ibid rec 52. However, as also pointed out by Jonathan Seymour and Steven Schwartz (see Seymour and Schwarcz (n 702) 29), it is not completely clear whether the choice may be made only between the liquidation scenario (which includes both piecemeal and going-concern-sale liquidation) and the next best alternative, or also within the former (between piecemeal liquidation and going-concern-sale liquidation).

857 See, eg, Riz Mokal and Ignacio Tirado 'Has Newton Had His Day? Relativity and Realism in European Restructuring' (2019) 4 JIBFL 233, 234; Giulia Ballerini, 'The Priorities Dilemma in the EU Preventive Restructuring Directive: Absolute or Relative Priority Rule?' (2021) 30 Intl Ins Rev 7, 10.

858 Madaus, 'Relative Priority Rule' (n 662) pt 1. For a discussion of different scenarios, see also Dominik Skauradszun, 'Restructuring Companies During and After the Covid-19 Pandemic: A Law & Economics Approach' (2021) 9 NIBLeJ 1 1 <https://www.ntu.ac.uk/media/documents/academic-schools/law/2021-9-NIBLeJ-1.pdf> accessed 21 October 2025, 18ff.

horizontal factor of the fairness assessment) and more favourable treatment than any class of more junior rank (the vertical factor of the fairness assessment).[859] In the literature, this priority model is often referred to as the relative priority rule ("RPR").[860] Member States can also opt for the APR, as discussed in the US context earlier, which requires that dissenting classes should be fully paid before any class of more junior rank receives anything under the plan.[861] Deviating from the APR is allowed under the PRD, provided that it is essential for achieving the objectives of the proposed plan and that affected parties are not unfairly prejudiced under the plan.[862]

As can be seen from the respective definitions, the key distinction between these two priority rules is that the RPR, unlike the APR, does not mandate full payment to senior claimants before more junior claimants can make some recovery under the plan. Providing better treatment of the former is sufficient in this context.

c) Academic Reception

The RPR has sparked controversy among scholars. Below, this work will briefly summarise the arguments for and against it.

aa) Arguments in Favour of the RPR

Stephan Madaus describes the RPR as a fairness test based on anti-discrimination.[863] In his opinion, the RPR rules out discrimination among pre-restructuring ranks of creditors by setting out a framework where dissenting classes are not treated worse than other classes of the same rank and are treated better than more junior classes, on the one hand.[864] On the other hand, says Stephan Madaus, the RPR allows some flexibility in distributing

---

859 PRD (n 15) art 11 (1) (c).

860 See generally Madaus, 'Relative Priority Rule' (n 662). It is essential to note the RPR is a different concept from the relative priority model suggested by Douglas Baird (see text to n 715). For a summary of the various approaches in the US scholarship associated with the term *relative priority*, see Krohn (n 662) 88-89 (en 4 therein and accompanying text).

861 PRD (n 15) art 11 (2).

862 ibid art 11 (2), sub-para 2.

863 Madaus, 'Relative Priority Rule' (n 662) pt 3.

864 ibid.

the reorganisation surplus[865] among classes within that framework, taking into consideration special circumstances.[866] Furthermore, he recommends assessing the RPR not separately but rather in conjunction with the EU BIT.[867]

According to Bob Wessels, the RPR will incentivise shareholders to initiate restructuring of viable businesses at an earlier stage, as it, unlike the APR, does not require their equity to be wiped out first.[868] He also underscores that in most Member States, there are a considerable number of creditor classes (such as employees, tax authorities, and tort victims) having a preferential status and, therefore, it would be challenging to fully settle the claims of these preferential creditors as required under the APR.[869] This, in turn, may lead to the failure of otherwise value-generating plans, according to Bob Wessels.[870]

Riz Mokal and Ignacio Tirado highlight the shortcomings of the APR, which, according to them, will probably be remedied by the RPR.[871] The APR, they say, encourages dissenting behaviour.[872] Besides, they argue that it is challenging to allocate value to existing shareholders under the APR, which can be a problematic issue, particularly in SME cases where shareholders' further participation may be necessary for the successful continuation of the business.[873] Riz Mokal refers to the RPR as a 'more realistic alternative' (to the APR), as it avoids encouraging holdout behaviour and allows old shareholders to retain equity stakes in SME cases.[874]

As far as SMEs are concerned, Axel Krohn underscores the difference in the focus of the PRD and that of Chapter 11.[875] That is to say, he argues that the PRD places considerable emphasis on SMEs,[876] which constitute

865 For the definition of the *reorganisation (restructuring) surplus*, see n 662 and accompanying text.
866 Madaus, 'Relative Priority Rule' (n 662) pt 3.
867 ibid pt 4. See also Krohn (n 662) 84-87.
868 Bob Wessels, 'The Full Version of My Reply to Professor De Weijs et al' (22 March 2019) Bob Wessels Blog (2019-03-doc10) <https://bobwessels.nl/blog/2019-03-doc10-the-full-version-of-my-reply-to-professor-de-weijs-et-al/> accessed 21 October 2025.
869 ibid.
870 ibid.
871 Mokal and Tirado (n 857) 235.
872 ibid.
873 ibid.
874 Mokal, 'Fairness' (n 571) s 9.
875 Krohn (n 662) 80.
876 ibid.

ninety-nine per cent of the business in the EU.[877] By contrast, says Axel Krohn, Chapter 11 was primarily designed for larger companies.[878] Hence, in his view, the APR, which ultimately requires existing equity to be wiped out first, was not entirely suitable for the intended focus of the European legislature.[879] He reinforces the respective argument by noting that the newly introduced Subchapter V of Chapter 11,[880] designed for restructuring small companies, does not necessitate adherence to the APR.[881]

bb) Arguments Against the RPR

Arguments against the RPR are also multi-fold. To begin with, critics argue that an unnecessary risk of changing the basis of private law is taken by opting for the RPR, which does not fully honour priority orders bargained for outside bankruptcy under private law (such as contract law and company law) rules.[882] One commentator notes that, for example, the very purpose of subordination agreements, which creditors bargained for (by also agreeing to different interest rates), would be undermined if subordinated creditors made some recovery from the insolvent debtor's estate before fully compensating senior creditors.[883] According to opponents, the RPR, which introduces the risk of a non-consensual deviation from a bargained priority order, will have practical implications, such as making debt financing less attractive and leading to higher interest rates.[884]

Additionally, critics argue that the RPR will encourage shareholders to increase leverage and, as a result, to undertake highly risky projects without

877 PRD (n 15) recs 17, 59.
878 Krohn (n 662) 80.
879 ibid.
880 BC (n 37) ss 1181-95.
881 Krohn (n 662) 80.
882 Roelf Jakob de Weijs, Aart Lambertus Jonkers, and Maryam Malakotipour, 'The Imminent Distortion of European Insolvency Law: How the European Union Erodes the Basic Fabric of Private Law by Allowing "Relative Priority" (RPR)' (11 March 2019) Amsterdam Law School Research Paper No 2019-10, Centre for the Study of European Contract Law Working Paper No 2019-05 <https://ssrn.com/abstract=3350375> accessed 21 October 2025, s 6.1; Ballerini (n 857) 12-13.
883 Ballerini (n 857) 12.
884 ibid 13; Seymour and Schwarcz (n 702) 27.

the fear of losing their entire equity if those projects fail.[885] It has been noted that this trend may undermine the stability of the entire economy.[886]

Furthermore, opponents of the RPR point out that it will lead to increased uncertainty and arbitrary outcomes, potentially encouraging opportunistic behaviours.[887] It has been argued that apart from the valuation uncertainty, which is also present in the APR, the RPR introduces additional uncertainty regarding *who* is entitled to the value and *to what extent*, as well as what is considered *fair*.[888] Critics stress that the APR encourages shareholders and senior creditors, albeit due to different reasons,[889] to avoid a cramdown scenario and come up with a consensual plan, thereby providing a clear framework for negotiations.[890] It has been noted that the RPR, by contrast, incentivises claimants, again for different reasons, to opt for a cramdown scenario and engage in fairness discussions in courts.[891]

It has also been pointed out that SMEs, whom the RPR claims to primarily protect, will suffer the most from it as creditors.[892] By referring to the original purpose of the APR, which was to protect junior creditors against the collusion of shareholders and senior creditors during the era of equity receiverships in the US, opponents argue that the RPR deprives intermediate creditors, who will be SMEs in most cases, of that protection.[893]

Finally, critics note that, despite all the concerns associated with it, the RPR does not address the problematic aspects of the APR and is mistakenly compared to the relative priority model advocated by US scholar Douglas

885 de Weijs, Jonkers, and Malakotipour (n 882) s 6.2, Ballerini (n 857) 12. See also Seymour and Schwarcz (n 702) 23-24.

886 de Weijs, Jonkers, and Malakotipour (n 882) s 6.2.

887 ibid s 6.3. See also Seymour and Schwarcz (n 702) 25-26.

888 de Weijs, Jonkers, and Malakotipour (n 882) s 6.3.

889 The rationale for shareholders is explained by the fact that under a cramdown plan, where the APR applies, shareholders would get nothing unless all creditors are fully paid. See ibid. Senior creditors do not bear that risk. On the contrary, they would be paid first under the APR. Their interest in avoiding a cramdown scenario is explained by a costly and inherently uncertain valuation that would be the case in that scenario under the realm of the APR. See Seymour and Schwarcz (n 702) 11-14. See also Ballerini (n 857) 17.

890 Seymour and Schwarcz (n 702) 14-16 (The authors refer to a valuation hearing under APR as a *penalty default rule* of Chapter 11 which encourages parties to avoid a cramdown scenario and to agree on a consensual plan). See also de Weijs, Jonkers, and Malakotipour (n 882) s 6.3; Ballerini (n 857) 17.

891 de Weijs, Jonkers, and Malakotipour (n 882) s 6.3.

892 ibid s 6.4.

893 ibid. See also Seymour and Schwarcz (n 702) 20-21.

Baird[894] as an alternative to the APR.[895] Unlike the RPR, say opponents, Douglas Baird's relative priority model fully respects the priority order among different ranks of creditors and aims to avoid the debtor's valuation during the confirmation stage.[896]

Nonetheless, opponents of the RPR acknowledge the issues linked to the APR, such as the challenges in retaining equity in SME cases or ensuring that trade creditors are fully paid.[897] That said, they suggest addressing these issues by designing carefully crafted exceptions to the APR instead of developing a new priority rule of a relative nature.[898]

4. Comparative Summary

In section E.II, this work examined restructuring frameworks and substantive fairness standards thereunder in the US and England as well as under the PRD. Both jurisdictions provide an extensive framework to ensure substantive fairness in restructuring proceedings. So does the PRD. However, there are several fundamental differences that may lead to different outcomes, even in cases with similar or identical facts.[899] To begin with, US law has a single hybrid restructuring mechanism (Chapter 11) for all corporations, whether insolvent or not yet insolvent. By contrast, English law offers numerous restructuring tools with different entry, voting, and confirmation requirements as well as fairness standards. For example, in a CVA process, creditors vote as a single class and can be treated in materially different ways, which is not the case in some other English restructuring tools and Chapter 11.

894 See text to n 715.

895 de Weijs, Jonkers, and Malakotipour (n 882) pt 5; Ballerini (n 857) 16.

896 ibid. Stephan Madaus points out that a valuation is inherent to all restructuring proceedings irrespective of a priority rule, at least for the purpose of the satisfaction of the BIT (See Madaus, 'Relative Priority Rule' (n 662), pt 4). However, Jonathan Seymour and Steven Schwartz argue that valuations for the purpose of the BIT are routine and require less extensive appraisal than those for the purposes of the cramdown. See Seymour and Schwarcz (n 702) 8 (fn 45 therein and accompanying text).

897 See, eg, de Weijs, Jonkers, and Malakotipour (n 882) pt 7; Ballerini (n 857) 18ff.

898 ibid.

899 See Paterson, 'A Qualified Defence of the Rule in Gibbs' (n 74) pt VI, where Sarah Paterson highlights certain differences between Chapter 11 and Part 26A, and argues that the plans sanctioned in some recent Part 26A cases would not have been confirmed under Chapter 11.

In addition, although both jurisdictions and the PRD agree that individual dissenting creditors cannot be worse off as a result of the restructuring, the baseline for comparison is not exactly the same. In the US, there is only one comparator: a liquidation scenario, which is a low bar. Under English law or the PRD, the bar is higher, and the respective baseline is not confined to the formal liquidation of the debtor.

More noticeable and fundamental differences are related to dissenting classes. That is to say, in the US, the APR strictly applies, subject to one exception. The rule prevents holders of more junior claims and interests from receiving anything unless dissenting classes of more senior claimants are fully paid. However, English law does not have a similar rule. In fact, existing shareholders' shares cannot be cancelled and creditors' claims cannot be extinguished without giving them something in return under Part 26 or Part 26A procedures. Recent EWCA cases have placed even greater emphasis on the fair treatment of out of money creditors in Part 26A plans. The PRD, in turn, introduces a new priority rule according to which better treatment of more senior claimants is sufficient. Besides, retention of equity by shareholders whose contribution to the continuation of the business does not constitute money's worth is not possible under Chapter 11 while being not impossible under English law or the PRD. The gifting doctrine, which allows senior classes to gift some part of their recovery under the plan to junior classes over intermediary classes, was rejected by some circuit courts in the US. In England, however, the doctrine received some endorsement in early Part 26A cases, although the initial case law was controversial in this regard. Furthermore, it remains to be seen whether this trend of endorsement will continue in light of recent EWCA decisions, which place greater weight than earlier cases on the position of out of the money creditors.

Finally, the statutory text grants English courts broader discretion than their US counterparts when sanctioning cross-class cramdown plans. That is to say, English courts still have discretion to sanction such plans under Part 26A, even if all statutory requirements have been met. It is also worth noting that English courts are still in the process of developing the principles guiding the exercise of this discretion on a case-by-case basis.

III. Summary

Part E was dedicated to the role of substantive fairness in restructuring in general, without considering cross-border elements. First, this work elaborated on the difference between insolvency and restructuring proceedings in terms of ensuring the fairness of outcome (substantive fairness) in these proceedings (E.I). It concluded that ensuring substantive fairness in restructuring proceedings is a more critical and multifaceted issue and should take into account the peculiarities of the case at hand.

This work then examined how the concept is implemented, using the examples of restructuring frameworks under US law, English law, and the PRD (E.II). It was observed that in some issues (e.g. priority rules and rewarding post-recognition contributions), these frameworks provide for different rules, which may lead to varying outcomes in cases with similar (if not identical) facts.

F. Ensuring Substantive Fairness in the Recognition of Restructuring Plans under the MLCBI

Part F will be dedicated to developing a framework to ensure substantive fairness in recognising restructuring plans under the MLCBI (substantive fairness framework under the MLCBI), which constitutes the main focus of this research. Section F.I will provide a normative justification and seek a legal basis for a substantive fairness review when considering the recognition of restructuring plans under the MLCBI. Section F.II will be dedicated to the essential aspects of the substantive fairness framework under the MLCBI. Section F.III will test the IBA plan against the framework suggested in this work. Section F.IV will outline several advantages of this framework. Section F.V will offer a summary of the points discussed in this Part.

I. Normative and Legal Foundations

This section will be dedicated to the justification of the need for a substantive fairness review in recognising restructuring plans in a system based on modifying universalism and seeking a legal basis for such a review in the text of the MLCBI. Subsection F.I.1 will be devoted to the justification, while subsection F.I.2 will examine the text of the MLCBI (as well as the MLIJ) to find a legal basis for a substantive fairness review.

1. Normative Justification

Below, this work will justify the need for a substantive fairness review in recognising foreign restructuring plans within a framework underpinned by modified universalism. It will first distinguish universalism from modified universalism in this context. Then, the matter will be examined under modified universalism, followed by an analysis of the correlation between the public policy exception and a substantive fairness review.

a) A Substantive Fairness Review under Universalism

This work will first examine whether a substantive fairness review is possible and necessary in achieving the cross-border effects of restructuring plans in a system underpinned by the principle of universalism. This work argues that such a review is unique to modified universalism and conducting it under universalism is neither feasible nor theoretically necessary or preferable.

To begin with, a system based on universalism does not require any recognition proceedings, as restructuring plans are automatically recognised and enforceable in such a system.[900] Hence, it is practically impossible to conduct a fairness review in this system. Any attempt to assess the fairness of foreign proceedings before granting recognition to foreign plans no longer upholds the underlying principle of *universalism* and effectively downgrades it to *modified universalism.*

Besides being a practical impossibility, a substantive fairness review is neither necessary nor preferable in this system from a normative perspective. In that regard, this work will analyse two scenarios of how universalism can be achieved:[901]

aa) A Single International Court and a Single International Law

In a first scenario, there is a single international court system and a single international law for cross-border restructuring cases. This means that the debtor's restructuring is administered by a transnational court applying a transnational law. Put another way, both the forum and the applicable law in question are not connected to any specific jurisdiction, and the proceedings are of a transnational nature. Hence, the restructuring plan cannot be categorised as a *domestic* or *foreign* plan in the eyes of any jurisdiction. The court and applicable law are neutral and all jurisdictions involved in the system have previously agreed to be bound by the outcome resulting from the application of that particular (transnational) law by that particular (transnational) court.[902] Accordingly, there is no need for two separate fairness reviews, one at the stage of plan confirmation and another

---

900 See sub-s B.II.3.b).

901 ibid.

902 Any system based on universalism requires consensus from all participants. See sub-s B.II.3.c).

at the stage of granting the cross-border effects. For the same reasons, public policy considerations do not arise in such a system

bb) A Uniform Set of Choice-of-Forum and Choice-of-Law Rules

A second scenario involves a system based on a uniform set of choice-of-forum and choice-of-law rules. To begin with, this does not represent true and full universalism, as is the case in the first scenario. Jay Westbrook notes that it 'would be far short of true universalism', potentially qualifying as 'the lowest form of universalism' or 'the highest form of ... modified universalism'.[903]

In this scenario, a forum and a law belonging to a jurisdiction determined in accordance with such uniform rules govern the debtor's restructuring and all other jurisdictions automatically and fully defer to and, thus, accept the outcome achieved in that jurisdiction. Therefore, no ancillary recognition proceedings are required. Setting aside the possibility of secondary (territorial) proceedings and exceptions concerning applicable law, the existing regional framework under the EIR offers a notable illustration of how this scenario might operate in practice:[904] once a proper forum (a Member State where the debtor has its COMI) and a proper law (the *lex fori concursus*) are identified, the said court and law function as a single court and a law, respectively, governing the debtor's restructuring throughout the EU.

The main difference from the first scenario mentioned above is that the respective court and law belong to a certain state within the system (under the EIR, to a Member State in the territory of which the debtor's COMI is situated). Hence, the respective court and law are not neutral to all participants of the system but rather belong to one of them. Accordingly, the restructuring plan can be viewed as *domestic* in one jurisdiction and *foreign* in all other jurisdictions that make up this system.

903 Westbrook, 'A Global Solution' (n 100) 2318.

904 For the avoidance of doubt, this work does not argue that the EIR establishes a fully universalist system. Despite its universalist ambitions, the EIR contains several exceptions in that respect, ie, those related to applicable law and the possibility of opening secondary (territorial) proceedings. See sub-s B.III.1. It is merely proposed to set these exceptions aside in order to use the EIR as an example of how the scenario discussed in the present subsection might function in practice.

Nonetheless, a substantive fairness review in a cross-border context is neither necessary nor preferable also in this scenario. Another principle of cross-border insolvency law, namely, the principle of mutual trust, plays a significant role in this respect.[905] By agreeing to be bound by uniform choice-of-forum and choice-of-law rules on the cross-border effects of restructuring proceedings with certain other states within a group, states within that group are generally presumed also to agree to mutually trust one another's legal system. That trust extends, *inter alia*, to substantive laws and fairness frameworks thereunder.[906]

A substantive fairness review in a cross-border context is unnecessary because states are presumed to generally assess and approve the legal systems of all other states within the group before forming a group with them. Unlike the framework provided for by the MLCBI, access to recognition is confined to mutually trusted (thus, generally pre-assessed and pre-approved) jurisdictions within a closed group. Nor is such a review preferable because its application in each case (when successfully invoked) can gradually undermine mutual trust and eventually destroy the entire system built on such trust.

Unlike the first scenario, public policy issues may arise in such a scenario due to the involvement of private international law rules. However, this is not necessary because a system based on full mutual trust does not require the public policy exception for substantially the same reasons mentioned above. Accordingly, it depends on the level of trust. The EIR, for example, includes the public policy exception. As Reinhard Bork puts it, a framework containing the public policy exception is based on *sceptical* mutual trust.[907] For substantially the same reasons that will be articulated later,[908] it is argued that even the presence of the public policy exception does not necessitate or justify a substantive fairness review with respect to foreign restructuring plans in this scenario.

---

905 See sub-s B.II.5.
906 See text to n 123.
907 See text to n 126.
908 See sub-s F.I.1.c).

b) A Substantive Fairness Review under Modified Universalism

aa) Difference from Universalism

Above, this work concluded that conducting a substantive fairness review of a foreign restructuring plan is neither practicable nor necessary or desirable in a universalism-based system. However, the situation is quite different under the principle of modified universalism. To begin with, a system underpinned by modified universalism does not benefit from a single transnational court and a single transnational law governing the debtor's restructuring globally as in the first scenario discussed above. As to the second scenario of achieving universalism, i.e. a uniform set of choice-of-forum and choice-of-law rules, a system based on modified universalism does not benefit from mutual trust, which is a basic pillar of the respective scenario.

Consider the MLCBI as an example. It provides the right of access to recognition in the enacting state to proceedings from all jurisdictions without the reciprocity requirement. Both Chapter 15 and the CBIR have adhered to this position without modification. Hence, it is difficult to speak about any level of trust here since jurisdictions (to which access is granted) have not been pre-assessed and pre-approved. Besides, any trust, if present, is not mutual since the MLCBI framework grants one-sided access and does not require reciprocity.

Now, envision a framework under which a group of states agree on uniform choice-of-forum and choice-of-law rules on cross-border restructuring cases. However, this framework does not provide for automatic recognition within the group (unlike the EIR). It rather requires ancillary recognition proceedings in each state. The fact that the states within the group did not agree to the automatic, group-wide recognition of the effects of restructuring proceedings governed by the court and law of one of them, even determined in accordance with the previously agreed choice-of-forum and choice-of-law rules, indicates the lack of sufficient mutual trust in one another's legal system. It is hard to argue for a sufficient level of pre-approval in this scenario.

bb) Case for a Substantive Fairness Review under Modified Universalism

(1) Practical Feasibility

To begin with, evaluating the substantive fairness of foreign plans is practically possible under the principle of modified universalism. The concept is termed *modified* universalism because it does not mandate foreign states to automatically defer to the proceedings in the debtor's home jurisdiction.[909] Instead, it sets a framework where such deference takes place after an initial review of such proceedings by foreign states. Hence, the process of evaluating foreign proceedings is not at issue. The primary concern lies in the scope and extent of such an evaluation.

(2) Necessity

This work argues that evaluating foreign restructuring proceedings should also include a review of the fairness of the distribution under the plan when recognition is contested on the respective grounds. Without elaborating on the need for such a review in the recognition of foreign insolvency proceedings, this work considers that a substantive fairness review is of particular importance and, therefore, necessary in the recognition of foreign restructuring plans for the reasons articulated below.

(a) Challenges in a Purely Domestic Context

In section E.I, this work has already identified the fundamental differences between restructuring and insolvency proceedings in terms of achieving substantive fairness in a purely domestic context. In that section, this work concluded that due to uncertainty related to several aspects of restructuring proceedings (such as the value available for distribution, restructuring measures, post-restructuring roles, and classification) and their ability to alter the substantive rights of participants, ensuring substantive fairness in these proceedings is a much more complex and important issue. That is to say, the fairness of outcome is assessed and (attempted to be) ensured in courtrooms within the provided legal framework after judges consider the individual circumstances of each case where the issue arises.

909 For a more detailed discussion of the principle of modified universalism, see sub-s B.II.4.

(aa) Examples from the US and England

In section E.II, this work examined how the concept of ensuring fairness functions in practice, using the examples of the US and England. Those examples have strengthened the argument mentioned above regarding the importance and complexity of the matter. Despite both jurisdictions being considered to have well-established statutory and case law in the respective area dating back to the 19th century, not all matters regarding the fairness of outcome in restructuring proceedings are fully settled in a domestic context. That is to say, not all courts interpret the general statutory framework and apply it to the facts of cases in the same way, particularly in the US. For example, this work observed that US courts have been following different approaches and applying different tests over the years on what constitutes *unfair discrimination* when confirming non-consensual plans.[910] In addition, there is no full consensus on whether gifting is allowed in a class cramdown scenario.[911] Furthermore, courts had split over the years on whether the new value exception survived the BC.[912] Not all legal matters end up being heard by the USSC to ensure the uniform application of the law. Some of them do, but after a while, with cases being decided on a daily basis. That is to say, it took the USSC more than twenty years after the adoption of the BC to (implicitly) acknowledge the survival of the new value exception to the APR.[913] The issue of non-consensual third-party releases is another example.[914] Matters like the ones mentioned are at the core of fairness frameworks in restructuring proceedings and can directly and materially affect the outcome of a restructuring. A split on one or another matter exists not only in courts but also in scholarship. For example, this work also noted that some scholars question the fairness of outcome under the APR, which is strictly applied in a cramdown scenario under Chapter 11.[915]

The examples of those two jurisdictions illustrate that ensuring substantive fairness is a complex matter that may require a thorough judicial assessment and is not always guaranteed in a purely domestic context, even in jurisdictions with established restructuring frameworks.

910 See nn 744, 745, 746 (and accompanying text) and text thereto.
911 See nn 728, 729 (and accompanying text) and text thereto.
912 See n 724 (and accompanying text) and text thereto.
913 See n 725 (and accompanying text) and text thereto.
914 See n 387 and accompanying text.
915 See, eg, nn 708, 715 (and accompanying text) and text thereto.

(bb) Jurisdictions with Less Developed Restructuring Frameworks

Ensuring fair outcomes in restructuring proceedings is an even more challenging task for judges in most other jurisdictions. Unlike the US and England, not all jurisdictions have well-established legal traditions and principles, particularly when it comes to debt restructuring.[916] Hence, an unbiased, transparent, and generally competent judge of a district court of Ruritania, where debt restructuring was not an option until recently, does not benefit from advanced statutory texts, countless previously decided cases (thus, well-established principles developed in these cases), and credible academic sources while hearing the first restructuring case, unlike a judge of the EWHC or the US Bankruptcy Court for the SDNY. The same holds if one compares judges of higher instances in the respective jurisdictions.

(cc) Interim Conclusion

To sum up this point, guaranteeing substantive fairness is a challenging issue even in transparent domestic proceedings and this holds even for jurisdictions with a long tradition of debt restructuring. In addition, not all jurisdictions are well-equipped to accomplish this task. In fact, most are not. This perspective alone, without considering the effect of the involvement of cross-border elements, justifies the core argument of the present work that outcomes reached in domestic proceedings should not be considered untouchable. Hence, blindly accepting, in other jurisdictions, the outcome achieved in the debtor's home jurisdiction in cases where the fairness of such outcome is contested cannot be justified.

(b) Incorporating Cross-Border Elements

Ensuring substantive fairness in restructuring proceedings becomes even more challenging when cross-border elements are added to the picture. Purely domestic restructuring plans are unlikely to require any action abroad, i.e. recognition in foreign jurisdictions. Therefore, if such action is required, it is likely due to the involvement of cross-border elements in the plan. A typical scenario in this respect involves the discharge of a

---

916 This point was also highlighted in the context of defending the Gibbs rule. See FMLC (n 332) para 4.9.

foreign law-governed debt under the plan. At least two main factors can be highlighted which justify that ensuring substantive fairness in domestic restructuring proceedings with cross-border elements is a more complex and sensitive issue and, therefore, the alarm level should be higher.

(aa) Risk of a Bias Towards Foreign Parties

A first factor is a possible bias towards foreign parties. Such a bias, if present, is not always obvious and is difficult to detect through a procedural fairness review. As this work noted in the example of the restructuring frameworks in the US and England (E.II), plan proponents (who are the debtor in most cases) may be granted some flexibility in certain matters, such as selecting which liabilities to be affected by the plan and which ones to remain totally unaffected as well as classifying creditors of the same rank into separate classes and treating them differently under the plan. The debtor may abuse this flexibility, possibly with the (active or passive) help of local courts, to unfairly discriminate against foreign creditors. Proving such discrimination is often difficult through a procedural fairness review.

Consider another aspect of fairness in restructuring cases as an example: the debtor's valuation. As Douglas Baird points out, even in the case of a non-biased judge, there is a degree of inherent variance in the debtor's valuation.[917] The value confirmed by the judge within the range of such variance may significantly impact the outcome for different parties when the APR applies: a senior creditor can receive the entire equity in one scenario, and a junior creditor can also receive a stake in another.[918] Thus, one or another value accepted by the judge may be in favour of the interests of one party and against those of another party. It is nearly impossible to find out whether the judge's decision on the debtor's value was influenced by factors that should, in theory, be irrelevant. For example, consciously or unconsciously, favouring a local creditor over a foreign creditor, who happens to be the senior and junior creditors in the scenario mentioned above, respectively, may (which, in theory, should not) be an influencing factor. Whether that was the case is hard to reveal through a procedural fairness review.

917 Baird, 'Priority Matters' (n 30) 821-22
918 ibid.

(bb) Potentially Unfamiliar Foreign Legal Concepts

A second factor is the likelihood of dealing with sophisticated foreign creditors and debt instruments, i.e. foreign law concepts that are unknown to the local jurisdiction. One of the main reasons for selecting a certain law (e.g. English law) to govern a certain complex debt instrument is the capability of that law to deal with various complex legal features of the instrument in question. Here, the instrument is subject to another law that might simply be not familiar with the respective features. Even if the bias issue is set aside, this aspect suffices to speak about a higher level of alert.

Recall the example of a non-biased (also towards foreign creditors), transparent, and generally competent Ruritanian judge. This time, the judge not only hears for the first time a restructuring case without any clear statutory guidelines and case law principles on substantive fairness but also, within the case, reviews a plan that provides for the restructuring of the obligations of a local company that are governed by different foreign laws. These obligations include, *inter alia*, different series of bonds issued on various foreign stock exchanges (involving different beneficial and legal owners, a foreign bank as a trustee, and so forth) as well as several sophisticated syndicated and subordinated loans from sophisticated foreign lenders. The concepts mentioned are not known under Ruritanian law. In a nutshell, an extremely exceptional day in the judge's career. The example speaks for itself.

(c) Ensuring Substantive Fairness Through the Entire Process

As already noted, substantive fairness refers to the fairness of outcome. If one speaks about the fairness of outcome, fairness should continue to be guaranteed until the outcome is fully achieved. In a cross-border scenario involving the non-consensual discharge of a foreign law-governed debt, such an outcome is achieved when cross-border substantive effects (e.g. binding the dissenting foreign creditor by the plan in the eyes of all affected jurisdictions) are in place. Otherwise, the outcome would not be final, as the dissenting foreign creditor can enforce its original claim against the debtor in jurisdictions that have not granted the recognition of the plan. Put another way, in the eyes of the *lex fori concursus* the plan might be final and binding on everybody once it has been confirmed by a local court (after conducting its fairness review) in the debtor's home jurisdiction. But from a global perspective, under modified universalism, the plan is final and binds everybody only when it has been given such effect in all affected jurisdictions. Hence, the process of ensuring substantive fairness should continue until such a global binding effect is obtained.

(d) Summary

To sum up, this work highlighted three points to justify the need for a substantive fairness review in contested cases under modified universalism: (i) the complexity of ensuring substantive fairness in domestic proceedings, particularly in jurisdictions with less developed restructuring frameworks; (ii) potential additional issues stemming from the involvement of cross-border elements, such as discrimination against foreign parties and challenges related to unknown foreign legal concepts; and (iii) the importance of ensuring fairness of restructuring plans until a globally binding effect is achieved.

c) Substantive Fairness and Public Policy

Below, this work will briefly examine whether ensuring substantive fairness of foreign plans at the recognition stage can be achieved under the public policy exception rather than conducting a separate substantive fairness review.

This work has already highlighted the importance of the protective role that the public policy exception plays in private international law generally (D.I.2) and under the MLCBI particularly (D.I.3). Hence, the cross-border effects of unfair (whether from a procedural or substantive perspective, or both) restructuring plans may be blocked under the public policy exception in some cases. As this work will discuss later,[919] fairness concerns may also affect the exercise of discretion under article 21 of the MLCBI pursuant to article 22. Hence, there may be an overlap. Nonetheless, this work argues in favour of a principle-based approach, given the significance of the issue identified thus far. Accordingly, it opposes assessing substantive fairness within the general public policy framework for the following reasons:

919 See sub-s F.I.2.b).

aa) Difference in the Purpose

To begin with, the public policy exception under the MLCBI and a substantive fairness review, despite the potential for overlap in the outcome of their invocation in some cases, have different functions. As already discussed in section D.I, the role of the former is to safeguard the most fundamental policies of the receiving state. The latter, as will be elaborated in greater detail as this work progresses, focuses on ensuring that the outcome under the foreign plan at hand is fair to a creditor (opposing creditor) opposing the recognition of the plan on the respective grounds. This work, thus, agrees with the arguments that the public policy exception under the MLCBI is not the appropriate safeguard to protect the interests of individual creditors in all cases.[920]

bb) Narrow Application of the Public Policy Exception

Additionally, as noted in this work, the public policy doctrine shall apply only in exceptional cases both in a general private international law context and the MLCBI framework.[921] A substantive fairness review, however, should be conducted in each case, subject to certain limitations, where the fairness of the plan is contested. Hence, the cross-border effects of foreign plans should be blocked in each case where such unfairness is established. That said, this work also argues against exploiting the substantive fairness framework under the MLCBI. This framework should have a limited application (but not as limited as the public policy exception) and the bar of what constitutes *unfair* in a cross-border context should not be low. This work will elaborate on these aspects of the respective framework in greater detail as Part F progresses.

cc) Proximity to the Forum

As noted, one of the dimensions of the public policy exception constitutes the proximity of the case at hand to the receiving state.[922] There may be cases with a weak connection with the state in which the recognition is

920 For a more detailed discussion, see sub-s D.I.3.c)bb).
921 See sub-ss D.I.2.c), D.I.3.c)aa).
922 See sub-s D.I.2.c)bb)(1).

sought. This could be due to factors such as the opposing creditor and the governing law of the contract belonging to a different jurisdiction and the recognition of the plan being sought merely to protect the debtor's assets in that state. Accordingly, courts of the respective state may not be keen to apply the public policy exception in such a case. For the purposes of a substantive fairness review, the proximity of the case to the state where the recognition is sought is irrelevant since the focus remains on the position of the opposing creditor.

2. Legal Basis under the MLCBI

This work will now examine whether the MLCBI, underpinned by the principle of modified universalism, provides for (or requires) a separate substantive fairness review, as justified in subsection F.I.1. This work will also refer to the text of the MLIJ to support its conclusions regarding the MLCBI.

a) Distinctive Approach to Restructuring Proceedings under the MLCBI

In general terms, the distinction between insolvency and restructuring proceedings extends to the cross-border effects of those proceedings under the MLCBI, as implemented in the jurisdictions examined in this work. That is to say, the automatic effects under article 20 of the MLCBI do not apply to restructuring proceedings under the British version.[923] The American version of article 20 (section 1520 of the BC), like the original version itself, applies also to restructuring proceedings. However, the effect of article 20 is limited in achieving the substantive goals of restructuring proceedings. That is to say, it is not possible to fully enforce foreign restructuring plans and, thus, bind dissenting creditors in the receiving state under this article. As already noted, this can be achieved under two articles of the MLCBI in the American version.[924] One option is through article 21 (section 1521 of the BC), which is of a discretionary nature. Additionally, any relief under article 21 is subject to article 22, which will be analysed in detail below. An alternative route is through article 7 (section 1507 of the BC), which is also discretionary and subject to the requirements of the American version of

923 For a more detailed discussion, see sub-ss C.II.1.a), C.II.1.b)cc).
924 See sub-s C.II.2.d).

this article. As can be generally observed, the MLCBI itself and its enacted versions tend to give local courts of the receiving state more control over the substantive cross-border effects of foreign restructuring plans. Given the analysis conducted in subsection F.I.1 of this work, it is not without reason.

b) The *Adequate Protection* Safeguard under Article 22 (1) of the MLCBI

Specifically, this work argues that a separate substantive fairness review may and should (given the use of *must*) be exercised under article 22 (1) of the MLCBI:

> Article 22. Protection of creditors and other interested persons
> 1. In granting or denying relief under article 19 or 21, or in modifying or terminating relief under paragraph 3 of this article, the court must be satisfied that the interests of the creditors and other interested persons, including the debtor, are adequately protected.

To begin with, the text of the MLCBI does not provide further details regarding this *adequate protection* safeguard, leaving a degree of uncertainty surrounding its application.[925] The Guide to the MLCBI generally underscores that the underlying idea of article 22 (1) is to strike a balance between the relief sought and the interests of the affected persons by that relief.[926] Accordingly, the matter is largely left to judicial discretion.[927] That said, this work argues that the protection granted by article 22 (1) of the MLCBI is primarily substantive. Below, it will thoroughly examine article 22 (1) to justify this argument.

---

925 Reinhard Bork, 'Article 22' in Reinhard Bork and Michael Veder (eds), *The UNCITRAL Model Laws on Cross-Border Insolvency and on the Recognition and Enforcement of Insolvency-Related Judgments: An Article-by-Article Commentary* (Edward Elgar 2025) paras 1.22.01, 1.22.03.

926 Guide to the MLCBI (n 17) para 196. See also Bork, 'Article 22' (n 925) paras 1.22.01, 1.22.03.

927 Bork, 'Article 22' (n 925) paras 1.22.01, 1.22.03.

aa) Language of Article 22 (1) of the MLCBI

To that end, this work first suggests focusing on the language used in the text of article 22 (1). This article provides for ensuring that the *interests* of all interested persons, with a specific emphasis on the creditors, are *adequately protected.*

Hence, the focus of the protection under article 22 (1) is the *interests*, not the *rights*, of the respective parties, particularly the creditors. The Oxford English Dictionary defines the noun *interest*, in its closest meaning to the context of article 22 (1) as follows: 'What is (most) advantageous or beneficial to a person or thing; an advantage, a benefit. Now esp. in **in a person's (best) interest**: to a person's advantage or benefit'.[928] As can be seen from this definition, the *interest* of a person in a particular context refers to the most advantageous or beneficial outcome in that particular context. With that definition in mind, parties involved in restructuring proceedings may have various, often conflicting, interests.[929] For example, shareholders may aim to retain their equity interests in the restructured company to the highest extent possible, if not entirely, which may result in reduced recovery for creditors. Creditors, on the other hand, may seek to achieve the satisfaction of their original claims to the greatest extent possible, if not fully, which may result in little or no equity for the existing shareholders in the restructured company. As this work observed in section E.II in the example of restructuring frameworks in the US and England, within the creditor side of the picture, too, different types of creditors may have competing interests, e.g. senior creditors versus more junior creditors or finance creditors versus trade creditors.

In order to *adequately protect* all those often-conflicting interests within a single restructuring case, the substantive outcome (rather than merely procedural aspects) should strike a fair balance among them. Hence, the *adequate protection* safeguard under article 22 (1) obliges the court of the receiving state, when giving effect to a foreign restructuring plan, to ensure that the distribution under the plan is fair and balanced *vis-à-vis* the interests of all affected parties, particularly the creditors. That is the exact aim of a substantive fairness review, too.

928 'interest, n, sense I.1.b' (*OED Online*, OUP December 2024) <https://www.oed.com/dictionary/interest_n?tab=meaning_and_use#260186> accessed 21 October 2025.

929 See Bork, 'Article 22' (n 925) para 1.22.01, where it is also mentioned in a general context that those interests are often conflicting.

The language of the analogous[930] article of the MLIJ, namely, article 14 *(f)*, which provides for a ground to refuse the recognition and enforcement of a foreign insolvency-related judgment, is clearer and supports the analysis made above with respect to the language used in article 22 (1) of the MLCBI. That is to say, the language of paragraph *(f)* of article 14 leaves little room for doubts regarding the substantive nature of the protection under the respective paragraph with respect to the recognition and enforcement of foreign restructuring plans (court orders confirming such plans):

> *(f)* The judgment:
> (i) Materially affects the rights of creditors generally, such as determining whether a plan of reorganization or liquidation should be confirmed, a discharge of the debtor or of debts should be granted or a voluntary or out-of-court restructuring agreement should be approved; and
> (ii) The interests of creditors and other interested persons, including the debtor, were not adequately protected in the proceeding in which the judgment was issued;

bb) Article 22 (1) in the Broader Context and Structure of the MLCBI

This work also suggests examining article 22 (1) within the broader context and structure of the MLCBI to justify its substantive nature. That is to say, article 6 of the MLCBI suffices to protect the public policy of the enacting state, which also encompasses assessing procedural fairness.[931] Additionally, courts may choose not to exercise their discretion to grant post-recognition relief under articles 7 or 21 in the cases involving procedural unfairness and other related issues, similar to the comity analysis of US courts.[932] Accordingly, there would be no necessity for an additional safeguard under article 22 (1) for merely procedural protection.

Again, the MLIJ, with its advanced context and structure, is of significant assistance. That is to say, the MLIJ contains separate provisions on the grounds for refusal, namely, public policy (article 7), procedural fairness (article 7), adequate notice (article 14 *(a)*), and fraud (article 14*(b)*). Accord-

930 See Rodriguez (n 594) para 2.14.44, where it is noted that article 14 *(f)* of the MLIJ 'is drafted in a manner and with the purpose to replicate Article 22 MLCBI ...'.

931 See text to nn 475, 476.

932 See text to nn 379, 380.

ingly, the *adequate protection* safeguard under article 14 *(f)* provides for an additional layer of (substantive) protection, particularly to creditors.

cc) Chapter 15 Case Law

Below, the American approach (upon which the model suggested in this work is built) will be analysed to support the argument on the substantive nature of article 22 (1) of the MLCBI.[933] In *Jaffé v. Samsung Elecs Co*, the Fourth Circuit was not convinced of the appellant's arguments that the protection under section 1522 (a) of the BC (the American version of article 22 (1) of the MLCBI) is 'merely a procedural' one and cannot be considered a safeguard against foreign substantive bankruptcy laws.[934] Instead, the court held that 'The analysis required by § 1522(a) is therefore logically best done by balancing the respective interests based on the relative harms and benefits in light of the circumstances presented, thus, inherently calling for application of a balancing test'.[935]

In fact, US courts developed three main principles regarding the satisfaction of the *sufficient protection*[936] requirement under section 1522 (a) of the BC:

> the just treatment of all holders of claims against the bankruptcy estate, the protection of U.S. claimants against prejudice and inconvenience in the processing of claims in the foreign proceeding, and the distribution of proceeds of the foreign estate substantially in accordance with the order prescribed by U.S. law.[937]

Among the three principles noted above, the last one is of particular importance for the purposes of the point discussed. Setting aside its problematic

933 For an analysis of the US case law regarding article of 22 (1), see also Bork, 'Article 22' (n 925) paras 1.22.09-16.

934 *Jaffé* (n 536) 27.

935 ibid 27-28. For a critical analysis of this balancing test, see Allan L. Gropper, 'The Curious Disappearance of Choice of Law as an Issue in Chapter 15 Cases' (2014) 9 Brook J Corp Fin & Com L 57, 78-79

936 The American text uses the adverb *sufficiently* instead of *adequately* as appears in the MLCBI. Bork, 'Article 22' (n 925) para 1.22.09.

937 *Bakrie* (n 375) 876 (square brackets and citations omitted).

aspects,[938] this principle expressly points to the distribution in foreign proceedings, i.e. whether or not the distribution in the foreign proceedings is substantially in line with that provided under US law. The same requirement is also set forth in section 1507 (b) (4) of the BC, which should be met when granting additional assistance under section 1507.[939]

dd) Existing Literature

It should be noted that the idea of a systematic substantive fairness review under article 22 (1) of the MLCBI (or article 14 *(f)* of the MLIJ) has not been extensively discussed in the literature so far. A few scholars have, nonetheless, touched on the subject. For example, Stephan Madaus highlights article 14 *(f)* of the MLIJ for refusing recognition on substantive grounds as part of the *sufficient connection* framework suggested by him.[940] Jay Westbrook leaves the door open for such a substantive review under article 22 of the MLCBI.[941] Irit Mevorach and Adrian Walters generally point to, *inter alia*, the *adequate protection* safeguard under article 22 (1) of the MLCBI for ensuring the fairness of cross-border pre-insolvency restructuring cases but also stress that additional clarification may be required in that respect.[942] Gerard McCormack generally highlights the importance of adequate protection of the interests of creditors under article 22 (1) of the MLCBI while supporting the implementation of Article X of the MLIJ in the UK and, thus, discontinuing the application of the Gibbs rule in its current form.[943]

3. Summary

In section F.I, this work first elaborated on the necessity of a substantive fairness review in recognising foreign restructuring plans in a system based on modified universalism (F.I.1). It concluded that, unlike universalism,

938 See sub-ss F.II.2.a)dd), F.II.2.b)aa).
939 Therefore, a separate analysis regarding section 1507 will not be provided further in this work.
940 Madaus, 'The Cross-border Effects of Restructurings' (n 3) 484-86. For a more detailed discussion, see sub-s B.I.2.b).
941 Westbrook, 'Chapter 15 and Discharge' (n 312) 517.
942 Mevorach and Walters (n 34) 878, 890-91.
943 McCormack 'UK Contracts and Modification under Foreign Law' (n 166) pts 6-7.

such a review is not only practically possible but also necessary in contested cases under the realm of modified universalism. This work highlighted three points in that regard: challenges of guaranteeing substantive fairness in domestic proceedings, particularly in jurisdictions with less developed restructuring frameworks; potential additional issues arising from the involvement of cross-border elements (bias against foreign creditors and unfamiliarity with foreign legal concepts); and the importance of ensuring the fairness of restructuring plans until they have a binding effect globally. By emphasising the importance of a principle-based approach in this context, it was also concluded that the general public policy framework does not fully address the respective issue, and a separate review should be conducted for that purpose.

Then, the text of the MLCBI (F.I.2) was examined. This work argued that the *adequate protection* safeguard under article 22 (1) requires such a review. This was supported by the analysis of its language, place in a general structure of the MLCBI, and interpretation under American case law, as well as by a summary of existing literature.

II. Essential Aspects of the Substantive Fairness Framework under the MLCBI

This work will now delve into the core aspects of the substantive fairness framework under the MLCBI. To begin with, like a domestic context, much should be done by courts after considering the peculiarities of each case to ensure substantive fairness when recognising foreign restructuring plans under the MLCBI, given the language used in article 22 (1). Nevertheless, the substantive fairness framework under the MLCBI significantly differs from domestic fairness frameworks, as will be evident as this section progresses.

This section will elaborate on the core features of the framework suggested in the present work. Subsection F.II.1 will be devoted to preliminary issues related to the limited scope and application of the substantive fairness framework under the MLCBI. In subsection F.II.2, this work will justify the necessity of a benchmark law under this framework and elaborate on the selection of the best law for that purpose. Subsection F.II.3 will be dedicated to the comparison with the benchmark law, while subsection F.II.4 will discuss the establishment of unfairness after the comparison has been conducted. Subsection F.II.5 will provide a summary.

In section F.II, this work will exclusively focus on substantive fairness. Therefore, it is assumed that public policy, due process, fraud, and other similar issues are not involved.

1. Limited Scope and Application

As mentioned earlier, the substantive fairness framework under the MLCBI should differ from domestic fairness frameworks. This work will emphasise and justify certain differences as Part F progresses while elaborating on various aspects of the former. Below, it will focus on one significant distinctive feature: its limited scope and application.

a) Reasons for the Limited Scope and Application

This work will outline two, albeit related, reasons for such limited scope and application.

aa) Private International Law Context

A first reason is linked to the general private international law nature of the matter. It is essential to remember that the matter involves recognising and enforcing a restructuring plan confirmed by a court order, which has become final in another state. The court of the receiving state does (and should) not act as a court of higher instance to conduct a full merits review (révision au fond) of a final decision of a foreign court having proper jurisdiction to administer the restructuring of the debtor.

bb) Modified Universalism

Second, the need for the limited scope and application also stems from the principle of modified universalism. As this work already noted, modified universalism has been suggested as an interim solution until universalism is fully achieved.[944] Its main idea is to achieve the objectives of universal-

944 For a more detailed discussion of modified universalism, see sub-s B.II.4.

ism (a single court and a single law governing the worldwide insolvency or restructuring of the debtor) through the collaboration of courts from different states rather than through automatic effects as envisioned by universalism. The MLCBI serves as an example of a framework for this type of collaboration. Under modified universalism, states retain some power to assess foreign restructuring proceedings before allowing their cross-border effects. Nonetheless, those powers should not undermine the central idea of a single court and a single law. Here, too, a single court and single law govern the worldwide restructuring of the debtor. The distinction lies in how cross-border effects are achieved. Therefore, any attempt to a full révision au fond would be inconsistent with that central tenet of modified universalism and, thus, jeopardise its main advantages.[945] So would assessing fairness in all cases.

b) Factors Ensuring the Limited Scope and Application

Although the matter will be returned to as Part F progresses, this work will below discuss several factors that it suggests will ensure the limited scope and application of the substantive fairness framework under the MLCBI.

aa) Effect on Substantive Rights

A substantive fairness review under the framework suggested in this work should only intervene when the action sought in the receiving state affects substantive rights. An obvious example is recognising and enforcing a foreign restructuring plan involving a non-consensual discharge. A permanent impediment to the enforcement of such rights should also be considered as affecting substantive rights.[946] The recognition of foreign proceedings and their automatic effects (temporary stays or moratoriums) and other actions of a procedural nature should not *per se* trigger a substantive fairness review. This is because substantive rights are not affected at that point in the eyes of the receiving state. Accordingly, a substantive fairness review is unnecessary at the respective stage.

945 For a discussion of the advantages of a concept based on a single court and a single law, see sub-s B.II.3.a).

946 See *IBA* (n 245) and its discussion in sub-s C.I.3.a).

bb) Opposition at the Recognition Stage

A substantive fairness review should be conducted only when the recognition of the plan is opposed on substantive fairness grounds. Dissenting behaviour in foreign proceedings alone does not suffice. Article 22 (1) of the MLCBI does not expressly state it. Rather, it generally requires ensuring the adequate protection of the interests of all parties. That said, reviewing the substantive outcome of the foreign proceedings by the court of the receiving state on its own initiative (ex officio) would be inconsistent with the private international law nature of the matter in general and the principle of modified universalism in particular. Accordingly, it should be presumed that the interests of a dissenting creditor have been adequately protected in the foreign proceedings if the creditor does not oppose the relief sought under the MLCBI in the receiving state.

cc) Exclusion of Local Creditors of Foreign Proceedings

The substantive fairness framework under the MLCBI does not apply to a creditor whose initial claim is governed by the *lex fori concursus.* By agreeing to be bound by that law at the outset, the creditor also agreed to any subsequent discharge of the debt under the respective law. The substantive outcome of the foreign proceedings, therefore, is final for local creditors of those proceedings.

dd) Exhaustion of All Remedies in Foreign Proceedings

In order to have standing to oppose the recognition of the plan in the receiving state, a dissatisfied creditor must first object to the confirmation of the plan in the original (foreign) proceedings. Again, mere dissenting behaviour during the voting process is not enough. The dissatisfied creditor should exhaust all remedies in the foreign proceedings in order to claim the unfairness of the distribution under the plan. That includes, *inter alia*, contesting the plan at the confirmation hearing, appealing the court order confirming the plan, and making further appeals on the respective grounds (as the case may be). That is to say, the focus of a substantive fairness review is on the *fairness of outcome.* The dissatisfied creditor, therefore, should first try to achieve the best possible outcome in the original proceedings, where courts are better equipped and have more extensive substantive and procedural powers for that. At that point, it is a matter of purely domestic substantive law, allowing the thorough assessment and assurance of fairness in the overall outcome, including with respect to that creditor. The recent case of *Adler*, where the EWCA dismissed a EWHC judgment sanctioning a Part 26A plan on the substantive fairness grounds upon the appeal of several dissenting foreign creditors, is a notable example of how the outcome can be more favourable for dissenting foreign creditors in domestic proceedings after successful contestation.[947] Accordingly, in order to question the outcome at the recognition stage, the dissenting creditor should first get a final verdict on the outcome in the domestic proceedings. Again, the respective court of the receiving state does not function as a higher court in this context.

As can be identified, this perspective is completely different from the English approach, according to which no protection is granted under the Gibbs rule to a creditor submitting to foreign proceedings.[948] The framework suggested in this work, by contrast, encourages dissenting creditors to actively engage and attempt to address any fairness concerns in domestic proceedings first. Besides the arguments mentioned above, this approach is also advantageous in terms of certainty and efficiency.

When considering this factor, parties with limited resources, such as SMEs and consumers, could be given an exception.

ee) Focusing on the Treatment of the Opposing Creditor

A substantive fairness review should assess the (un)fairness of the foreign plan only in relation to the opposing creditor. Whether the overall outcome reached in the foreign proceedings in question is fair should not be a matter to decide for the court of the receiving state. Nor is it the business of that court to evaluate the fairness framework under the *lex fori concursus* in general. This is something to be revisited as this work progresses.

---

947 *Adler* (n 622). For a more detailed discussion of the case, see sub-s E.II.2.c)bb)(2)(b).

948 See text to n 276.

ff) Burden of Proof

Another factor is related to the burden of proof. A substantive fairness review is an additional layer of protection for creditors and should be operational only when invoked by the opposing creditor. Therefore, it should be the opposing creditor who bears the burden of proving that the outcome under the plan is unfair in relation to that creditor. Arguing otherwise would unfairly disadvantage the debtor (the foreign representative). As identified earlier, the foreign representative already carries the burden of proving the fulfilment of requirements for recognition under Chapter 15.[949] With that in mind, requiring the foreign representative to prove that the substantive outcome of the foreign proceedings is fair in relation to the opposing creditor only because the latter argues otherwise would be illogical, unfair, and open to abuse. One should also remember that article 22 (1) aims to protect the interests of the debtor, too, i.e. to strike a fair balance between the respective interests.

Against this backdrop, a creditor opposing the relief sought on substantive fairness grounds should present credible evidence in that respect. Depending on the method of comparison, as will be discussed later in this work, the evidence should illustrate a significant deterioration of the position of that creditor in the respective foreign jurisdiction. These matters (comparison, the deterioration of position, and so forth), too, will be examined later in this work. At this point, it suffices to note that the burden of proof of unfair treatment should be on the opposing creditor. Once the opposing creditor has met this burden, it is up to the foreign representative to challenge the arguments and evidence of the opposing creditor. This factor will also help to prevent abuse by creditors with ill-founded claims, for example, those attempting to delay the cross-border effects of the plan in question. It goes without saying that time can be of the essence for a successful restructuring.

An exception for vulnerable creditors could be made regarding this factor, too.

gg) Costs

Finally, the unsuccessful party should bear all costs of a substantive fairness review, including the winning party's costs. Such costs may include court

949 See text to n 375.

fees, legal costs, and the costs associated with obtaining evidence, which can be quite high depending on the case. This factor, too, may significantly deter creditors with unfounded claims. Besides, it may have an *ex ante* deterrence effect on the plan proponent, who is typically the debtor. The possibility of losing the case due to a substantive fairness review at the recognition stage and, thus, having to bear all costs would discourage the plan proponent from devising a plan that may survive a domestic substantive fairness review but not a potential one at the recognition stage. Instead, it would encourage the plan proponent develop a fair plan that would survive the latter, too. Therefore, the deterrence effect on both sides will lead to the limited application of the substantive fairness framework under the MLCBI.

Again, a different treatment could be considered for vulnerable creditors.

2. Benchmark Law

This work argues that one of the key components of the substantive fairness framework under the MLCBI is a benchmark law. Below, this work will justify its necessity and elaborate on selecting the best law for that purpose.

a) Case for a Benchmark Law

Several factors necessitate a benchmark law for a substantive fairness review under article 22 (1) of the MLCBI, as will be summarised below:

aa) Difference Between a Full Révision au Fond and a Substantive Fairness Review

To begin with, the overall fairness of the *lex fori concursus* or the foreign proceedings at hand should not be a concern for the respective court of the receiving state. The establishment of a framework to ensure fairness in restructuring proceedings in a particular jurisdiction is determined by its national law. Ensuring of the overall fairness of restructuring proceedings within the legal framework of that jurisdiction is the responsibility of its national courts. As already noted, assessing fairness in this context should be distinguished from a full révision au fond. The court of the receiving state has only one task in this context: to assess and be satisfied with the fairness of the distribution under the foreign plan at hand in relation to the opposing creditor. That said, there is no universally accepted test for assessing substantive fairness in a cross-border context. Hence, despite its limited nature, the respective task of the court of the receiving state may not be straightforward and may require a complex assessment.

bb) Relative Nature of Substantive Fairness

Even if the issues of assessing the overall fairness of the *lex fori concursus* and a full révision au fond are set aside, solely focusing on the jurisdiction of the original proceedings as part of a substantive fairness review will take the matter nowhere. Unlike procedural fairness, universal standards do not exist to assess the fairness of foreign restructuring laws in a substantive context. For example, the right to a fair trial (due notice, right to be heard, and so forth) is widely recognised and is found in many international conventions.[950] Hence, it is relatively straightforward to establish at least certain aspects of the procedural (un)fairness of foreign proceedings.

That cannot be said about substantive fairness. To begin with, there is no widely recognised standard to evaluate substantive fairness frameworks under restructuring laws across different jurisdictions. These fairness frameworks are designed with different policy considerations behind them. For example, some may favour debtors, while others may be creditor-oriented. These competing policies may also include favouring different types of claims, such as tax or employment claims, as well as prioritising trade creditors over financial creditors. The level of creditor support and the enforcement of private law priority rules (strict application versus flexible one) may also vary and so forth. In subsection E.II.4, this work has already summarised the differences in the main aspects of the fairness frameworks under Chapter 11, English law, and under the PRD. As already mentioned, these differences may lead to different outcomes in cases with similar, if not identical, facts. The fact that distribution rules are not similar in two jurisdictions, which, in turn, may lead to different outcomes when applied to the same facts, does and should not mean that one framework is fairer than the other. It is a matter of policy for each state to design a fairness framework that suits its needs and a judge of the receiving state should not be concerned with the assessment of policies of foreign states. Furthermore,

950 See text to n 578.

even in jurisdictions with a relatively long history of restructuring and creditor protection, such as the US (which has influenced many other jurisdictions), certain aspects of the fairness framework are far from ideal and have been roundly criticised in the literature.[951] Accordingly, it would be inaccurate to assert that the fairness of outcome is a guaranteed matter in all Chapter 11 proceedings. Additionally, the recent academic debate on two competing priority rules under the PRD (the RPR versus the APR) once again demonstrates that the fairness of outcome in restructuring proceedings is a relative matter. That is to say, supporters of each priority model present arguments in favour of their preferred model and against the other model based on, *inter alia*, fairness concerns. As mentioned above, the design of a fairness framework under restructuring law is a policy matter for each state, and whether the adopted framework in one state will lead to fair outcomes can be evaluated from different angles. This work, thus, argues that there is no absolute affirmative answer to that question. Consequently, no jurisdiction exists where there is an absolute guarantee of the fairness of outcome under the existing restructuring framework.

cc) Comparison with Another Jurisdiction

The question then arises as to how the court of the receiving state should assess the fairness of the foreign plan with respect to the opposing creditor. As Sarah Paterson correctly puts it, substantive fairness in the context of debt restructuring is a notion that is generally linked to 'some sort of imbalance' and to the comparison of different indicators (comparison of the treatment of participants, comparison of efforts and gains, and so forth).[952] This work also observed it in the examples of restructuring frameworks discussed in section E.II, e.g. horizontal and vertical comparisons and rewarding post-restructuring contributions. The need for a comparison also holds for assessing substantive fairness at the recognition stage, particularly considering the relative nature of substantive fairness in restructuring, as stated above.

Another question concerns the proper reference point for comparison in assessing the substantive fairness of the foreign plan in relation to the opposing creditor. Confining the reference point to within the foreign jurisdiction in question (comparing the actual outcome for the opposing

951 See text to n 708.

952 See n 644 and accompanying text.

creditor with possible outcomes of alternative scenarios available in that jurisdiction, comparing the treatment of the opposing creditor with the treatment of other participants in the foreign proceedings, and so forth) is not preferable. This would be identical to a fairness review in a domestic context and ultimately involve a full révision au fond. Therefore, the respective reference point should not be within the foreign jurisdiction in question. Besides, the private international law nature of the matter also underlines the need to extend the reference point beyond that foreign jurisdiction.

One feasible solution, therefore, could be to compare the treatment of the opposing under the foreign plan at hand with a hypothetical treatment of that creditor in a restructuring in another jurisdiction. Hence, the reference point for comparison is a hypothetical treatment of the opposing creditor in another jurisdiction. This solution addresses the concerns noted above. First, a fairness review in that scenario is confined to the position of the opposing creditor only. Thus, assessing the fairness of the overall outcome of the foreign proceedings and a full révision au fond can be avoided. Second, there is no need to evaluate the fairness framework under the *lex fori concursus.*

It should also be noted that the concept of comparing with another jurisdiction is not new in the context of cross-border insolvency and restructuring. In the literature, 'rough similarity' has been referred to as a pre-requisite for deference to a foreign jurisdiction under the principle of modified universalism.[953]

dd) Chapter 15 Case Law

This work will below turn to the American approach first to support the conclusion mentioned above and then highlight the shortcomings of the American approach. As already noted, such a comparison is required under Chapter 15.[954] That is to say, one of the principles followed by courts in determining a fair balance between the respective interests under section 1522 (a) of the BC is the substantial conformity of the distribution in the foreign proceedings with the one provided for under US law.[955] The

953 Westbrook, 'A Global Solution' (n 100) 2301. See also van Zwieten (ed), *Principles of Corporate Insolvency Law* (n 29) para 16-06 (fn 20 therein and accompanying text).

954 See sub-s F.I.2.b)cc).

955 See text to n 937.

following sentence from a decision of the Fifth Circuit provides a concise summary of Chapter 15 case law in that respect: 'In considering whether to grant relief, it is not necessary that the result achieved in the foreign bankruptcy proceeding be identical to that which would be had in the United States. It is sufficient if the result is comparable'.[956] This perspective under Chapter 15 case law supports the general idea of comparison with another jurisdiction in cross-border cases.

Nonetheless, the American approach has two shortcomings. A first issue is the lack of clarity. A second problematic aspect is related to requiring conformity of the distribution in the foreign proceedings with US law, which will be discussed below. Returning to the first issue, American courts do not expressly refer to a substantive fairness review but rather conduct their analysis on substantive matters mainly within a procedural framework, as already underscored in this work.[957] Given that this work has already made the case for a separate substantive fairness review in contested cases, that cannot be considered an entirely preferable approach.

As to the requirement of the substantial conformity of the distribution in the foreign proceedings with US law under the American version of article 22 (1) of the MLCBI specifically, no guidelines or principles exist under case law on how to conduct such a comparison and when the distribution under a foreign plan should be considered *substantially* in accordance with US law. This has the potential to lead to inconsistency in the application of the respective requirement in contested Chapter 15 cases. This work will attempt to address the respective matters, too.

b) Governing Law of the Contract as a Benchmark Law

After justifying the need for a benchmark law to compare the treatment of the opposing creditor under the foreign plan, this work will now focus on selecting the most suitable law for that purpose. As already noted, under Chapter 15, similarity is required with US substantive law, i.e. the law of the receiving state.[958] According to this work, the respective aspect constitutes one of the shortcomings of the American approach with respect to the assessment of substantive fairness under the American version of article 22 (1) of the MLCBI. That is to say, this work argues that a benchmark law for

956 *Vitro* (n 87) 1044 (citations omitted).
957 See sub-s C.III.2.b).
958 See sub-ss C.III.2.b), F.I.2.b)cc).

that purpose should be the governing law of the contract rather than the law of the receiving state.

aa) Justification

(1) Non-Discrimination of Creditors

To begin with, these two laws may, and perhaps do, overlap in most cases. In some cases, however, they may not. For example, as noted earlier in this work, there may be cases where the recognition of a foreign plan is sought to protect the assets of the debtor in the receiving state with the governing law of the contract belonging to a third country, i.e. a country other than the receiving state and the debtor's home country. Perhaps there are other scenarios, too. This work argues in favour of a principle-based approach in relation to the respective aspect of the substantive fairness framework under the MLCBI. That is to say, a substantive fairness review should be conducted not only with respect to local creditors of the receiving state but rather in relation to any creditor who has standing. This position is also supported in the Guide to the MLCBI, which recommends not confining article 22 (1) of the MLCBI to local creditors of the enacting state and, thus, not discriminating against foreign creditors.[959] Prioritising the law of the receiving state for the purposes of article 22 (1) has the potential (and should be seen as) to favour local creditors.

(2) Purpose of Article 22 (1)

Why should the governing law of the contract be a benchmark law? To answer this question, one should look at the purpose of the *adequate protection* safeguard under Article 22 (1) of the MLCBI. As already identified, it aims to strike a fair balance between the respective interests. On one side of the picture, there is the debtor seeking the recognition of a plan confirmed in its home jurisdiction. On the other side, there is a dissenting

959 Guide to the MLCBI (n 17) para 198. This argument is further strengthened by contrasting article 22 (1) with article 21 (2), which expressly refers to local creditors of the receiving state. See Bork, 'Article 22' (n 925) paras 1.22.02, 1.22.05, 1.22.06 (US cases discussed therein). For a similar view, albeit in a different context, that the protection under the US version of article 22 should not be limited to US creditors and should extend to all creditors globally, see Gropper (n 935) 72.

creditor claiming that the distribution under the plan is unfair in relation to that creditor and a benchmark law is necessary to find out whether this opposition is well-grounded. The law most suitable for balancing these conflicting positions is the law that the respective parties (the debtor and the opposing creditor) agreed to be bound by from the outset.

(3) Debt-Oriented Nature of Restructuring Proceedings

More generally, the debt-oriented nature of restructuring proceedings speaks for the governing law of the contract, too. As stated in different contexts earlier in this work, one factor differentiating restructuring proceedings from asset-oriented insolvency proceedings is the debt-oriented nature of the former.[960] To reiterate, unlike insolvency proceedings, marshalling and realising the entire asset pool of the debtor to satisfy creditors is not the aim of restructuring proceedings. Rather, it focuses on restructuring the debtor's debts so that the debtor can continue to trade, with the existing assets mainly remaining untouched. Hence, if one talks about a benchmark law that will be used to compare the treatment of the opposing creditor in the proceedings that primarily affect claims against the debtor rather than its assets, the governing law of the contract is a better fit than the law of the state where the recognition is sought due to the existence of assets or any other reason.

bb) Consideration of a Potential Counter-Argument

A potential counter-argument may be made against the idea of the governing law of the contract as a benchmark. That is to say, one may argue that by agreeing to engage with a foreign party (the debtor) the opposing creditor assumed the risk of being bound by the restructuring law of a foreign country (the debtor's home jurisdiction) and the governing law of the contract should not be relevant. In fact, this is one of the core arguments of critics of the Gibbs rule.[961] Using the same argument, potential opponents may question the necessity of a benchmark law or a substantive fairness review under the MLCBI at all. Therefore, the justification of the

960 See sub-s B.I.3.a).
961 See n 319 and text thereto.

need for a substantive fairness review in recognising foreign plans[962] and a benchmark law for that purpose[963] generally suffice to address this potential counter-argument. However, a few additional points will be highlighted below that signify the role of the governing law of the contract in this context.

(1) Potential COMI Shift

As already noted, the location of the debtor's COMI plays a decisive role in determining whether a restructuring proceeding commenced in a given jurisdiction may be recognised as a foreign main proceeding under the MLCBI. However, it shall not be forgotten that the COMI of the debtor is not fixed and can be subject to changes several times without the consent of creditors.[964] Accordingly, a German creditor engaging with a debtor which, at the time of the conclusion of the contract, had its COMI in Japan may end up being bound by the restructuring law of Albania due to the subsequent COMI shift from Japan to Albania. Can it be argued that the German creditor in that scenario assumed the risk of being bound by the restructuring law of Albania? According to this work, that is not the case. In addition, modern restructuring lawyers have been devising various methods to artificially bring restructuring cases into jurisdictions where the desired outcome for plan proponents (who, in most cases, are the debtor) will be yielded (forum-shopping). For example, this may involve creating a *substitute obligor* or *co-obligor* company in the desired jurisdiction, similar to what happened in the *Adler* case.[965] It can be concluded that, in this context, the only law that both parties (the debtor and the opposing creditor) agreed to be bound by and cannot be subsequently changed without their mutual consent, particularly without the consent of the opposing creditor, is the governing law of the contract.

962 See sub-s F.I.1.

963 See sub-s F.II.2.a).

964 This point was also highlighted in the context of defending the Gibbs rule. See Paterson, 'A Qualified Defence of the Rule in Gibbs' (n 74) s VII.A. See also FMLC (n 332) para 4.9.

965 *Adler* (n 622) [29]-[33]. The issue was not considered in that case, as it had not been raised in the appeal. See ibid [34]-[35]. For a more detailed discussion, see Madaus, 'The Cross-border Effects of Restructurings' (n 3) 481; van Galen, 'The Scheming Brits' (n 291) pt V.

(2) Recent Proposals for Flexible Choice-of-Forum Rules

Recently, a group of scholars proposed replacing the COMI concept under the MLCBI with even more flexible concepts regarding the selection of a forum for the debtor's insolvency proceedings.[966] Their preferred approach, which they refer to as the *Commitment Rule*, suggests that the debtor should be allowed to commit *ex ante* to a specific forum in its articles of association for possible insolvency proceedings.[967] The authors agree that such commitment may generally be changed *ex post* by the debtor by altering the articles of association and offer certain safeguards in that respect.[968] Their next best approach (if the COMI concept is retained) suggests that the debtor should be allowed to initiate insolvency proceedings in any foreign jurisdiction (without having its COMI or an establishment in that jurisdiction) that provides such an opportunity for foreign companies.[969] Proceedings in the debtors' home jurisdiction and any other foreign jurisdiction selected by the debtor should have similar cross-border effects under the MLCBI, provided that the debtor illustrates that creditors as a whole benefit from the selection of the forum, say the authors.[970]

Without further analysing those approaches, this work argues that, in light of such proposals, the respective potential counter-argument becomes even less convincing.[971] The idea of the governing law of the contract as a benchmark law in considering the recognition of restructuring plans, on the contrary, gains more relevance.

cc) Reconciling the Gibbs Rule and Modified Universalism

Under a framework where the governing law of the contract serves as a benchmark, the rhetorical questions of Lord Esher in *Antony Gibbs* ('Why should the plaintiffs be bound by the law of a country to which they

966 Anthony J Casey, Aurelio Gurrea-Martínez, and Robert K Rasmussen, 'A Commitment Rule for Insolvency Forum' (23 January 2024) ECGI Law Working Paper No. 754/2024 <https://ssrn.com/abstract=4704029> accessed 21 October 2025.

967 ibid s 3.1.

968 ibid sub-s 3.1.2.

969 ibid s 3.2.

970 ibid.

971 For similar concerns, albeit in the context of defending the Gibbs rule, see Paterson, 'A Qualified Defence of the Rule in Gibbs' (n 74) s VII.A.

do not belong, and by which they have not contracted to be bound')[972] and Lord Collins in *Rubin* ('why should the seller/creditor be in a worse position than a buyer/debtor?')[973] would become less relevant. That is to say, the framework suggested in this work favours neither the debtor nor the dissenting foreign creditor and provides some protection for each. On the one hand, the dissenting foreign creditor is bound by the outcome of the restructuring proceedings in the debtor's home jurisdiction and does not have vetoing power from the outset. On the other hand, the protection granted to the creditor under the governing law of the contract is not completely disregarded, at least in achieving the cross-border effects of the plan.

Accordingly, the framework suggested in this work aligns the main advantage of the Gibbs rule with modified universalism. However, this approach departs from the Gibbs rule (mainly from its oft-criticized aspects) in a substantial way. First, this framework does not oppose the discharge of a foreign law-governed debt in restructuring proceedings in the debtor's home jurisdiction. Second, unlike the Gibbs rule, it does not ultimately require parallel or main proceedings under the governing law of the contract. Third, the approach suggested in this work does not give vetoing power to foreign creditors from the outset. Rather, it encourages them to fight for the best possible outcome in the debtor's home jurisdiction instead of merely relying on the protections granted by the governing law of the contract.

dd) Support in the Literature

The idea of the governing law of the contract serving as a benchmark law enjoys scholarly support. While considering a distinctive framework for cross-border restructuring cases, Stephan Madaus highlights the necessity of respecting 'substantive limits' of the governing law of the contract in restructuring proceedings, thus securing a 'sufficient connection' to that law.[974] According to him, such sufficient connection is required in the cases when it is not possible to determine a law with the 'closest connection' (e.g. the law governing an absolute majority of the debts to be restructured or

972 See text to n 271.
973 See text to n 350.
974 See text to n 70.

agreed by most of the affected creditors) to govern the restructuring of the debtor.[975]

As already noted, this work suggests using the governing law of the contract as a benchmark under a framework underpinned by modified universalism (the MLCBI), thus, for all eligible cross-border restructurings. This work will also elaborate on the extent to which the governing law of the contract should be given consideration.

ee) Difference from Virtual Territoriality

Although there is a similarity in the idea that the governing law of the contract should be considered in a restructuring context, the framework suggested in this work should not be confounded with Edward Janger's *virtual territoriality* approach[976] as part of a broader concept of *universal proceduralism*,[977] which he suggested as an alternative to modified universalism.

(1) Overview

Virtual territoriality provides for 'one case under many laws' for the global insolvency (restructuring) of the debtor.[978] That is to say, the *lex fori concursus*, which is determined through the harmonised choice-of-forum rules, should be confined to the procedural matters of the case only, while general rules of private international law should determine the law applicable to the substantive matters.[979] Put another way, virtual territoriality suggests that the court administering the case in the debtor's home country should, to the extent possible, directly apply the law governing each debt affected by the plan to the substantive issues (e.g. priority of claims) relating to that debt.

975 See text to n 69.
976 See generally Edward J. Janger, 'Virtual Territoriality' (2010) 48 Colum J Transnatl L 401
977 See n 115 and accompanying text.
978 Janger, 'Virtual Territoriality' (n 976) 408.
979 ibid 408-09, 432ff.

(2) Distinction and Critical Analysis

The concept of virtual territoriality substantially differs from the framework suggested in this work in several ways. Firstly, assessing fairness during the recognition stage, with the governing law of the contract as a benchmark, is suggested not as a replacement for but rather to take place within modified universalism. The difference lies not only in the name of the concept but also in its essence. As mentioned earlier, virtual territoriality supports, to the greatest possible extent, the direct application of the governing law of the contract by the court of the debtor's home jurisdiction to substantive matters concerning the restructuring of the debt in question. This work does not go that far. Nor does it support this approach since virtual territoriality takes away most of the advantages that modified universalism offers.[980]

Below, this work will briefly scrutinise the concept of virtual territoriality.

(a) Doctrinal Aspect

To begin with, virtual territoriality reinforces the Gibbs rule while eliminating the ultimate need for restructuring proceedings to take place in the jurisdiction whose law governs the contract. While this is a step forward, virtual territoriality does not fully address the rule's significant weaknesses. Therefore, the main doctrinal issue with the Gibbs rule[981] holds for virtual territoriality. That is to say, like the Gibbs rule, virtual territoriality treats discharge in restructuring proceedings as a merely contractual matter between the contracting parties. Hence, the insolvency-related background of and broader policy considerations behind restructuring frameworks are mostly disregarded.

(b) Practical Difficulties

Even if its doctrinal aspect is set aside, implementing virtual territoriality would pose significant practical challenges. Virtual territoriality, as the name suggests, combines multiple *parallel* proceedings into one without

980 Jay Westbrook also criticises an approach under which the governing law of the contract determines the bankruptcy law applicable to the contract. See Westbrook, 'Comity and Choice of Law' (n 12) 266.

981 See sub-s C.III.1.b).

significantly addressing the issues posed by such parallel proceedings while raising problems of its own.

Imagine a restructuring plan in the debtor's home jurisdiction that involves, *inter alia*, the non-consensual discharge of debts governed by ten different foreign laws. These laws provide for restructuring frameworks that are similar in some ways but fundamentally different in other aspects, such as priority rules. Based on a comparative analysis of Chapter 11, English law, and the PRD in subsection E.II.4, it is quite possible to argue that this scenario could occur in the real world. Consequently, reconciling the respective rules of those ten foreign laws in one plan, which is necessary due to the implementation of virtual territoriality, would be difficult and possibly unachievable. Otherwise, the proceedings would no longer be collective.

Apart from the reconciliation problem mentioned above, it would be exceptionally challenging for the court in the debtor's home jurisdiction to examine and apply (to the extent possible) ten foreign laws in the above scenario. To begin with, section E.II of this work illustrated that not all significant matters are settled and competing approaches are in place regarding one or another aspect of restructuring frameworks at a domestic level. As identified in section E.I, such uncertainty is inherent to restructuring frameworks to maintain their flexibility. Hence, it would not always be straightforward to even determine what the position with respect to a certain matter under foreign laws in question is before applying those foreign laws in *one case* under virtual territoriality. A foreign court is not the best venue to resolve an uncertainty under one law.

In addition, having to examine and apply multiple foreign laws (as many as ten in the above scenario) would lead to the need for numerous expensive expert opinions on various legal and evidential matters, potentially conflicting with one another. As can be concluded, the process of examining, applying, and reconciling various foreign laws in one case would be both costly and time-consuming. Another set of potential practical challenges pertains to differences in language, legal systems, and legal traditions, among other things. Thus, the primary issues associated with parallel proceedings, such as costs, time, and efficiency, would still exist in virtual territoriality. It goes without saying that costs and efficiency are crucial in restructuring proceedings.

(3) Advantages of the Substantive Fairness Framework under the MLCBI Compared to Virtual Territoriality

The framework suggested in this work is different from virtual territoriality in terms of in what form (benchmark) and when (at the recognition stage) the governing law of the contract should intervene. Each of these two factors offers several advantages, which will be summarised below.

(a) Benchmark Function of the Governing Law of the Contract

The primary function of the governing law of the contract is to serve as a benchmark for comparing the treatment of the opposing creditor rather than governing the substantive issues of the restructuring of the debt in question. Accordingly, a deviation from the governing law of the contract to a certain extent (beyond minor) is acceptable,[982] considering the benefits of the concept of a single set of proceedings with universal effect governing the global restructuring of the debtor under modified universalism.[983] Such a deviation is also justifiable when considering the background circumstances (the debtor's distress) and the alternative to an unsuccessful restructuring (most likely, the debtor's liquidation) and the law applicable in that alternative (the *lex fori concursus*).

Besides, the benchmark function will not require a detailed examination of the governing law of the contract as opposed to the direct application of that law.

(b) Intervention at the Recognition Stage

In addition, the governing law of the contract weighs in not from the outset but only at the recognition stage. A single law (the *lex fori concursus*) applies to both procedural and substantive matters in the original proceedings, as modified universalism suggests. As a result, the uncertainty and practical difficulties as well as cost and efficiency concerns associated with the detailed examination and application (and reconciliation, if necessary) of multiple foreign laws, do not arise during the confirmation of the plan.

At the recognition stage, some of the concerns mentioned above may not arise at all, while others may arise to a much lesser extent. That is to say,

982 For a more detailed discussion, see sub-s F.II.4.

983 For a more detailed discussion, see sub-ss B.II.3.a), B.II.4.

there will be no need to reconcile different foreign laws, as the plan will be assessed solely with respect to the opposing creditor. Accordingly, the comparison will be conducted solely with the governing law of the contract between the debtor and the opposing creditor. If the recognition is opposed by several creditors whose claims are governed by various foreign laws, there will be multiple separate substantive fairness reviews with respect to each opposing creditor, again, without reconciling those laws.

In addition, the substantive fairness framework under the MLCBI has only limited application. In order to have standing, the opposing creditor should fulfil the requirements outlined earlier in this work. If its benchmark function (as opposed to its direct application) and, thus, the possibility of a deviation from the governing law of the contract and *ex ante* effects[984] are also added to the picture, it can be assumed that a substantive fairness review will not be invoked extensively and will be confined to the cases with gross violation of foreign creditors' substantive rights in the original proceedings. The IBA restructuring proceedings demonstrated that several foreign dissenting creditors subsequently agreed to receive new entitlements under the IBA plan and, thus, did not oppose its recognition abroad.[985] Finally, in most cases, although not necessarily, recognition will be opposed in the jurisdiction whose law governs the respective creditor's claim. Accordingly, the judge will make a comparison with the law of its own jurisdiction.

Against this backdrop, it is noteworthy that any potential recognition abroad and, consequently, any comparisons with the laws governing the claims of dissenting creditors should be reflected in some form in the original proceedings. However, this should primarily be a matter for the plan proponent and the supporting majority. As the key stakeholders of a successful restructuring with worldwide effects, they must devise a plan capable of withstanding potential substantive fairness reviews during recognition in foreign jurisdictions. The judge in the original proceedings should not be preoccupied with potential future comparisons with different foreign laws and should instead apply a single law.

984 For a more detailed discussion, see sub-s F.IV.4.

985 See *IBA* (n 245) [21].

3. Comparison with the Benchmark Law

Below, this work will focus on the process of comparing the actual treatment of the opposing creditor under the foreign plan with the hypothetical treatment under the restructuring framework of the governing law of the contract. To begin with, selecting a suitable method for the comparison is one of the most complex issues associated with the substantive fairness framework under the MLCBI. On the one hand, the method selected should accurately illustrate the difference in the treatment of the opposing creditor. On the other hand, it should not be overly burdensome considering the objectives of the MLCBI. Specifically, one of the central objectives of the MLCBI is administering cross-border cases in an efficient manner.[986] As this work already noted, under modified universalism, the designated court of the receiving state can evaluate foreign plans in deciding whether to recognise them. Any type of review, including a substantive fairness review, however, should not overshadow the respective objective.

Hence, there should be a balance between efficiency and accuracy. Below, this work will outline several comparison methods and discuss the advantages and possible shortcomings of each, given the need for maintaining the balance mentioned. It should be noted that one aspect will remain constant in all methods: the actual distribution under the plan at hand. The *lex fori concursus* (or the opposing creditor's position under the *lex fori concursus*) in a general context should not be examined for the purpose of the comparison, as a substantive fairness review focuses on the fairness of the distribution under the plan, which is already known. The difference in methods concerns the reference point for comparison, i.e. the governing law of the contract (benchmark law).

a) General Restructuring Framework of the Governing Law of the Contract as a Benchmark

A first method is to generally review the restructuring framework of the benchmark law to determine the degree of conformity of the distribution under the plan with the distribution rules under that framework, focusing on the position of the opposing creditor. This method primarily corre-

986 MLCBI (n 17) preamble *(c)*.

sponds to the approach taken in Chapter 15 cases.[987] The main advantages of this method are its efficiency and cost-effectiveness. Determining the content of the benchmark law and the position of the opposing creditor under that law will take less time and lower expenses than the third method that will be discussed below. This method will work best when the position of the opposing creditor under the benchmark law is relatively clear. This can occur, for example, when the opposing creditor's claim cannot be adjusted through restructuring mechanisms or when the position of the creditor is straightforward to determine (e.g. due to the priority of the claim) by analysing distribution rules and principles under the benchmark law without resorting to hypothetical proceedings.

That said, this may not always be the case. As this work outlined in section E.I and explored in section E.II, most restructuring laws deliberately establish a broad framework for distribution and the ultimate decision within that framework is made by the court, considering the specific circumstances of each case. Hence, in some cases, as opposed to the cases described above, analysing the benchmark law will only yield a broad picture as to the position of the opposing creditor. The broader the picture, the lower the accuracy will be. That may be considered as the main shortcoming of this method. That said, as already noted, the accuracy of the comparison is not the only factor to consider and should be balanced against efficiency and costs.

b) Overriding Mandatory Provisions of the Governing Law of the Contract as a Benchmark

A second method is similar to the first one but has one important distinctive feature. The difference lies in limiting the comparison to the overriding mandatory provisions of the benchmark law.[988] Thus, the comparison will aim to determine the extent of a derogation only from the overriding mandatory provisions of the benchmark law that affect the opposing creditor in the context of debt restructuring. An additional challenge associated

987 See sub-ss F.I.2.b)cc), F.II.2.a)dd).

988 For a discussion of the role of overriding mandatory provision in private international law, see sub-s D.I.2.a)bb). For an example of its use in a private international law instrument, see Regulation (EC) No 593/2008 of the European Parliament and of the Council of 17 June 2008 on the law applicable to contractual obligations (Rome I), art 9.

with this method might occur in determining provisions of the benchmark law with an overriding mandatory status. The advantages of the first method also remain true for this method. However, this method limits the scope of the substantive fairness framework under the MLCBI by setting a higher threshold for determining a deviation from the benchmark law. Depending on one's perspective, it can be criticised or supported for that. Ultimately, it is a matter of policy choice.

c) Hypothetical Proceedings under the Governing Law of the Contract as a Benchmark

A third method involves comparing the treatment of the opposing creditor under the foreign plan with the treatment that creditor would receive in hypothetical restructuring proceedings under the benchmark law. This method is advantageous because it provides a relatively accurate picture of how much the actual treatment deviates from the benchmark law for the opposing creditor. It is in line with the spirit of substantive fairness review as it compares different scenarios of the treatment of the opposing creditor and, thus, corresponds to, *mutatis mutandis,* fairness tests used in different jurisdictions (such as the BIT[989], the *no worse off* test,[990] and the EU BIT[991]) to assess the fairness of the plan in relation to dissenting creditors.[992]

The method is not without shortcomings. Achieving greater accuracy requires increased complexity, time, and costs, therefore leading to less efficiency. To begin with, even in a domestic context, it is a complex matter to determine what the relevant alternative is and to calculate the hypothetical outcome of that alternative.[993] The same holds, *mutatis mutandis,* for the current method. The first difficulty that may arise is determining which restructuring framework under the benchmark law should be selected as the most suitable comparator. This may occur when multiple restructuring mechanisms (within insolvency proceedings or as stand-alone procedures)

989 See text to nn 691, 692.
990 See text to nn 803, 804.
991 See text to nn 854, 855.
992 To briefly and generally recap, the aim of those tests is to determine what the outcome for a dissenting creditor would be without the proposed plan and compare this outcome with the treatment of the creditor under the proposed plan. It is also noteworthy that the baseline for comparison may differ depending on the test.
993 See text to n 809.

exist in the benchmark jurisdiction, such as in England.[994] After determining the appropriate comparator, difficulties may arise when calculating the hypothetical recovery rate for the opposing creditor. This calculation is typically not straightforward and may involve complex legal and factual issues.

Additionally, the hypothetical recovery rate may sometimes be presented as a range due to the same considerations mentioned in connection with the second group of cases when discussing the first method above. However, the accuracy will be much higher in this method. Finally, although the comparison mainly focuses on the opposing creditor, it should consider all relevant circumstances that would affect the outcome in the hypothetical proceedings. For example, to determine whether the opposing creditor would represent a minority or majority in the corresponding class in the hypothetical proceedings, the potential behaviour of the other creditors should be taken into account based on their actual behaviour in the foreign proceedings in question.

4. Establishment of Unfairness

a) Material Difference

In order to establish unfairness, a comparison should first identify a deviation from the benchmark law that adversely affects the position of the opposing creditor. However, a substantive fairness review does not conclude merely upon finding such a deviation, regardless of which of the methods discussed above (or any other possible ones) is applied. That is to say, a mere deviation from the benchmark law does not suffice to establish unfairness for the purposes of the substantive fairness framework under the MLCBI.

The fact that the treatment of the opposing creditor differs from that which would be received under the benchmark law should not come as a surprise. Substantive laws of different states may vary and can lead to different outcomes when applied to the same facts. That is the reason why choice-of-law rules exist in the first instance.[995] A single court and a

994 See text to n 750. In jurisdictions with a single centralised restructuring framework (like Chapter 11 under US law) the issue will not arise.

995 Fletcher (n 27) para 28-013.

single law approach to cross-border restructurings under the principle of modified universalism acknowledges the risk of such a difference in the substantive treatment of a creditor, which is outweighed by the benefits of the respective approach.[996] Accordingly, jurisdictions applying modified universalism, whether through regional or international frameworks or in their domestic legislations, also accept the possibility of such differences.

As previously mentioned in various contexts in this work, an initial evaluation is conducted under modified universalism before deferring to a single court and single law governing the worldwide restructuring of the debtor. This work has also concluded that such an evaluation should also include a separate review of the (substantive) fairness of the plan in relation to the opposing creditor. According to this work, the most feasible approach in that regard is to compare the treatment of the opposing creditor under the plan with the hypothetical treatment under the governing law of the contract. Considering any adverse difference in treatment as constituting an unfair outcome for the opposing creditor would be tantamount to denying modified universalism and, consequently, all its benefits. Furthermore, as noted in various contexts throughout this work, discharge in restructuring proceedings is not merely a contractual matter between the parties to a contract. Accordingly, some degree of derogation from the governing law of the contract must be tolerated. That said, there should be a balance between the advantages of a single forum and single law approach and the sacrifices of foreign creditors.

Hence, unfairness should be established only when there is a *material* difference in the respective treatments that adversely affects the opposing creditor. Once the court of the receiving state has established the material difference in question, it should complete the respective substantive fairness review in favour of the opposing creditor and deny the recognition and enforcement of the plan with respect to that creditor.

b) Flexible Approach

What constitutes *material* should be left to the discretion of the court and will likely depend on the facts of each case. However, one point should be emphasised in this context: *material* denotes significantly more than merely *minor*. For example, this work does not consider the difference as material

996 For a discussion of the benefits, see sub-s B.II.3.a).

in a scenario where the opposing creditor receives eighty-five per cent of the outstanding debt under the plan, while that creditor would be paid in full under the benchmark law. Accordingly, the court should determine the extent to which it is reasonable to expect the opposing creditor to forgo what that creditor is entitled to receive under the governing law of the contract for the sake of modified universalism and its associated benefits.

Drawing a strict line in this context is not a straightforward matter, nor is it desirable given the need to maintain flexibility. A general threshold might be around thirty per cent, though this figure could be higher in some cases and lower in others, depending on the facts. This work has, in various contexts, emphasised the role of individual circumstances in restructuring proceedings and possible reasons for that. The recognition stage is no exception in this regard. Furthermore, factors such as variance in the accuracy of comparison, the potential need to consider the protection-worthiness of the opposing creditor, and the possibility of applying different methods underscore the necessity of a flexible approach. Accordingly, the question of whether a difference is material should be resolved on a case-by-case basis, taking into account the specific circumstances of each case.

Nonetheless, this work considers that some general patterns can be determined in case law for the sake of clarity, certainty, and consistency in application. Below, it will make some suggestions in that respect. First, it is important to consider the type of creditor involved. When dealing with sophisticated institutionalised creditors, the permitted level of derogation should be higher than for trade creditors or consumers. Several factors can justify this differentiation, including differences in risk appetite, bargaining power at the time of contract conclusion, tolerance for potential loss, and worthiness of protection, among others. Second, the tolerance for deviation from the overriding mandatory provisions of the benchmark law should be lower than that for non-overriding provisions. Third, the extent of tolerable derogation may depend on the range of the hypothetical recovery rate, where applicable. If the actual recovery rate falls within the hypothetical recovery range but is close to its lower end, it generally should not raise concerns, provided the range is not too wide. But if the actual recovery rate falls below the hypothetical recovery range, the wider the range, the less deviation from the lower end should be tolerated. For instance, the difference may be considered material where the actual recovery rate is thirty per cent and the hypothetical range is fifty to ninety per cent, but not material if the hypothetical range is fifty to sixty per cent. These factors should, of course, be balanced against one another.

5. Summary

Section F.II was devoted to an in-depth analysis of the key aspects of the substantive fairness framework under the MLCBI. This work first underscored its limited scope and application, outlining several factors to ensure this objective (F.II.1).

Then, it made the case for a benchmark law to compare the treatment of the opposing creditor under the plan, which is one of the essential components of the substantive fairness framework under the MLCBI and elaborated on the selection of this law (F.II.2). It concluded that the most suitable law for this purpose is the governing law of the contract, due to factors such as the need to protect all creditors, the purpose of article 22 (1) of the MLCBI, and, more generally, the debt-oriented nature of restructuring proceedings. This work also reviewed the existing literature to support the respective conclusion and to underscore the differences from the concept of virtual territoriality.

Finally, it examined other important components of the substantive fairness framework under the MLCBI: the process of comparison with the benchmark law (F.II.3) and the establishment of unfairness (F.II.4). It was concluded that the unfairness of the plan should be established when there is a material adverse deviation from the position of the opposing creditor under the governing law of the contract.

III. Application of the Substantive Fairness Framework under the MLCBI to the IBA Plan

After discussing the key components of the substantive fairness framework under the MLCBI in the previous section, the IBA plan will be tested below against this framework. More specifically, this work will analyse the fairness of the IBA plan with respect to one of the English law creditors who opposed a permanent moratorium in England, namely, Sberbank of Russia ("Sberbank").[997] This work will analyse the outcome of the attempts to secure the recognition of the substantive effects of the IBA restructuring proceedings in both jurisdictions (England and the US). This analysis is

997 This selection stems from the fact that Sberbank, as opposed to the other opposing creditor, was the sole lender and was not involved in any ancillary issues. See *IBA* (n 245) [12], [21].

predicated on the fact that no public policy and procedural fairness issues arose with respect to the IBA restructuring proceedings and, therefore, will exclusively focus on substantive fairness. This is because the applicable Azerbaijani law generally ensures procedural justice for participants of proceedings,[998] and the respective matters were found to be an issue by neither the English nor the US courts in considering the recognition of the IBA restructuring proceedings.[999]

1. England

There is not much room for analysis of the outcome in England, as it was based on the strict application of the Gibbs rule,[1000] with which this work disagreed. The reason that the substantive effects of the IBA plan in relation to Sberbank were impossible to achieve in England was not the unfairness of the IBA plan with respect to Sberbank. It was merely because the English courts did not have jurisdiction on the matter since an Azerbaijani restructuring plan discharged an English law-governed debt. Accordingly, substantive fairness was not a central issue before the English courts. Such an approach is not in line with the framework suggested in this work.

2. The US

In the US, the Gibbs rule (or a similar rule) did not apply. However, in order to examine the outcome in the US under the framework suggested in this work, several pre-conditions should have been met.[1001] To begin with, Sberbank should have exhausted all remedies in Azerbaijan, which it did not[1002] in order not to engage the exception to the Gibbs rule (submission).[1003] Besides, Sberbank should have opposed the recognition of the IBA plan in the US and provided some evidence to support the argument that the distribution under the IBA plan was unfair to Sberbank. These

998 See sub-s C.I.1.d).
999 See sub-s C.I.3.
1000 See sub-s C.I.3.a).
1001 See sub-s F.II.1.b).
1002 *IBA* (n 245) [12].
1003 For a more detailed discussion of the exception, See nn 276, 277 (and accompanying text) and text thereto.

pre-conditions were not satisfied either. Assume a scenario where Sberbank did meet all those pre-conditions.

It was argued that the English law-governed claims would have constituted a separate class if the IBA had chosen to promulgate a Scheme (the appropriate route) in England.[1004] Assuming this argument to be accurate, the English law creditors of the IBA would then have been able to veto the Scheme since a cross-class cramdown is not possible under a Scheme if used as a stand-alone procedure.[1005] Hence, the English law claims would have remained unaffected (unless the respective class had assented), meaning a potential hundred per cent recovery for Sberbank (with its claim potentially remaining untouched) in the hypothetical English proceedings. Without further analysis and based on the assumption mentioned above, this number is taken as a benchmark for comparison.

It should then be compared to the actual treatment of Sberbank under the IBA plan. This work was unable to obtain this information from public sources, so it will make assumptions here as well. Given the elaborations made in subsection F.II.4, if Sberbank was offered more than seventy per cent of the outstanding amount of its original debt under the IBA plan, the plan would likely pass a substantive fairness review under the framework suggested in this work. It, however, should be noted that this work does not endorse all aspects of the applicable Azerbaijani law since it grants excessively broad powers to the debtor and lacks clarity on substantive protection of dissenting creditors.[1006] That said, as mentioned earlier, the actual distribution under the foreign plan rather than the content of the foreign law in question is a factor that matters for the purposes of the substantive fairness framework under the MLCBI.

IV. Advantages of the Substantive Fairness Framework under the MLCBI

This section will outline several advantages of the framework suggested in the present research. It is noteworthy that due to the shared idea of respecting the governing law of the contract (despite fundamental differences on

---

1004 *IBA* (n 245) [88].

1005 See text to n 781. For the purposes of this section, English law is examined as it stood in 2017, the year when the IBA restructuring proceedings were launched and the recognition in England was sought. Hence, the analysis does not include Part 26A plans.

1006 For a more detailed discussion of the applicable Azerbaijani law, see sub-s C.I.1.

how, at what stage, and to what extent), some of these advantages are, in a similar form, also attributable to the Gibbs rule[1007] or the concept of virtual territoriality.[1008] However, unlike them, the framework suggested in this work offers these benefits within a system underpinned by modified universalism, i.e. without recourse to multiple parallel proceedings or direct application of multiple laws in one case.

1. Certainty

One key benefit is, albeit relative, certainty. Creditors get assurance that, in case of the debtor's restructuring, their entitlements under the law they agreed to be bound will be respected to some extent, irrespective of a jurisdiction where the restructuring is conducted and a substantive law governing the restructuring. Otherwise, the restructuring will not have global effects. Such a relative degree of certainty minimises the risk associated with lending to foreign debtors, and its *ex ante* effects (e.g. reduction of risk premiums in the form of lower interest rates) will lead to greater cooperation in global commerce.

2. Forum Shopping

Another benefit is related to the issue of forum shopping.[1009] The framework suggested in this work would cause a decline in the number of cases involving bad-faith forum shopping. Whatever jurisdiction is selected, for whatever reasons, for the debtor's restructuring, the governing law of the contract will follow (as a benchmark) the proceedings. Accordingly, forum shopping aimed at materially worsening the position of foreign creditors will likely lead to problems in global recognition, outweighing its benefits for the initiating party.

1007 eg, certainty. See n 332 (and accompanying text) and text thereto.
1008 eg, addressing forum shopping. See Janger, 'Virtual Territoriality' (n 976) 432.
1009 For a discussion of forum shopping in the insolvency and restructuring context, which also includes historical comparisons, see Paulus, 'European and Europe's Efforts' (n 851) 96-98.

3. Fraud

Additionally, the framework suggested in this work would effectively address fraud and similar procedural irregularities, such as latent or unconscious discrimination against foreign creditors (or favouring local parties). This kind of irregularities in foreign proceedings is extremely difficult to uncover or prove through a procedural fairness review. The primary advantage of the substantive fairness framework under the MLCBI is that it solely focuses on the fairness of outcome. All the irregularities mentioned occur, in one form or another, to influence and achieve the *desired* outcome. Therefore, if an outcome is significantly tainted by such irregularities, in most cases, it will be uncovered as a result of a substantive fairness review without the need to expressly prove their existence.

4. Fairness in Domestic Proceedings

Finally, the prospect of a substantive fairness review at the recognition stage may, in most cases, influence the earlier stages of restructurings involving foreign law-governed debts. That is to say, it may encourage stakeholders to come up with a plan that would pass not only a fairness assessment of a local court but also a possible substantive fairness review of a foreign court.

Imagine a restructuring case of an American company under Chapter 11. The company has only four creditors. Two of the claims are governed by Albanian law, while the other two are US (New York) law-governed claims. The Albanian law-governed claims have more junior status than those governed by US law under the BC. The Albanian law law-governed claims together constitute a separate class. So do the US law-governed claims. The debtor has assets in Albania, the value of which suffices to fully satisfy the Albanian law creditors. The recovery rate for each of the Albanian law creditors under Albanian law is approximately fifty per cent. The debtor's going-concern value suffices to partly satisfy only the US law creditors and no party disputes this. Based on these facts, now consider two scenarios of a plan confirmation under Chapter 11.

In a first scenario, the class of the Albanian law creditors receive nothing and that of the US law creditors gets the whole going-concern value under the plan. The former rejects the plan, while the latter votes for it. Under the APR, which applies in such a non-consensual plan scenario,[1010] a US court will not reject the plan based on the mere opposition of the Albanian law creditors. However, such a plan would unlikely survive a substantive fairness review of an Albanian court under the framework suggested in this work. The Albanian law creditors, therefore, would not be bound by the plan confirmed in the US in the eyes of Albanian law. Therefore, the Albanian law creditors would likely seek to enforce their claims against the debtor's assets in Albania, which, in turn, might jeopardise the entire restructuring process. The American court confirming the plan should not be blamed for this potential failure because it is strictly bound by the APR.

In a second scenario, the class of the Albanian law creditors is offered twenty per cent of the outstanding amount of the original claims (which comes at the expense of the US law creditors consensually giving up some portion of their entitlements) under the plan. The classes exhibit the same voting behaviour as in the first scenario mentioned above. Again, a US court will not reject the plan on fairness grounds. This time, however, the plan would likely pass a substantive fairness review in Albania, too. Therefore, the prospect of the failure of the entire endeavour would be avoided.

This hypothetical example based on a basic model illustrates how the possibility of a substantive fairness review of a foreign court can encourage parties to come up with a fairer plan in domestic proceedings and, thus, create a fair balance among the respective interests. However, it is not the only benefit in this context. By negotiating a fairer plan, parties would also avoid a time-consuming, costly, and uncertain non-consensual plan scenario in most cases. Besides, the more equitable the plan is, the less opposition it would face during the confirmation and recognition stages. This would significantly improve the overall efficiency of restructuring proceedings.

To summarise the point, the mere possibility of a substantive fairness review in a foreign jurisdiction may lead to a fair outcome from the outset. The *ex ante* effect mentioned would also eventually reduce the number of cases with actual substantive fairness reviews at the recognition stage.

1010 See sub-s E.II.1.b)bb).

V. Summary

Part F focused on the development of a framework to ensure substantive fairness in recognising restructuring plans under the MLCBI. First, it made the case for a substantive fairness review under modified universalism in general and the MLCBI in particular (F.I). The *adequate protection* safeguard under article 22 (1) of the MLCBI was highlighted in that regard. It was concluded that the fairness of foreign plans should be separately evaluated in contested cases.

This work then analysed the key aspects of the substantive fairness framework under the MLCBI (F.II). After arguing for its limited scope and application, this work examined the essential components of the framework. This included a benchmark law for comparing the treatment of the opposing creditor under the plan, the process of comparison with the benchmark law, and the establishment of unfairness. This work concluded that the most suitable law for the benchmark role is the governing law of the contract, and that unfairness should be established when the position of the opposing creditor under the benchmark law has materially deteriorated under the plan.

Against the backdrop of those insights, this work assessed the fairness of its exemplary case, the IBA restructuring proceedings, in a cross-border context with respect to one of the dissenting creditors (F.III). The recognition proceedings in the US were examined, as the American approach (as opposed to the English approach) generally allows the application of the framework suggested in this work. It was concluded that, based on the assumptions made in that section, the IBA plan could be considered fair in relation to the dissenting creditor.

Finally, this work touched on the advantages of the framework suggested in the present research (F.IV). This work highlighted its *ex ante* effects, including encouraging stakeholders to agree upon a fair solution at the earlier stages of restructurings.

G. Conclusion

This work examined the matter of striking a fair balance between the interests of the debtor and dissenting foreign creditors in recognising restructuring plans under the MLCBI. It consisted of five main parts.

Part B was devoted to the foundations of debt restructuring with a particular focus on cross-border aspects. It discussed the nature of restructuring proceedings and concluded that their cross-border effects could be achieved through the existing cross-border insolvency frameworks, such as the MLCBI, provided that the interests of all parties are balanced. Therefore, it also examined several principles underlying the cross-border insolvency system as well as three notable instruments in this area, including the MLCBI.

In Part C, this work first examined two leading jurisdictions that have already implemented the MLCBI: England and the US. This examination demonstrated that these jurisdictions apply substantially different approaches to recognising restructuring plans under the national versions of the MLCBI. This work analysed both approaches and considered neither to be entirely preferable despite possessing certain fairly advantageous features. That is to say, the English approach sees discharge in restructuring proceedings as a strictly contractual matter. Therefore, initiating restructuring proceedings under the governing law of the contract is effectively required to bind a dissenting foreign creditor. While this approach provides certainty for creditors, it is not consistent with the principle of modified universalism, which offers multi-fold advantages. Additionally, it does not reflect the spirit of the MLCBI. The American approach is generally in line with modified universalism, but it primarily evaluates the substantive fairness of foreign restructuring proceedings within a procedural context, which can potentially lead to inconsistency. Furthermore, the American approach is designed to protect mainly the interests of local creditors. Nonetheless, this work noted that the American approach offers a more robust framework, which also aligns with the spirit of the MLCBI. As a result of the analysis, this work suggested a model that, to the extent possible, combines the advantageous aspects of the respective approaches while eliminating their disadvantages. That is to say, this work argued that the American approach needs to raise the bar for fairness review to expressly include the substantive fairness of foreign restructuring plans in contested cases.

As part of the model suggested in this work, Part D analysed the traditional safeguards in recognising foreign judgments (public policy and procedural fairness), particularly in the context of recognising foreign plans under the MLCBI. This work highlighted and joined the arguments for the limited application, particularly when it comes to the public policy exception. It also underscored that the primary purpose of the public policy exception is the protection of the most fundamental policies of the receiving state, not the interests of local creditors.

The rest of this work was dedicated to substantive fairness in restructuring proceedings. Part E explored substantive fairness in a domestic context without considering cross-border issues. It concluded that due to inherent uncertainty around certain aspects of restructuring frameworks and their ability to modify substantive rights against the will of their holders, ensuring substantive fairness is a much more complex and vital issue in restructuring proceedings and many matters depend on the peculiarities of each case (as compared to insolvency proceedings). The analysis of the fairness frameworks under Chapter 11, English law, and the PRD confirmed this conclusion.

Part F focused on developing a framework to ensure substantive fairness in recognising restructuring plans under the MLCBI (substantive fairness framework under the MLCBI) as part of the model suggested in this work. In that Part, this work thoroughly analysed and justified the need for a substantive fairness review in recognising foreign plans under modified universalism. It then examined the MLCBI in that regard. It concluded that the *adequate protection* safeguard under article 22 (1) of the MLCBI provides for and requires such a substantive fairness review. This work also discussed critical aspects of the substantive fairness framework under the MLCBI, starting with its limited scope and application. Most importantly, this work argued and justified that a benchmark law is required to evaluate the fairness of the plan in relation to the opposing creditor, and the most suitable law for that purpose is the governing law of the contract. It also elaborated on the process of comparison with the benchmark law and the establishment of unfairness. This work concluded that the unfairness of the plan in relation to the opposing creditor should be established when the position of that creditor under the governing law of the contract has materially worsened under the plan. In that Part, this work also outlined several advantages of the respective framework.

Bibliography

— — 'Bankruptcy in English Private International Law. II: Foreign Adjudications' (1955) 4 Intl & Comp LQ 1 (published online by CUP in 2008)

Abbasov A, 'Protection of Dissenting Creditors' Interests: Direct Application of the "Substantive Fairness" Test While Considering the Recognition of Foreign Restructuring Plans' (2022) Richard Turton Award Paper 2021 <https://insol.azureedge.net/cmsstorage/insol/media/documents_files/richard%20turton%20award%20papers/richard-turton-award-final-paper-2021.pdf> accessed 21 October 2025 (Overview: Eurofenix [Aut 2022] 32; INSOL World [4th qtr 2022] 42)

Adams ES, 'Toward a New Conceptualization of the Absolute Priority Rule and Its New Value Exception [1993] Det C L Rev 1445

— — and Finche JK, 'Coordinating Cross-Border Bankruptcy: How Territorialism Saves Universalism' (2008) 15 Colum J Eur L 43

Akkermans B, 'Public Policy (Orde Public): A Comparative Analysis of National, Private International Law, and EU Public Policy' (2019) 8 EPLJ 260

Baird DG, 'The Uneasy Case for Corporate Reorganizations' (1986) 15 J Legal Stud 127

— — 'Priority Matters: Absolute Priority, Relative Priority, and the Costs of Bankruptcy' (2016) 165 U Pa L Rev 785

— — and Bernstein DS, 'Absolute Priority, Valuation Uncertainty, and the Reorganization Bargain' (2006) 115 Yale LJ 1930

Ballerini G, 'The Priorities Dilemma in the EU Preventive Restructuring Directive: Absolute or Relative Priority Rule?' (2021) 30 Intl Ins Rev7

Bork R, *Principles of Cross-Border Insolvency Law* (Intersentia 2017)

— — 'Article 22' in Reinhard Bork and Michael Veder (eds), *The UNCITRAL Model Laws on Cross-Border Insolvency and on the Recognition and Enforcement of Insolvency-Related Judgments: An Article-by-Article Commentary* (Edward Elgar 2025)

Boshkoff DG, 'United States Judicial Assistance in Cross-Border Insolvencies'(1987) 36 Intl Comp LQ 729

Brady J, 'Investor Protections in England: The Non-Recognition of the Foreign Discharge of English Law-Governed Debt' (2019) 15 Pratt's J Bankr L 22

Briggs J, 'Bars to Common Law Recognition' in Richard Sheldon (ed) *Cross-Border Insolvency* (4th edn, Bloomsbury Professional 2015)

Brubaker R, 'Bankruptcy Injunctions and Complex Litigation: A Critical Reappraisal of Non-Debtor Releases in Chapter 11 Reorganizations' [1997] U Ill L Rev 959

Brunstad GEJ and Sigal M, 'Competitive Choice Theory and the Unresolved Doctrines of Classification and Unfair Discrimination in Business Reorganizations under the Bankruptcy Code' (1999) 55 Bus Law 1

Buckel E, 'Curbing Comity: The Increasingly Expansive Public Policy Exception of Chapter 15'(2013) 44 Geo J Intl L 1281

Carnevale M, 'Is Gifting Dead in Chapter 11 Reorganizations? Examining Absolute Priority in the Wake of the Second Circuit's No-Gift Rule in re DBSD' (2012) 15 U Pa J Bus L 225

Carter PB, 'The Role of Public Policy in English Private International Law' (1993) 42 Intl & Comp LQ 1

Casey AJ, 'Chapter 11's Renegotiation Framework and the Purpose of Corporate Bankruptcy' (2020) 120 Colum L Rev 1709

— —, Gurrea-Martínez A, and Rasmussen RK, 'A Commitment Rule for Insolvency Forum' (23 January 2024) ECGI Law Working Paper No. 754/2024 <https://ssrn.com/abstract=4704029> accessed 21 October 2025

— — and Macey JC, 'Purdue Pharma and the New Bankruptcy Exceptionalism' (2025) [2024] Sup C Rev 365

Chng K, 'A Theoretical Perspective of the Public Policy Doctrine in the Conflict of Laws' (2018) 14 J Priv Intl L 130

Chung JJ, 'In Re Qimonda AG: The Conflict between Comity and the Public Policy Exception in Chapter 15 of the Bankruptcy Code' (2014) 32 BU Intl LJ 89

Coco D, 'Third-Party Bankruptcy Releases: An Analysis of Consent Through the Lenses of Due Process and Contract Law' (2019) 88 Fordham L Rev 231

Collins (of Mapesbury, Lord) and Harris J (eds), *Dicey, Morris & Collins on the Conflict of Laws* (16th edn, Sweet & Maxwell 2022)

Committee on Bankruptcy and Corporate Reorganization of the Association of the Bar the City of New York (ABCNY), 'Making the Test for Unfair Discrimination More "Fair": A Proposal' (2002) 58 Bus Law 83

Davies DJL, 'The Influence of Huber's De Conflictu Legum on English Private International Law' (1937) 18 Brit YB Intl L 49

de Weijs R, 'Too Big to Fail as a Game of Chicken with the State: What Insolvency Law Theory Has to Say About TBTF and Vice Versa' (2013) 14 EBOR 201

— —, Jonkers AL, and Malakotipour M, 'The Imminent Distortion of European Insolvency Law: How the European Union Erodes the Basic Fabric of Private Law by Allowing "Relative Priority" (RPR)' (11 March 2019) Amsterdam Law School Research Paper No 2019-10, Centre for the Study of European Contract Law Working Paper No 2019-05 <https://ssrn.com/abstract=3350375> accessed 21 October 2025

Dodge WS, 'International Comity in American Law' (2015) 115 Colum L Rev 2071

Eberhart AC, Moore WT, and Roenfeldt RL, 'Security Pricing and Deviations from the Absolute Priority Rule in Bankruptcy Proceedings' (1990) 45 J Fin 1457

Eidenmuller H, 'What Is an Insolvency Proceeding' (2018) 92 Am Bankr LJ 53

Financial Markets Law Committee (FMLC), 'The Rule in Gibbs: Exploring its Value and Practical Use in the Financial Markets as a Guarantor of Legal Predictability' (29 February 2024) <https://fmlc.org/wp-content/uploads/2024/02/Paper-The-Rule-in-Gibbs-Exploring-its-value-and-practical-use-in-the-financial-markets-as-a-guarantor-of-legal-predictability-29-February-2024.pdf)> accessed 21 October 2025

Fisher TCG and Martel J, 'Does It Matter How Bankruptcy Judges Evaluate the Creditors' Best-Interests Test' (2007) 81 Am Bankr LJ 497

Fletcher IF, *The Law of Insolvency* (5th edn, Sweet & Maxwell 2017)

Garza MA, 'When Is Cross-Border Insolvency Recognition Manifestly Contrary to Public Policy' (2015) 38 Fordham Intl LJ 1587

Ghodoosi F, 'The Concept of Public Policy in Law: Revisiting the Role of the Public Policy Doctrine in the Enforcement of Private Legal Arrangements' (2016) 94 Neb L Rev 685

Glosband DM, 'Common Law Perspective on UNCITRAL Instruments on Insolvency Law' in Ángel María Ballesteros Barros and David Amable Morán Bovio (eds), *Insolvency Law in UNCITRAL: Instruments and Comments* (Editorial Aranzadi 2023)

Godwin A, Howse T and Ramsay I, 'The Inherent Power of Common Law Courts to Provide Assistance in Cross-Border Insolvencies: From Comity to Complexity' (2017) 26 Intl Ins Rev 5

Grohsgal B, 'How Absolute Is the Absolute Priority Rule in Bankruptcy: The Case for Structured Dismissals' (2017) 8 Wm & Mary Bus L Rev 439

Gropper AL, 'The Curious Disappearance of Choice of Law as an Issue in Chapter 15 Cases' (2014) 9 Brook J Corp Fin & Com L 57

Grossman A, 'Conflict of Laws in the Discharge of Debts in Bankruptcy' (1996) 5 Intl Ins Rev 1

Hicks J, 'Foxes Guarding the Henhouse: The Modern Best Interests of Creditors Test in Chapter 11 Reorganizations' (2005) 5 Nev LJ 820

Ho LC, *Cross-Border Insolvency: Principles and Practice* (Sweet & Maxwell 2016)

Insolvency Service (UK), 'Implementation of Two UNCITRAL Model Laws on Insolvency Consultation' (published 7 July 2022, updated 10 July 2023) <https://www.gov.uk/government/consultations/implementation-of-two-uncitral-model-laws-on-insolvency/implementation-of-two-uncitral-model-laws-on-insolvency-consultation> accessed 21 October 2025

— — 'Implementation of Two UNCITRAL Model Laws on Insolvency: Summary of Consultation Responses and Government Response' (updated 10 July 2023 <https://www.gov.uk/government/consultations/implementation-of-two-uncitral-model-laws-on-insolvency/outcome/implementation-of-two-uncitral-model-laws-on-insolvency-summary-of-consultation-responses-and-government-response#:~:text=On%207%20July%202022%20the,Law%20> accessed 21 October 2025

International Bank of Azerbaijan, 'ABB Launches Debt Restructuring Offer to its Creditors' (2017) <https://abb-bank.az/en/maliyye-ve-investisiya/diger-melumatlar/press-relizler/londonda-azerbaycan-beynelxalq-bankinin-xarici-kreditorlari-ile-gorus-kecirilib> accessed 21 October 2025

— — 'Reports' <https://abb-bank.az/en/hesabatlar> accessed 21 October 2025

Jackson TH, 'Bankruptcy, Non-Bankruptcy Entitlements, and the Creditors' Bargain' (1982) 91 Yale LJ 857

Janger EJ, 'Universal Proceduralism' (2007) 32 Brook J Intl L 819

— — 'Virtual Territoriality' (2010) 48 Colum J Transnatl L 401

Johnson MM, 'The Not-So-Settled Absolute Priority Rule: The Continued Threat of Priority-Deviation Through Interim Distributions of Assets in Chapter 11 Bankruptcy' (2017) 13 Seton Hall Cir Rev 291

Klee KN, 'All You Ever Wanted to Know about Cram Down under the New Bankruptcy Code' (1979) 53 Am Bankr LJ 133

Krohn A, 'Rethinking Priority: The Dawn of the Relative Priority Rule and the New "Best Interests of Creditors" Test in the European Union' (2021) 30 Intl Ins Rev 75

Lobo ED and Soltman DJ, 'Azeri Restructuring Could Test Limits of Chapter 15 Foreign Plan Enforcement' (2018) 5 (Winter 2017-2018) Emerg Mark Rest J 37

LoPucki LM, 'Cooperation in International Bankruptcy: A Post-Universalist Approach' (1998-1999) 84 Cornell L Rev 696

Lubben SJ, 'The Overstated Absolute Priority Rule' (2016) 21 Fordham J Corp & Fin L 581

Madaus S, 'Leaving the Shadows of US Bankruptcy Law: A Proposal to Divide the Realms of Insolvency and Restructuring Law' (2018) 19 EBOR 615

— — 'The Rule in Gibbs, or How to Protect Local Debt from a Foreign Discharge' (OBLB 19 December 2018) <https://blogs.law.ox.ac.uk/business-law-blog/blog/2018/12/rule-gibbs-or-how-protect-local-debt-foreign-discharge> accessed 21 October 2025

— — 'Is the Relative Priority Rule Right for Your Jurisdiction? A Simple Guide to RPR' (18 January 2020) <https://papers.ssrn.com/sol3/papers.cfm?abstract_id=3827696> accessed 21 October 2025

— — 'Corporate Reorganisation Law and the Shaping Powers of Market Realities and Doctrinal Concepts' (2022) 42 OJLS 1195

— — 'The Cross-border Effects of Restructurings' in Katharina de la Durantaye and others (eds), Festschrift für Christoph G. Paulus zum 70. Geburtstag (CH Beck 2022)

— — 'Are Non-EU Preventive Restructuring Plans Effective in Germany?' (2025) 22 Int Corp Res 198

— — 'Article 25: Cooperation and Direct Communication Between a Court of This State and Foreign Courts or Foreign Representatives' in Reinhard Bork and Michael Veder (eds), *The UNCITRAL Model Laws on Cross-Border Insolvency and on the Recognition and Enforcement of Insolvency-Related Judgments: An Article-by-Article Commentary* (Edward Elgar 2025)

Mankowski P and Langenhagen S, 'Germany' in Olaf Meyer (ed), *Public Policy and Private International Law: A Comparative Guide* (Edward Elgar Publishing 2022)

Markell BA, 'A New Perspective on Unfair Discrimination in Chapter 11' (1998) 72 Am Bankr LJ 227

— — 'Slouching Toward Fairness: A Reply to the ABCNY's Proposal on Unfair Discrimination' (2002) 58 Bus Law 109

— — 'The International Two-Step: Recognizing Domestic Chapter 15 Reorganizations' (2024) 98 Am Bankr LJ 1

McCormack G, 'US Exceptionalism and UK Localism? Cross-border Insolvency Law in Comparative Perspective' (2016) 36 Legal Studies 136

— — 'UK Contracts and Modification under Foreign Law: Time to Consign the Gibbs Rule to Legal History?' (2024) 2023 (4) J Bus L 290 (a repository copy: <https://eprints.whiterose.ac.uk/198398/3/Modification%20of%20English%20law%20contracts.pdf> accessed 21 October 2025

— — and Wan WY, 'The UNCITRAL Model Law on Cross-Border Insolvency Comes of Age: New Times or New Paradigms' (2019) 54 Tex Intl L J 273

Metreveli L, 'Toward Standardized Enforcement of Cross-Border Insolvency Decisions: Encouraging the United States to Adopt UNCITRAL's Recent Amendment to Its Model Law on Cross-Border Insolvency' (2017) 51 Colum JL & Soc Probs 315

Mevorach I, 'On the Road to Universalism: A Comparative and Empirical Study of the UNCITRAL Model Law on Cross-Border Insolvency' (2011) 12 EBOR 517

— — *The Future of Cross-Border Insolvency: Overcoming Biases and Closing Gaps* (OUP 2018)

— — 'Overlapping International Instruments for Enforcement of Insolvency Judgments: Undermining or Strengthening Universalism?' (2021) 22 EBOR 283

— — and Walters A, 'The Characterization of Pre-Insolvency Proceedings in Private International Law' (2020) 21 EBOR 855

Meyer O, 'A Flexible System in Flux: On the Realignment of Public Policy' in Olaf Meyer (ed), *Public Policy and Private International Law: A Comparative Guide* (Edward Elgar Publishing 2022)

Mills A, 'The Dimensions of Public Policy in Private International Law' (2008) 4 J Priv Intl L 201

Mokal RJ, 'On Fairness and Efficiency' (2003) 66 MLR 452

— — *Corporate Insolvency Law: Theory and Application* (OUP 2005)

— — 'Shopping and Scheming, and the Rule in Gibbs' [2017 March] South Square Digest 58

— — 'Fairness' in Lorenzo Stanghellini and others (eds), *Best Practices in European Restructuring: Contractualised Distress Resolution in the Shadow of the Law* (Wolters Kluwer 2018)

— — 'The Goals, Contents, and Structure of the Plan' (with help from Case CG and Stanghellini L) in Lorenzo Stanghellini and others (eds), *Best Practices in European Restructuring: Contractualised Distress Resolution in the Shadow of the Law* (Wolters Kluwer 2018)

— — 'The Two Conditions for the Pt 26A Cram Down' (2020) 11 JIBFL 730

— — 'The Court's Discretion in Relation to the Pt 26A Cram Down' (2021) 1 JIBFL 12

— — 'What is an Insolvency Proceeding? *Gategroup* Lands in a Gated Community' (2022) 31 Intl Ins Rev 418

— — 'Cram Dos, Don'ts, and Darn Its: The 'Too Much Unfair Value' Approach to the UK Cramdown' [2025 April] South Square Digest 36

— — and Tirado I, 'Has Newton Had His Day? Relativity and Realism in European Restructuring' (2019) 4 JIBFL 233

— — and others, 'The Cramdown: A Conceptual Framework' in Jennifer Payne and Kristin van Zwieten (eds), *Corporate Restructuring Law in Flux* (Hart Publishing 2025)

Mund SC, '11 U.S.C. 1506: U.S. Courts Keep a Tight Rein on the Public Policy Exception, but the Potential to Undermine Internationals Cooperation in Insolvency Proceedings Remains' (2010) 28 Wis Intl LJ 325

Nadelmann KH, 'Solomons v. Ross and International Bankruptcy Law' (1946) 9 MLR 154

— — 'Compositions: Reorganizations and Arrangements: In the Conflict of Laws' (1948) 61 Harv LR 804

— — 'Introduction - The Comity Doctrine' (1966) 65 Mich L Rev 1

Nelson TG, 'Down in Flames: Three U.S. Courts Decline Recognition to Judgments from Mexico, Citing Corruption' (2010) 44 Intl L 897

Neville DS, 'The New Value Exception to the Chapter 11 Absolute Priority Rule' (1995) 60 Mo L Rev 465

Noirault L, 'Rule in Gibbs: The Continuation of Territorialism by Other Means?' (2025) 15 Harv Bus L Rev 325

Olivares-Caminal R and others, *Debt Restructuring* (3rd edn, OUP 2022)

Omar PJ, 'The Landscape of International Insolvency Law' (2002) 11 Intl Ins Rev 173

Oxford English Dictionary, 'interest, n, sense I.1.b' (*OED Online*, OUP December 2024) <https://www.oed.com/dictionary/interest_n?tab=meaning_and_use#260186> accessed 21 October 2025

Paterson S, 'Rethinking the Role of the Law of Corporate Distress in the Twenty-First Century' (2014) LSE Law, Society and Economy Working Papers 27/2014 <https://eprints.lse.ac.uk/60583/1/WPS2014-27_Paterson.pdf> accessed 21 October 2025

— — 'Debt Restructuring and Notions of Fairness' (2017) 80 MLR 600

— — 'Reflections on English Law Schemes of Arrangement in Distress and Proposals for Reform' (2018) 15 ECFR 472

— — 'Judicial Discretion in Part 26A Restructuring Plan Procedures' (24 January 2022) <https://papers.ssrn.com/sol3/papers.cfm?abstract_id=4016519> accessed 21 October 2025

— — 'The Conceptual Foundation of Cross-class Cramdown (18 September 2024) < https://papers.ssrn.com/sol3/papers.cfm?abstract_id=4959732> accessed 21 October 2025

— — 'A Qualified Defence of the Rule in Gibbs' (15 April 2025) LSE Legal Studies Working Paper 6/2025 <https://papers.ssrn.com/sol3/papers.cfm?abstract_id=5218429> accessed 21 October 2025

Paul JR, 'Comity in International Law' (1991) 32 Harv Intl L J 1

Paulus CG, 'Global Insolvency Law and the Role of Multinational Institutions' (2007) 32 Brook J Intl L 755

— — 'European and Europe's Efforts for Attractivity as a Restructuring Hub' (2021) 56 Tex Intl L J 95

— — 'Civil Law Codificationalism vs. UNCITRAL's Soft Law Approach in the Context of Insolvency Law' in Ángel María *Ballesteros Barros and* David Amable *Morán Bovio (eds), Insolvency Law in UNCITRAL: Instruments and Comments (*Editorial *Aranzadi 2023)*

Payne J, 'Debt Restructuring in English Law: Lessons from the US and the Need for Reform' (30 January 2014) Oxford Legal Studies Research Paper No 89/2013 <https://papers.ssrn.com/sol3/papers.cfm?abstract_id=2321615> accessed 21 October 2025

— — 'The Role of the Court in Debt Restructuring' (2018) 77 CLJ 124

— — Schemes of Arrangement: Theory, Structure and Operation (2nd edn, CUP 2021)

Polivy DR, 'Unfair Discrimination in Chapter 11: A Comprehensive Compilation of Current Case Law' (1998) 72 Am Bankr LJ 191

Pottow JAE, 'Greed and Pride in International Bankruptcy: The Problems of and Proposed Solutions to Local Interests' (2006) 104 Mich L Rev 1899

Ramesh K, 'The Gibbs Principle - A Tether on the Feet of Good Forum Shopping' (2017) 29 SAcLJ 42

Rasmussen RK, 'Debtor's Choice: A Menu Approach to Corporate Bankruptcy' (1992) 71 Tex L Rev 51

— — 'A New Approach to Transnational Insolvencies' (1997) 19 Mich J Intl L 1

Rodriguez R, 'Article 14: Grounds to Refuse Recognition and Enforcement of an Insolvency-related Judgment' in Reinhard Bork and Michael Veder (eds), *The UNCITRAL Model Laws on Cross-Border Insolvency and on the Recognition and Enforcement of Insolvency-Related Judgments: An Article-by-Article Commentary* (Edward Elgar 2025)

Rogerson P, *Colliers's Conflict of Laws* (4th edn, CUP 2013)

Sachdev V, 'Choice of Law in Insolvency Proceedings: How English Courts' Continued Reliance on the Gibbs Principle Threatens Universalism' (2019) 93 Am Bankr LJ 343

Seymour JM and Schwarcz SL, 'Corporate Restructuring under Relative and Absolute Priority Default Rules: A Comparative Assessment' [2021] U Ill L Rev 1

Shahid O, 'The Public Policy Exception: Has Sec. 1506 been a Significant Obstacle in Aiding Foreign Bankruptcy Proceedings' (2010) 9 J Intl Bus & L 175

Skauradszun D, 'Restructuring Companies During and After the Covid-19 Pandemic: A Law & Economics Approach' (2021) 9 NIBLeJ 1 1 <https://www.ntu.ac.uk/media/documents/academic-schools/law/2021-9-NIBLeJ-1.pdf> accessed 21 October 2025

— — and Nijnens W, 'Brussels Ia or EIR Recast? The Allocation of Preventive Restructuring Frameworks' (2019) 16 Int Corp Res 193

— — and Nijnens W, 'The Toolbox for Cross-Border Restructurings Post-Brexit - Why, What & Where?' (2019) 7 NIBLeJ 1 1 <https://www.ntu.ac.uk/media/documents/research-documents/1.pdf> accessed 21 October 2025

— —, Schröder J, and Kümpel J, 'Why a Sanction Order Pursuant to Part 26A UK CA Cannot Be Recognised in Germany: Part One' (2024) 21 Int Corp Res 349

— —, Schröder J, and Kümpel J, 'Why a Sanction Order Pursuant to Part 26A UK CA Cannot Be Recognised in Germany: Part Two' (2025) 22 Int Corp Res 7

Smith T, 'Recognition of Foreign Corporate Insolvency Proceedings at Common Law' in Richard Sheldon (ed) *Cross-Border Insolvency* (4th edn, Bloomsbury Professional 2015)

Timm A, 'The Gift That Gives Too Much: Invalidating a Gifting Exception to the Absolute Priority Rule' [2013] U Ill L Rev 1649

Tirado I, 'Examining and Confirming Plans' in Lorenzo Stanghellini and others (eds), *Best Practices in European Restructuring: Contractualised Distress Resolution in the Shadow of the Law* (Wolters Kluwer 2018)

Tung F, 'Is International Bankruptcy Possible' (2001) 23 Mich J Intl L 31

UNCITRAL, *Legislative Guide on Insolvency Law, Parts One and Two* (UN 2005) <https://uncitral.un.org/sites/uncitral.un.org/files/media-documents/uncitral/en/05-80722_ebook.pdf> accessed 21 October 2025

— — *Model Law on Cross-Border Insolvency with Guide to Enactment and Interpretation* (UN 2014) <https://uncitral.un.org/sites/uncitral.un.org/files/media-documents/uncitral/en/1997-model-law-insol-2013-guide-enactment-e.pdf> accessed 21 October 2025

— — *Model Law on Recognition and Enforcement of Insolvency-Related Judgments with Guide to Enactment* (UN 2019) <https://uncitral.un.org/sites/uncitral.un.org/files/media-documents/uncitral/en/ml_recognition_gte_e.pdf> accessed 21 October 2025

— — 'Digest of Case Law on the Model Law on Cross-Border Insolvency' (UN 2021) <https://uncitral.un.org/sites/uncitral.un.org/files/media-documents/uncitral/en/20-06293_uncitral_mlcbi_digest_e.pdf> accessed 21 October 2025

— — 'Status: UNCITRAL Model Law on Cross-Border Insolvency (1997)' <https://uncitral.un.org/en/texts/insolvency/modellaw/cross-border_insolvency/status> accessed 21 October 2025

van Galen R, 'The Scheming Brits' in Katharina de la Durantaye and others (eds), Festschrift für Christoph G. Paulus zum 70. Geburtstag (CH Beck 2022)

van Zwieten K (ed), *Goode on Principles of Corporate Insolvency Law* (5th edn, Sweet & Maxwell 2018)

— — 'Mid-Crisis Restructuring Law Reform in the United Kingdom' (2023) 24 EBOR 287

— — 'Article 6: Public Policy Exception' in Reinhard Bork and Michael Veder (eds), *The UNCITRAL Model Laws on Cross-Border Insolvency and on the Recognition and Enforcement of Insolvency-Related Judgments: An Article-by-Article Commentary* (Edward Elgar 2025)

— — 'Article 7: Additional Assistance under Other Laws' in Reinhard Bork and Michael Veder (eds), *The UNCITRAL Model Laws on Cross-Border Insolvency and on the Recognition and Enforcement of Insolvency-Related Judgments: An Article-by-Article Commentary* (Edward Elgar 2025)

Veder M, 'Article 2: Definitions' in Reinhard Bork and Michael Veder (eds), *The UNCITRAL Model Laws on Cross-Border Insolvency and on the Recognition and Enforcement of Insolvency-Related Judgments: An Article-by-Article Commentary* (Edward Elgar 2025)

Walters A, 'Giving Effect to Foreign Restructuring Plans in Anglo-US Private International Law' (2015) 3 NIBLeJ 20 375 <https://irep.ntu.ac.uk/id/eprint/11905/1/220288_2492.pdf> accessed 21 October 2025

— — 'Modified Universalisms & the Role of Local Legal Culture in the Making of Cross-Border Insolvency Law' (2019) 93 Am Bankr LJ 47

Wan WY, 'Article 7: Public Policy Exception' in Reinhard Bork and Michael Veder (eds), *The UNCITRAL Model Laws on Cross-Border Insolvency and on the Recognition and Enforcement of Insolvency-Related Judgments: An Article-by-Article Commentary* (Edward Elgar 2025)

Wessels B, 'The Full Version of My Reply to Professor De Weijs et al' (22 March 2019) Bob Wessels Blog (2019-03-doc10) <https://bobwessels.nl/blog/2019-03-doc10-the-full-version-of-my-reply-to-professor-de-weijs-et-al/> accessed 21 October 2025

— — 'Should Parties Have the Right to Appeal a Restructuring Plan?' (7 August 2023) Bob Wessels Blog (2023-08-doc1) <https://bobwessels.nl/blog/2023-08-doc1-should-parties-have-the-right-to-appeal-a-restructuring-plan/> accessed 21 October 2025

— — and Madaus S, *Rescue of Business in Europe: A European Law Institute Instrument* (OUP 2020)

Westbrook JL, 'A Global Solution to Multinational Default' (2000) 98 Mich L Rev 2276

— — 'Chapter 15 and Discharge' (2005) 13 Am Bankr Inst L Rev 503

— — 'Chapter 15 at Last' (2005) 79 Am Bankr LJ 713

— — 'Ian Fletcher and the Internationalist Principle' (2015) 3 NIBLeJ 30 565 <https://ssrn.com/abstract=3064868> accessed 21 October 2025

— — 'Interpretation Internationale' (2015) 87 Temp L Rev 739

— — 'Global Insolvency Proceedings for a Global Market: The Universalist System and the Choice of a Central Court' (2018) 96 Tex L Rev 1473

— — 'Comity and Choice of Law in Global Insolvencies' (2019) 54 Tex Intl L J 259

— — and others, *A Global View of Business Insolvency Systems* (World Bank and Brill 2010)

World Bank, 'Principles for Effective Insolvency and Creditor/Debtor Regimes' (World Bank 2021) <https://documents1.worldbank.org/curated/en/391341619072648570/pdf/Principles-for-Effective-Insolvency-and-Creditor-and-Debtor-Regimes.pdf)> accessed 21 October 2025

Wurmnest W, 'Public Policy in European Private International Law' in Olaf Meyer (ed), *Public Policy and Private International Law: A Comparative Guide* (Edward Elgar Publishing 2022)

Yntema HE, 'The Comity Doctrine' (1966) 65 Mich L Rev 9

Zander K, 'Application of the Public Policy Exception in the UNCITRAL Model Law on Cross Border Insolvency: Issues and Challenges' (December 2022) INSOL International, Technical Paper Series 54 <https://insol.azureedge.net/cmsstorage/insol/media/document-library/technical%20paper%20series/application-of-the-public-policy-exception-in-the-uncitral-model-law-on-cross-border-insolvency.pdf> accessed 21 October 2025